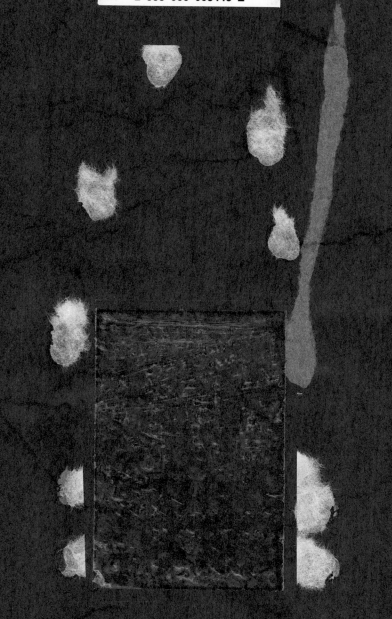

Black Society

GERRI MAJOR'S

Black Society

with DORIS E. SAUNDERS

 Johnson Publishing Company Inc.   Chicago: 1976

First printing, 1976
Library of Congress Cataloging in Publication Data
Main entry under author:
Major, Geraldyn Hodges, 1894-
Black Society.
1. Negroes—Biography. 2. Negroes—Genealogy.
3. Upper classes—United States. I. Saunders, Doris E.,
joint author. II. Title.
E185.96M22   929′.373   75-39546
ISBN 0-87485-075-4

Norman L. Hunter Layout and Design

12/13 Kenntonian—Baltic—Helvetica

Printed in the United States of America.

However laudable an ambition to rise may be, the first duty of an upper class is to serve the lowest classes. The aristocracies of all peoples have been slow in learning this, and perhaps the Negro is no slower than the rest, but his peculiar situation demands that in his case this lesson be learned sooner.

William E. B. DuBois
The Philadelphia Negro, 1899

Introduction

*I*n these days when the black revolution has swept aside most shibboleths, and when black consciousness is at its highest, it may seem ludicrous to talk of Black Society. Outside the black community, its actual existence would probably be challenged. One doubting Thomas asked how there could be such a thing as Black Society, when black people have rarely had two nickels to rub together. Society to him was synonymous with wealth, not necessarily an accurate reflection of the truth.

To others, society is little more than an anachronism—a nineteenth century institution trying desperately to preserve its exclusive status in a decreasingly class-conscious twentieth century.

It is to put the record straight that I have been persuaded to write this chronicle of Black Society. I have lived it for over eighty years, and before me, my family lived it.

The aristocracy of which I write is based on birth. It is a club whose passwords are "Who are your people?" As the nation celebrates its 200th anniversary, it is well to remember these dark aristocrats whose genealogy provides the other side of the coin in America's family tree.

The names may be strange to the outsider's ear: Syphax, Cook, Craft, Tanner, Wormley, Jones, Trotter and others. These names belong to some of the "first families" of black America. For every family noted in these pages, ten families, equally notable, are unfortunately omitted. It is hoped that the practice followed by many families of naming a family historian in each generation will be emulated by others. It is our history and we must preserve it.

Geraldyn Hodges Major

October 28, 1976

Acknowledgments

I would like to express fond appreciation to my cousins, the late Dr. Raymond Farrow Powell and Mrs. Herman Moore, and my dear friend, Pauline Kigh Reed who reminisced with me about the good old days of our youth. I have talked to people throughout the United States who either belong to old families or who are my stringers and who know all of the old families. Many of my oldest and dearest friends may not find their names in this book. It is intended to be a guide to the nature of Black Society, not a directory.

I'm grateful to Rose Morgan, Thelma Gorham, Anita Pope, Ella Ascher, Agnes Davis, Gretchen Jackson, Johnetta Kelso, Louise Fischer Morse, Margaret Richardson, Leontyne King, Lois Caesar, Morris Speed, Jesse Adams, and others.

In addition, Doris Saunders has interviewed and borrowed material from a wide number of descendants of old families. We are indebted to Ms. Denise Denison Morris, Mrs. Harvey Russell, Mr. and Mrs. George Denison, Lloyd Wheeler, Mrs. Russell Minton, Mrs. Maurice Clifford, Mercer Cook, Hugh Cook, Alice Conners Coleman, Mrs. Ellen Craft Dammond, Sue Barnett Ish, Mrs. J. Newton Hill, Clarence Holte, Dr. Stanton Wormley, Dr. Lowell Wormley, Mrs. Mary Gibson Hundley, Ellen Terry, William C. Syphax, Mrs. Dorothea Scurlock Dedmon, William T. Syphax, Jetta Norris Jones, Mr. and Mrs. Byron C. Minor, and Mrs. Eloise Flory.

Arlean Vauthier, Jerry Dibblee, Larry McGee, Pamela Cash, Ruth Zielinski, Paula Materre, Michael Winston, Joseph Semper, Jean Brannon, Johnny Marie Brannon, M. Fannie Granton, Maurice Sorrell, Ellen Tarry, and Norman L. Hunter have all contributed immeasurably to the final product. We cannot fail to express thanks to Patrick O'Conner, editor-in-chief of Popular Library Publishing Company. His interest and encouragement have been invaluable.

Finally, without the heartfelt cooperation and support of our publisher, John H. Johnson, this project which began in January, 1973, could not have been completed. We thank him.

Table of Contents

Table of Contents

Photographs

Black Society

Black Society

Beginnings

"*L*ight, bright and damned near white" was one of the prerequisites for admission to black society back in the old days.

Black society today has been shaken by a virtual revolution. Wealth and accomplishment have replaced family background as the criterion of "Who's Who" in the top-rung social set.

The miscegenated family tree has been supplanted by stocks, bonds, bank accounts, real estate, and/or high professional standing as a standard for acceptance. The result has been that where once black society was firmly rooted in a dozen or so cities where the "blue-veined" social elite knew how many generations back they could count their free-black ancestry and how much "aristocratic" white blood they had, today, black society is nation-wide. From the smallest town to the largest metropolis you will find leading citizens ruling as social arbiters strictly according to financial and pro-fessional status, and proclaiming their black identity proudly. Many have never heard of the "paper bag test," wherein a woman whose skin was darker than a Kraft paper bag was not admitted to the most exclusive so-cieties and social clubs. Up to fairly recent times, Washington, D. C. was noted for its adherence to the code of color.

Unquestionably, the old social lines have shifted. In many ways the old guard has relaxed its attitudes and has a new concept of itself. But then, let's face it, a large number of social arbiters, who made black society *really* society, are dead. In many cases, their children are not interested in perpetuating the carefully structured arrangement and have gone far afield in mate selection. The doors to the clubhouse, while not wide open, are at least ajar.

From the earliest days of black men and women in America, there existed a group of people who had status and were "society" in the very traditional sense of breeding, education and leadership position. I suspect that this innate sense of class came with the kidnapped Africans on the slave ships. Many who were stolen were themselves, or were the children of, chiefs and rulers in their native tribes. Knowing who they were, they brought with them a quality of leadership and sense of being. Many unmixed blacks were early leaders and doers.

Because of the accidents of fate and the slave owners' desire for the bodies of black women, many other aristocrats, who frequently traced their ancestry back to America's founding fathers, were highly conscious of their identity. It was like a union card. Whether casually conquered in a transient relationship or the recipient of the questionable status of concubine, mistress or house servant, the women thus used produced children who, considering the options, stood a better chance for survival in the society than the enslaved African whose lot was hard labor and no future outside the terms of the slave owner's whim. Again, in many cases, children of mixed unions were the product of free white mothers and slave fathers. The mother was sometimes the owner, as was the case in Benjamin Banneker's family where the grandmother bought her husband and her daughter's husband off the slave block.

Whatever the philosophical argument, the fact remains; a new race had been created by miscegenation. In 1790, the free colored population in the United States was 59,000; by 1860, it had skyrocketed to 488,000.

A new class had been born, standing lower on the socio-economic ladder than the free white, but above the depressed and still enslaved black. Those who were inside this circle of free colored people were conscious of the differences of status. They were members of a special club with its own requirements and obligations. They were the progenitors of Black Society. *in the U.S.*

In order to try to understand what it was and why it was, it is necessary to go back to the beginning, or at least to the early days of the nation, when words which dealt with the spirit of liberty and equality and fraternity were still fresh with meaning. It will be necessary to examine the historical record in a new frame of reference to see who some of the people were that constituted the bedrock upon which the black upper class was formed. What set these people apart and made them different from the thousands of others whom the outside observer would have considered to be the same? Among those to consider are Absalom Jones, Richard Allen, Peter Williams, Sr., Samuel Cornish, James Varick, and James Forten.

Foremost in this group is James Forten of Philadelphia, perhaps one of the least known of the great Americans whose ancestors were captured in their African homeland and brought in chains to America. In 1833, when nearly sixty years of age, Forten, manufacturer, inventor, philanthropist, organizer and financial supporter of abolition and the Underground Railroad, said, "My great grandfather was brought to this country as a slave from Africa. My grandfather obtained his own freedom. My father never wore the yoke. He rendered valuable service to his country in the War of our Revolution, and I, though then a boy, was a drummer in that war . . ." Forten was, in 1833, a fourth generation American and a grandfather himself, so that his granddaughter, Charlotte Forten, the educator, had six generations of American history behind her. During the Civil War, she wrote about her black charges at Port Royal, St. Helena Island, S.C., where she went as a teacher for the Freedmen's Aid Bureau, in the following words; "My heart gave a great throb of happiness as I looked at them, and thought, 'They are free! So long downtrodden, so long crushed to the earth, but now in their old homes, forever free!' And I thanked God that I had lived to see this day." "They" were freed; she had been born free.

Freedom had been on the tongues of blacks since they had first known the chains of slavery. Nearly a century earlier, the slave poet Phillis Wheatley had articulated the soul's longing for freedom. In 1772, four years before the Declaration of Independence, she addressed a poem to the Earl of Dartmouth, secretary of state for the American colonies. A portion says:

> "Should you, my lord, while you peruse my song
> wonder from whence flow these wishes for the
> common good,
> by feeling hearts alone best understood,
> I, young in life, by seeming cruel fate
> was snatch'd from Afric's fancy'd happy seat;
> What pangs excrutiating must molest,
> What sorrows labour in my parents' breast?
> Steel'd was that soul
> and by no misery mov'd
> That from a father seiz'd his babe belov'd;
> Such, such my case.
> And can I then but pray
> Others may never feel such tyranic sway?"

The freedom fever had been caught by slave and free alike.

On January 6, 1773, slaves in Boston petitioned the governor and the court in behalf of their fellows: ". . . who have had every Day of their Lives imbittered with this most intollerable Reflection, That, let their Behaviour be what it will, not their Children to all Generations, shall ever be able to do, or to possess and enjoy any Thing, no not even *Life itself,* but in a Manner as the *Beasts that perish.* We have no Property! We have no Wives! No Children! We have no City! No Country . . ."

Shortly thereafter, a printed letter was sent to the delegates in the House of Representatives, signed by four slaves—Peter Bestes, Sambo Freeman, Chester Joie and Felix Holbrook—which stated, "We expect great things from men who have made such a noble stand against the designs of their fellow-men to enslave them. . . . Now, at least, allow the Africans . . . one day in a week to work for themselves to enable them to earn money so that they can buy their freedom."

In 1782, after the surrender of Cornwallis, George Washington wrote to a member of his staff regarding a plan for the abolition of slavery: "That spirit of freedom which, at the commencement of this contest, would have gladly sacrificed everything to the attainment of its object, has long since subsided, and every selfish passion has taken its place. It is not the public but private interest which influences the generality of mankind; nor can Americans any longer boast an exception."

Five years later, that spirit had not only subsided in political and social matters regarding the blacks who had fought by the side of, and in place of, the colonists, it was dead. Crispus Attucks, Peter Salem, Salem Poor were forgotten. In the institution of the church, the spirit of freedom and compassion was also dead and forgotten.

In Philadelphia, in November, 1787, the prayers of Absalom Jones, Richard Allen, William White, and Downs Jinnings were halted. The black men, having been removed from the first floor, were snatched from their knees in the gallery of St. George's Methodist Episcopal Church and ordered to their feet. But, like Rosa Parks, the accumulation of indignities became too heavy to be borne an instant longer. Absalom Jones, Richard Allen and their friends, now on their feet, walked out of the church promising that "they would not be plagued further." This was the end of a long chain of insults to those black Christians in Philadelphia.

They had been compelled to sit in the rear seats; they had been sent up to the dusty galleries; they had been required to take communion separate from the rest of the congregation—after the white communicants had been served the bread and wine; they had been proscribed from vocal worship—no amens could come from the black occupied pews; then the final indignity, the physical interference with them as they knelt in prayer in the House of the Lord.

In withdrawing from St. George's Church, Allen said, "We are determined to seek out for ourselves. The Lord being our Helper . . ."

It would be several years before they would be in a position to start the church, but while preparing, Jones and Allen organized the Free African Society in Philadelphia in 1787 for the purpose of looking after the sick and poor, and burying the dead among them. Similar self-help groups started up and down the seaboard.

In Charleston, S. C., in 1790, the Brown Fellowship Society was founded with such a discreet and non-threatening operation that even when other black organizations were broken up by whites, they permitted the Brown Fellowship, composed of mulattoes, to continue.

In 1789, the Constitution of the United States was adopted, counting members of the slave population as three-fifths of a man. And, in Massachusetts, Prince Hall and his colleagues petitioned the General Court of Massachusetts for "the restoration of the enjoyment of freedom which is the natural right of all men. . . . So may the inhabitants of this State, no longer chargeable with the inconsistency of acting themselves the part which they condemn and oppose in others, be prospered in their . . . struggle for liberty."

And then in 1793, with the invention of the cotton gin, the entire agricultural/industrial operation was revolutionized. It was now immensely profitable to grow cotton. Slave labor, almost on the way out, was now a necessity in the new economic balance.

By 1794, the Abolition Society, which had been organized in Philadelphia in 1775 with Benjamin Franklin as president, acted to prohibit the transfer of slaves to a foreign country. But on December 30, 1799, the black community of Philadelphia was stirred to action by the repeated violation of the rights of free black people of Maryland and Delaware who were being kidnapped and sold into slavery in the South. A petition was drawn up in protest.

The petition signed by Absalom Jones and seventy-five other "people of Colour, free men of Philadelphia" charged, "If the Bill of Rights or the Declaration have any validity, we beseech, that as we are men, we may be admitted to partake of the liberties and unalienable rights therein held forth." The House viewed the petition as a "tendency to create disquiet and jealousy."

Who were these petitioners, these men who were determined to "seek for themselves?"—the Absalom Joneses, the Prince Halls, the Richard Allens, and the James Fortens.

James Forten, we have already learned, had been born free in Philadelphia, as had his father and mother. He had studied for a year or so at the Quaker school run by Anthony Benezet before his father died and he had to go to work. He was enterprising and was described by a contemporary as having "an open and honest countenance . . . Strong and of excellent intelligence."[2]

He had served on a privateer during the Revolution, been captured, and was a prisoner on the ship *Jersey* for several months before being released to walk from New Jersey back to Philadelphia.

By 1880, he was already a leader in the Philadelphia community of free colored people. Because he hired some twenty or so black and white men in his sail shop, he had the attitudes of a businessman, and thus he could converse on something of a parity basis with white people. Usually, when Forten spoke, it was interpreted that he was speaking for the group.

Older than Forten by some twenty years, Absalom Jones, quiet and rather introspective, has been described as the mediator type. He was born a slave in Sussex County, Delaware, and separated from his mother, four brothers and a sister while still a young boy. He had been brought to Philadelphia by his owner and put to work in a store where he acted as stock boy and delivery boy. He was ambitious, and so he learned to read from the spelling book he bought with a few pennies and from the New Testament.

The white clerk in the store taught him to count and to write. Later, his owner permitted him to go for a time to a night school where he learned more arithmetic and sharpened up his other skills. He worked overtime, saved his money and married a slave woman whose father's name was John Thomas, but whose own name has not been recorded. He bought his wife's freedom, and several years later bought his own, continuing all the while to work for the same man. He bought his own home and built two rent houses on the same property which provided him extra income.

By the early 1800s, Absalom Jones was nearing the half-century mark. He was a man of property, dignity, and standing in the community. Philadelphia could not forget that he and Richard Allen had buried the dead and cared for the sick in the epidemic that struck Philadelphia in 1793. They had earned their leadership roles.

Richard Allen had been born a slave owned by the Chew family in Philadelphia. His entire family had been sold to a Delaware farmer where he grew up. During the war, he and his brother hauled salt for the troops. At sixteen or seventeen, he was converted to Methodism and started to preach. His sermons were so effective that he converted his master, who then became convinced of the evils of slaveholding with regard to his immortal soul. Allen and his brother were permitted to buy their freedom, which they did with Continental currency.

Richard Allen in Philadelphia preached four or five times a day "to his brethren who had been a long forgotten people." He worked as a master shoemaker, and soon had journeymen and apprentices in his employ.

By the last decade of the eighteenth century, he, too, was a man of property, influence and with a vast constituency among his people.

Now comes the point at which the first division along class lines is made in the black or free colored community.

The Free African Society, which had been created by Absalom Jones and Richard Allen, did not see eye-to-eye with Allen on the need for a separate denomination. Allen was absent from a number of meetings and, with Absalom Jones abstaining from the vote, Allen was "discontinued" as a member in June, 1789. He was reinstated in 1790, but he had already made the emotional separation, and was determined to have an African church.

Finally, in 1791, an election was held by the membership of the Free African Society to determine which doctrine should be accepted, the Methodist or that of the Church of England. Two voted in favor of the Methodist, Richard Allen and Absalom Jones. The majority favored the Church of England. But when offered the pastorate of the Protestant Episcopal church, Allen refused the call, saying, ". . . I was confident that there was no religious sect or denomination [which] would suit the capacity of the colored people as well as the Methodist; for the plain and simple gospel suits best for any people. . . ."

Although Jones would have followed Allen, he could not ignore the wishes of the majority to identify with the Episcopal doctrine. Absalom Jones accepted the offer and became the first rector of the African Episcopal Church of St. Thomas. Ten years later, he became the first black ordained priest in the United States. St. Thomas Episcopal Church, organized in 1791, opened formally on July 17, 1794. James Forten, Sr. was a member of the first vestry. The other vestrymen were closely identified with what was then called "the better people."

Richard Allen then set about organizing Bethel Methodist Episcopal Church, under the leadership of Bishop Asbury who dedicated Bethel in the white denomination. Bethel remained affiliated with this group for several years. Allen's African church was still in the future.

From that early day in our history, there was an invisible line which set black people who attended Episcopal churches, and later Presbyterian and Congregational, a little apart from the masses who attended the Methodist, Baptist and other denominations. Jones had joined that group which believed that to be a part of the larger framework, though subordinate within it, was more important than to be part of a separate institutional framework run by blacks for blacks with all of the decision-making power vested in blacks.

Autonomy

*R*ichard Allen was not alone in his desire for autonomy. While most of the free colored people had been worshipping in separate churches since before the turn of the century, the need for absolute autonomy had become increasingly clear to men like Allen in Philadelphia, James Varick and Peter Williams in New York, and Daniel Coker in Baltimore.

Although the traumatic provocation was absent in New York City, still in 1796, Peter Williams, Sr. and James Varick had led a group of New Yorkers from the John Street Church to form the Mother Zion Church, the first black church in New York. Money for the land and a great deal of the cost of construction was donated by Peter Williams, who had served so long as sexton at the John Street Church but in his later years was financially very well off from the income from property and his tobacco shop. He laid the cornerstone for the Zion Church in 1800. The exodus continued and in 1808 the Gold Street First Baptist Church in New York City lost their black worshippers who left to establish the Abyssinian Baptist Church.

Allen continued to dream of his African church, and the idea of a conference had now crystallized. By April, 1816, having determined that the only viable route was to separate completely from the domination of the white Methodist Episcopal church, he invited representatives of the larger congregations outside the South to Bethel in Philadelphia. There, they set about the business of organizing a denomination along the lines of the Methodist Episcopal discipline but catering to the problems of the free and enslaved black. The men meeting there were Richard Allen, Jacob Tapsico, Clayton Durham, James Champion, and Thomas Webster of Philadelphia; Daniel Coker, Richard Williams, Henry Harden, Stephen Hill, Edward Williamson, and Nicholas Gaillard of Baltimore; Jacob Marsh, Edward Jackson, and William Andrew of Attleborough, Pennsylvania; Peter Spencer of Wilmington, Delaware; and Peter Cuffe of Salem, New Jersey. The New York representation was conspicuously absent.

In addition to Allen, one of the most interesting persons present was Daniel Coker. Born in Maryland, he was the son of a white, English indentured servant mother, and a slave father owned by the same master. Although his mother was not a slave, but indentured, Daniel was still considered to be a slave and treated as one.

Coker, who had learned to read and write as a result of taking his master's young son to school daily, finally escaped and ran away to New York City. He came under the influence of James Varick and the Methodist Episcopals and was ordained a deacon by Bishop Asbury. Upon returning to Baltimore, he worked under an assumed name as a teacher in the school operated by Bethel Church. Baltimore's Bethel had been established at about the same time as the Philadelphia church, and there was a degree of rivalry as to which was the oldest. Coker's freedom was finally purchased from his former master, and he took his rightful place at the head of the Baltimore congregation, leading the delegation of six members to the historic meeting in Philadelphia.

On April 7, 1816, when the first general convention of the new denomination was opened in Philadelphia, the New Yorkers under Varick had voted not to attend. Two days later, on April 9, Coker from Baltimore was elected bishop. Richard Allen, the host minister, was absent from the election and cast no ballot. The following day, for reasons clouded in speculation and gossip, Coker either resigned or declined to accept the office. Some said it was because a vocal group took exception to Coker's non-African appearance. Allen, though also of mixed parentage, was darker in complexion than Coker. Others alluded to a scandal of more recent vintage. Following a closed hearing, Coker removed himself from the convention, and the next day Richard Allen was elected bishop. He served in the post until his death on March 26, 1831.

Following the election of bishop, the convention resolved that ministers coming from another denomination into the African Methodist Episcopal fold should not lose rank or status by making such a move, but would carry the same rank as previously held in the earlier connection. The body of rules under which they would operate were the principles which had been earlier established by the Wesleyan Methodists. In establishing the African Methodist Episcopal church, these men had gone a long way to set up a basic institution to deal with the needs of black people.

Daniel Coker returned to Baltimore, and although he attended the 1818 convention, he no longer played an active role in the leadership of the church. In February, 1820, in the employ of the American Colonization Society, he went as a missionary with the first group of emigrés to Liberia.

Bishop Allen had received into the church at the 1816 meeting an itinerant minister from Charleston, South Carolina named Morris Brown. Brown, a boot and shoe maker, had been born free in Charleston on January 8, 1770, of mulatto parents. Brown was so concerned about the plight of those around him who were in slavery that he used as much of his income as possible to provide assistance to slaves seeking freedom. Some he gave their purchase price; others he gave money to help as they made their way North as fugitives. He finally came to the attention of the authorities, was arrested, charged and convicted of aiding escaping slaves, and sentenced to one year in jail. Following his release from prison, Morris Brown organized his own church, and soon as many as one thousand people were following his leadership. In 1818, he was made an elder. His church was growing, and he presided over congregations throughout the Charleston area. Some said he preached freedom as much as he preached gospel. On the eve of the Vesey revolt in 1822, the Reverend Morris Brown counted three thousand souls in his faithful flock.

On August 11, 1820, the Zionites, as the New York group was called, met to determine whether they should reunite with the white Methodist Episcopalians, or join the Allenites, as the larger black group was known. The decision was to take steps to establish a firm church organization of their own, and under the leadership of James Varick, Christopher Rush and others, the African Methodist Episcopal Zion church was organized in 1821, electing James Varick the first bishop in 1822. Rush was elected bishop, succeeding Varick, who died in 1827.

On another level of organization, and with its own religious overtones, the development of freemasonry took place in the centers of free black population. This development was concurrent with the self-help and church movements, and the pioneer was Prince Hall.

Six weeks before Lexington and Concord, March 6, 1775, while the British were stationed in Boston, Prince Hall and fourteen other free blacks applied for and were instituted a lodge by members of a British Army lodge of Free and Accepted Masons. The qualified permit which these black men were given enabled them to meet as a lodge. The actual charter did not come from England until after the war had ended.

Meanwhile, the provisional lodge survived, the members celebrating the traditional feast of St. John with a parade and other observations, and "burying our dead in manner and form," according to a letter Prince Hall addressed to the English lodge. In the spring of 1787, African Lodge #1, which had been the name of the young lodge, upon receipt of the charter, was reorganized as Lodge #459. Prince Hall was elected Grand Master; Boston Smith, Senior Warden; and Thomas Sanderson, Junior Warden.

By June of 1797, Absalom Jones, Richard Allen, and James Forten had laid the groundwork and were ready to bring the discipline of Masonry to their Philadelphia brothers. Accordingly, Prince Hall came down from Boston to install Absalom Jones as Worshipful Master and Richard Allen as treasurer of the new lodge. On the same trip, nine Masons who had been members of Boston's African lodge were instituted under the name of Hiram Lodge #4 at Providence, Rhode Island, with a warrant dated June 25, 1797. At the beginning of the nineteenth century, three Masonic lodges were active in the United States among the free colored population.

In 1808, to commemorate the tenth anniversary of the Philadelphia lodge's formation, a special service was held at St. Thomas Protestant Episcopal Church honoring the rector and the Worshipful Master, Absalom Jones. His old friend, Reverend Richard Allen, delivered the sermon, and a Liverpool pitcher, bearing the silhouette of Jones and the insignia of the Masonic order, was created to mark the occasion.

Prince Hall was not in Philadelphia for the celebration. He had died on December 7, 1807 in Boston at the age of seventy-two. Reports differ on his birth. According to some authorities, he was born in Bridgetown, Barbados, the son of a free colored woman and a Britisher named Thomas Prince Hall. He is said to have migrated to the United States around 1765. Other sources indicate that, while he may have been born in the West Indies, he was in Boston and a slave in the household of William Hall in the 1740s. He joined the Congregational church on School Street and in 1762 married a slave woman named Sarah Ritchie. In the spring of 1770, shortly after the Boston Massacre and the death of Crispus Attucks, Hall was given his freedom. With his first wife now dead, he married Flora Gibbs of

Gloucester. Whether he actually participated in the war is not documented, but as a skilled leather worker, he did supply leather drumheads to Colonel Crafts of the Boston Regiment of Artillery in 1777, so the possibility of his having been in combat at the same time is remote.

His son, Primus Hall, was, however, active in several campaigns. He enlisted in January, 1776 in Captain John Butler's company and later was a servant to Colonel Timothy Pickering, Commissary General of the Army. After the war, he became a reputable citizen of Boston where he was in the coal boiler business, and accumulated real estate and personal property sufficient to place him in the class of leading citizens. He was married on October 29, 1817 to Anna Clark of Boston, and, by a special act of Congress, was pensioned on June 28, 1838. He died in 1855.

There is no indication that he took the same leadership role in the activities of the Masons as his father. On July 24, 1808, representatives from the Providence, Philadelphia, and Boston lodges met in Boston and elected Nero Prince, who had served as Deputy Grand Master under Prince Hall, as Grand Master. At the same time, the name of the lodge was changed to Prince Hall Grand Lodge in honor of its first Grand Master. George Middleton served as Grand Master from 1808 until 1811, and Barzillai Lew's son, Peter Lew, was the Grand Master from 1811 to 1817. It was under Lew's leadership that the New York lodge was established in 1812 and that the Laurel Lodge #2 and the Phoenix Lodge #3 were established in Philadelphia.

On December 27, 1815, St. John's Day, a convention of three Pennsylvania lodges of Master Masons was held at the Masonic Hall on Lombard Street, and the Grand Lodge of Pennsylvania was constituted. The Grand officers included Reverend Absalom Jones, Grand Master; Richard Parker, Deputy Grand Master; Thomas Depree, Senior Grand Warden; Prim Clover, Junior Grand Warden; and Peter Richmond, Grand Secretary.

The original warrants were surrendered to the Mother Lodge in Massachusetts, and the First African Independent Grand Lodge of Free and Accepted Masons of North America for the State of Pennsylvania was established. This was the second Grand Lodge in the United States to be a direct descendant of Prince Hall's original group.

The Mulatto Infusion

*I*n this multi-faceted account of Black Society, one element cannot be overlooked, and that is the effect of the Haitian revolution (1790-1803) and the subsequent immigration of mulatto refugees to seaboard communities.

The mulatto class had a significantly different background in Santo Domingo, as Haiti was known before independence, than the same class in the United States. In the 17th and 18th centuries, there was little racial prejudice among the French and Spanish people. During the early days of the island's history, the laws of the island were the same for the white *engagés,* the indentured servants, as they were for the Negroes. The Negro Code of 1685 authorized marriage between white men and black women who had children, the ceremony freeing the women and children. The Code gave free mulattoes and free blacks equal rights with the whites. Not until 1768 was marriage between the whites and blacks forbidden by law. Many of this group, which constituted the colored aristocracy, looked down upon the *petite blancs,* the white working class. The colored aristocracy despised them for their poverty.

As a group, the mulattoes were, for the most part, both highly literate and more than reasonably prosperous. They could own and inherit property, bear arms, exercise any profession, and marry whomever they pleased. They amassed property, were conservative to the point of frugality, and by 1776, were said to have owned one-third of the land and the slaves.

This was a group that working-class whites feared almost as much as the slave group. For while they feared the slave, they hated the mulattoes with a passion. By 1789, laws had been passed barring the mulatto from entering the priesthood, practicing medicine, pharmacy, law or becoming an officer in the military. He could no longer hold public office or wear a sword. Further, he was denied the use of the same surnames as white families. Intermarriage was forbidden, dress codes were established and travel to France was forbidden. On reaching their majority, mulattoes were compelled to join the *maréchaussér,* a police organization for arresting fugitive blacks, capturing dangerous blacks, and fighting the *maroons,* those escaped slaves who had taken to the mountains and become fierce warriors. After three years' service in this organization, they were then forced to join the local militia, forced to provide their own weapons and ammunition, and without pay or allowance, serve at the discretion of the white commanding officer. All of these restrictions and harassment only served to stimulate the mulattoes to a greater acquisition of real property and wealth, since this right had not been limited.

The mulattoes organized a revolt following the defeat of their claims to the Rights of Man at the French National Assembly, where they had offered the constituent assembly six million francs as security for the national debt. It was the refusal of the mulatto to be downgraded to the condition of the blacks that ultimately set the stage for Haitian independence. However, in the process, the mulatto as well as the white was warred upon by the aroused slaves, who were determined to be their own masters and to look up to no man, mulatto or white.

The United States looked uneasily at the successful revolt of slaves against their masters and the Absalom Jones petition to the legislature praying for immediate abolition of slavery. The petition by the Absalom Jones group to Congress praying for prospective emancipation for all Negroes, which was presented by Congressman Waln, created such an uproar in the House of Representatives that it was charged that the entire petition had been instigated by the Haitian revolutionaries. The persons who had signed it were censured for their participation in drawing up the document.[1]

Toussaint L'Ouverture, at the head of the black army, outwitted the French who had been sent out to save the colony by accepting their protection against Spain and England and declaring Haiti an independent nation. And in the War of the Castes (1800–1802), the civil war between the blacks and mulattoes, the United States's supplies and equipment helped Toussaint defeat Rigaud, the leader of the mulattoes.

Many of the mulattoes, fearing for their lives, fled Haiti and sought sanctuary in the other colonial islands of the West Indies, such as Cuba, Guadaloupe and Martinique. However, they were forced from these islands because of the fear that Napoleon would reinstitute slavery, which had been abolished during the French Revolution and the increased hostility between France and Spain. The United States was safer, so they came, these *gens de colour,* to all of the cities along the seaboard but particularly to those in the "free" states. They came primarily to New York City, Philadelphia and New Orleans where there was a population sophisticated enough to appreciate their skills as hairdressers, barbers, copiers of elegant French designed gowns, and masters of the *haute cuisine.* Many came bringing some wealth; others brought whatever they could salvage; a few brought the clothes on their backs; but all brought a great deal in the way of presence and style. These were no ordinary colored people, and they knew it.

In Philadelphia, one of these immigrants was Peter Augustin, who started a catering business that made Philadelphia catering famous all over the country. It was the Augustin establishment that set the standards that were emulated by those who entered the field afterward, such as the Prossers, the Joneses, the Dorseys, and the Mintons. But Augustin was the one who made it "in" to be served by "caterers of color." The best families of the city and the most distinguished foreign guests were handled by the Augustins. He bought out the Robert Bogle catering business which had been established in the early 1800s. Bogle, a free black, is credited with creating the industry. Augustin and his successors refined it.

St. John Appo, the confectioner, was at 6th and Spruce Streets in 1804. His French wife had an original recipe for ice cream which was the *specialité de maison.* Their sons, William and Joseph Appo, played in Frank Johnson's band and in the orchestra of the Walnut Street Theatre as early as 1824. Frank Johnson's band was internationally known and played a command performance for Queen Victoria at Windsor Castle in 1838. Ann Appo, also a musician, was organist for St. Thomas Episcopal Church, the first black church in the United States to have a pipe organ. John Francis Cook, II married Helen Elizabeth Appo, the daughter of William and Elizabeth Brady Appo. Their son, John Francis, III, married Elizabeth Rebecca Abele, a descendant of the Abele family which, along with the Baptistes, the Cuyjets, the Montiers, the Dutrieuilles, the Dutertes, and the Le Counts, were held in very high esteem. Incidentally, John F. Cook, I's second wife was Jane Le Count, by whom he had one son, Samuel Le Count Cook.

Members of another distinguished black family with French connections are the Fishers: Orpheus, Leon, and George II. They are the descendants of

Photographs

"I, young in life . . . was snatch'd from Afric's fancy'd happy seat," wrote slave poet Phillis Wheatley in 1772.

20

PHILLIS WHEATLEY, NEGRO SERVANT to Mr. JOHN WHEATLEY, of BOSTON.

A hero of the Boston Massacre, Crispus Attucks was the first person shot by the British soldiers on March 5, 1770.

21

*Philadelphia was a major
center for blacks during Revolutionary
War. Market (above) was site for selling produce
and slaves. Continental currency (top, r.) was used to
buy freedom by such slaves as Richard Allen and Absalom Jones.
James Forten as a youth was familiar with the Arch Street Ferry (r.).*

22

23

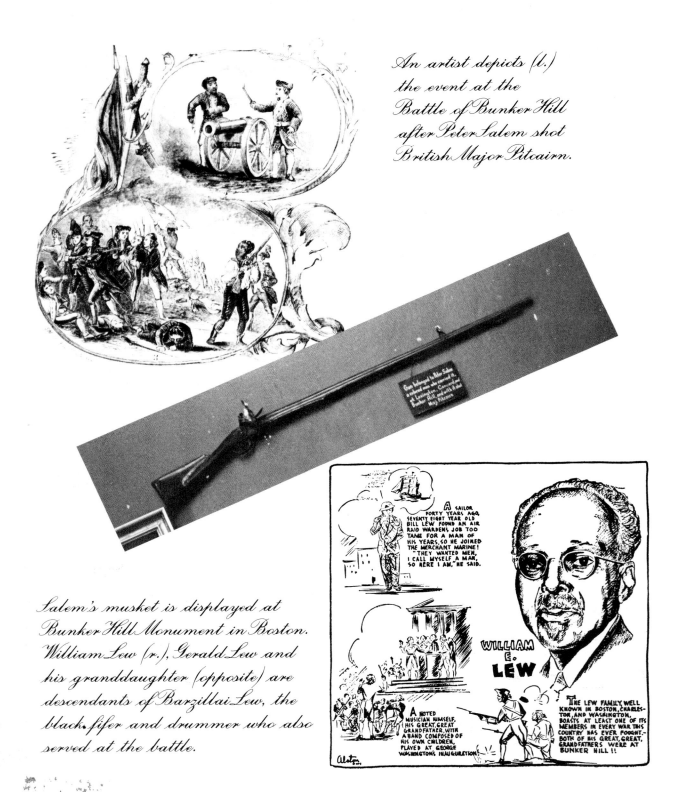

An artist depicts (l.) the event at the Battle of Bunker Hill after Peter Salem shot British Major Pitcairn.

Salem's musket is displayed at Bunker Hill Monument in Boston. William Lew (r.), Gerald Lew and his granddaughter (opposite) are descendants of Barzillai Lew, the black fifer and drummer who also served at the battle.

24

A SAILOR FORTY YEARS AGO, SEVENTY EIGHT YEAR OLD BILL LEW FOUND AN AIR RAID WARDENS JOB TOO TAME FOR A MAN OF HIS YEARS, SO HE JOINED THE MERCHANT MARINE! "THEY WANTED MEN, I CALL MYSELF A MAN, SO HERE I AM," HE SAID.

WILLIAM E. LEW

A NOTED MUSICIAN HIMSELF, HIS GREAT GREAT GRANDFATHER, WITH A BAND COMPOSED OF HIS OWN CHILDREN, PLAYED AT GEORGE WASHINGTON'S INAUGURATION

THE LEW FAMILY, WELL KNOWN IN BOSTON, CHARLESTON, AND WASHINGTON, BOASTS AT LEAST ONE OF ITS MEMBERS IN EVERY WAR THIS COUNTRY HAS EVER FOUGHT. BOTH OF HIS GREAT, GREAT, GRANDFATHERS WERE AT BUNKER HILL!!

25

Prince Hall (above), the first black Mason, organized the African lodge in 1787. The Grand Masters (opposite) visit gravesite of Prince Hall in Boston during 1950 conference. Group of prominent Masons (below opposite) includes Supreme Court Justice Thurgood Marshall (third from left).

27

St. Thomas P. E. Church, Phila.

The first rector of the African Episcopal Church of St. Thomas, Absalom Jones, created the Free African Society with Richard Allen. Jones's silhouette on the Liverpool pitcher (l.) was created in 1808 to mark the commemoration of the tenth anniversary of the formation of the first black Philadelphia lodge of Masons.

29

Richard Allen, outraged by the abuse of blacks in white churches, co-founded the Free African Society, and later realized his dream of the Bethel African Methodist Episcopal Church in Philadelphia. Daniel Coker (r.) eventually broke with the church and joined the first group of emigres to Liberia.

31

The internationally
famous Fraunces's Tavern
(above) was located in New
York where James Varick became the first bishop of the
African Methodist Episcopal
Zion church. Peter Williams, Sr.
was one of the church's founders.

P. Williams, Sr.   J. Varick

Registre contenant Les Proclamation, Ordonnance & Les Adresse du Général Toussaint L'ouverture Depuis Le 18 Germinal An 9 jusqu'au ...

New York City provided refuge for many Haitian mulattoes after L'Ouverture's victory in Haiti. Many blacks withdrew from New York's John Street Church (below) to form the A.M.E. Zion church of which Christopher Rush was an organizer. Peter Williams, Jr. was the first ordained priest in the Protestant Episcopal church in New York.

C. Rush   P. Williams, Jr.

George Albert Fisher, a mulatto of Irish and Negro descent who settled in Lincoln, Pennsylvania during the nineteenth century. He married the beautiful Pauline Conklin who was herself a blood relative of Josephine Beauharnais, Empress of France and the wife of Napoleon Bonaparte. The Conklins and Empress Josephine came from the French West Indian island of Martinique.

Opheus Fisher, the architect, is married to the famed Marian Anderson; his brother Leon is a wealthy Texas rancher; and George, II is a member of the Protestant Episcopal clergy.

Another was Edward de Roland, the musician and composer who also played with Johnson's Band and was bugler for the mounted troops that preceded the local parades. De Roland (later called Edward D. Roland) had been born in Haiti in 1804 and brought to Philadelphia by his parents who had been forced to leave as a result of the insurrection. They had spent some time in Martinique before coming to Philadelphia. He was educated at the Quaker school in Willings Alley, which Forten had also attended and which had been founded by Anthony Benezet. His natural talent for music dominated his entire life, and he played and taught piano, organ, violin, guitar, cello, double bass, as well as every wind instrument, although his chosen instrument was the violin. In the command performance at Windsor Castle, Roland not only played as a part of the group but also had a solo part.

He was married very late in life to Eugenie Augusta de Neully, who had been born and raised in St. Croix in the then Danish West Indies. She married and lived on St. Croix in the great House of the Diamond-Ruby Plantation. Her first husband was a member of the prominent Farrelly family. Widowed and with two daughters, Mme. Farrelly came to Philadelphia in 1867 and married Edward de Roland in 1872. They were the parents of two children—a son and a daughter. Roland died in 1894 at the age of ninety. His widow lived on until 1924. Her daughter, Henrietta R. Farrelly, and their daughter, Marian E. Roland, both became supervising school principals in Philadelphia. Miss Farrelly was the first woman of her race to become a supervising principal in the Philadelphia school system when she received her certificate in 1897. She died in 1946. Their son, Edward J. Roland, born in 1876, was married to Lelia N. Keene, who died five years after their wedding in 1900. Their daughter, Marian, was married to Russell F. Minton in 1927. He was a grandson of Henry Minton, the caterer.

In New York City, where a West Indian colony had earlier gained a foothold, Samuel Fraunces's Tavern had become internationally famous as General George Washington's choice for his farewell to his officers. Here the refugees were welcomed. Samuel Fraunces had presided over the first presidential mansion as steward after the election of George Washington as president. Fraunces, a black from the French West Indies, had purchased the tavern in 1762 for two thousand pounds. It became the gathering-place for the mercantile interests of New York City, and during the Revolution, he fed and housed many of the American troops. Fraunces's daughter, Phoebe, was Washington's housekeeper during the period he was stationed in New York City. When Fraunces died in 1795, his will revealed that the United States government was still in his debt for services rendered during the Revolution.

Theodore Duplessis became famous for his superlative ice cream, while Pierre Toussaint, a hairdresser of Chapel Street, was noted for the quality of his workmanship and for the piety of his devotion to the Catholic Church. One of the first communicants at St. Peter's Catholic Church, Toussaint could generally be found in pew #25 which he owned.

In one period of sixty days between May and July of 1809, 34 vessels from Cuba landed in the Port of New Orleans with 5,800 refugees, 4,000 of whom were free coloreds and blacks. Other ships from Guadaloupe and neighboring islands brought more, until more than 10,000 people had been transplanted to the American continent. Many of these "cordon bleus," by the outbreak of the Civil War, constituted a major force in the free colored community, owning some $15 million worth of taxable property and having established a reputation for philanthropy, education, refinement and culture.

Many others, such as Jean Baptiste Savary who fled from Santo Domingo, took the leadership in forming the Battalion of Free Men of Color to fight for their new flag in the War of 1812. Quite a few of the prominent Creole families trace their lineage back to these heroes, among them Dolliole, Forneret, Populus, Trevigne and Roudenez. Paul Trevigne, the co-editor of the *New Orleans Tribune,* the French-English newspaper of the Reconstruction period, was the son of a veteran of the Battle of New Orleans.

The Federal City

Boston, Philadelphia, New York, and Baltimore were all old cities when Washington, D. C. came into being. Charleston, Wilmington, Richmond, and New Orleans all had their free colored communities and their old established families before the act of Congress authorized the new Federal City.

Benjamin Banneker was fifty-nine years old when Major Ellicott informed him that the commission had approved naming him as assistant on the planning project for the new Federal City. The year was 1790, and the astronomer-mathematician was no doubt honored to receive a commission from President George Washington to survey the ten-mile area on the banks of the Potomac which had been designated as the site. The distinguished French city planner, Major Pierre Charles L'Enfant, had been appointed by Thomas Jefferson to prepare drawings of the site where the buildings and major arteries were to be located. Little did Banneker know that L'Enfant would become angered midway in the project, pack his bags, and return to France leaving the Americans high and dry. Nor did he imagine that he would be called upon to recreate from memory the master plan which L'Enfant had been careful to keep secret from the others on the project.

By 1800, the city was a reality and had been named Washington in honor of the nation's first president, George Washington. Of the 4,024 black or mulatto persons in the city, only 783 were free; the rest were in slavery. But those slaves had the hope that they would not be slaves forever. Many of those free had once been slaves, but had been able to "buy their time."[1]

Letitia Woods Brown has reasoned that, "One reason for the hope that existed in the District of Columbia may have been the fact that the District's population was faced more often with the contradiction in terms of reality and goals. Since service for life made the person a slave, by commuting life service to service for a term, the slaveowners escaped completely the onus and moral responsibility for ownership of property in human flesh. The relationship between master and slave became an arrangement for service, which left room for God-given, natural rights in the slave. Whatever deprivation of rights occurred during the period of service was temporary and could be compensated for by the slave's eventual freedom to enjoy his natural liberty."[2]

In any event, the president occupying the White House in the new city at the turn of the century was a widower, Thomas Jefferson. The gossips held that, although he was without a legal wife, the mistress of the Monticello plantation was Sallie Hemmings, a mulatto slave reputed to be the half-sister of Jefferson's deceased wife. His political enemies made capital out of his relationship with the lovely young woman who had accompanied his youngest daughter to Paris during the period that he served as ambassador to France, returning pregnant with their first child. Thomas Callender, one of Jefferson's critics, wrote in the *Richmond Recorder* in 1802:

> "By this wench Sallie, our President has had several children. There is not an individual in the neighborhood of Charlottesville who does not believe the story, and not a few who know it. The African Violet is said to officiate as housekeeper at Monticello."[3]

But Jefferson kept his own counsel in the bitter presidential campaign, neither affirming nor denying his relationship with the woman who came to be known as "Black Sal," even though her skin was creamy white and her hair lustrous and dark. Two of their older children were said to have found refuge in Washington where, with the transient population, they took new identities and their mixed racial heritage became lost.

Sallie Hemmings's other children did not lose their racial identity, and neither did the black son of Charles Carroll of Carrollton, William Becraft. Becraft maintained the mementoes of the Carroll family for his lifetime in his Georgetown residence. He was born at Carrollton, while his mother, a free woman of color, worked as housekeeper on the vast Maryland estate of the signer of the Declaration of Independence. He came to Georgetown as a young man of eighteen, and secured a position as steward at the Union Hotel, where he worked all of his life, ending his career as chief steward when he was in his sixty-fifth year. His daughter, Marie Becraft, born in 1805, was so well educated that by the time she was fifteen years of age, she was able to open a school for girls in Georgetown, which she operated until she was twenty-two. At that time, fearing that her beauty would lead her to a tragic end, she joined the convent of Baltimore of the Oblate Sisters of Providence. Here, under the name of Sister Aloyons, she worked for the next few years, dying at the untimely age of twenty-eight years in 1833.

The Costin family also had connections, theirs to Mount Vernon. William Costin, the father, was the son of Ann Dandridge, the half-sister of Martha Washington. Ann and Martha Dandridge grew up on the same plantation. Ann, after giving birth to a son fathered by a white Virginian, married a Mount Vernon slave named William Costin whose name she gave her infant son. In 1800, young Costin married his cousin, Philadelphia Judge, at Mount Vernon where they both had been born in 1780. Philadelphia had been given to Eliza Parke Custis Law after her grandmother Martha Dandridge Custis Washington's death, but William, who had been considered free because of his mother's Indian blood, was permitted to bring his wife to Washington where she was manumitted. Their seven children, five daughters and two sons, were born free. The Costins started a school for colored children on Capitol Hill.

But the very first school in Washington for colored children was started in 1807 by three men who had been slaves: George F. Bell (Beall), Nicholas Franklin, and Moses Liverpool. They hired a white man named Lowe to teach their children. Bell (Beall) had been a slave in the home of Anthony Addison, "who lived a few rods beyond Eastern Boundary, D. C."[4] His wife was Sophia Browning, who was in the service of the Bell family and saved four hundred dollars from the money she earned truck gardening to purchase her husband's freedom. He had in turn purchased her from Mrs. Pratt before 1909.

Sophia Browning Bell was one of the three Browning girls held in slavery on the plantation of Mrs. Rachel Bell Pratt. The other two girls were Alethia and Laurena. Alethia Browning was perhaps one of the most unusual women of her time. A slave on the Pratt plantation, she had saved enough to buy her own freedom by 1810, and by 1826, she had enough to purchase the freedom of her older sister, Laurena Cook, and five of Laurena's children, four boys and a girl. One of the boys was John Francis

Cook, the distinguished educator and minister. In 1828, Alethia purchased
the freedom of the rest of the Cook family: Hannah Ferguson and her four
children; Annette and her one child; and George and Daniel Cook. Alto-
gether, she was responsible for the freedom of her sister, ten children, and
seven grandchildren—a total of eighteen persons, not counting herself. She
paid $800 for her sister and approximately $300 for each child.[5]

At about the same time that the Brownings, Bells, Cooks, and Costins
were getting established in the new city of Washington, two other families
were sinking their roots on the other side of the Potomac from their native
Virginia. They were the Syphax and Wormley families.

Peter Leigh Wormley and his wife Mary came to Washington in 1814
from the Virginia plantation where they had been born and where they had
lived "as free people." According to legend, Peter, or Pere as he was sometimes called, was very dark-skinned with straight black hair. He was sometimes referred to as a Madagascan. Mary Wormley, his wife, was very fair
in skin color with fine, Caucasian features. They were the parents of five
children; William, Mary, Betsey, Andrew, and James. Peter started operating a livery stable with his eldest son, William, working with him as
a hacker.

The Syphax family of Washington and Alexandria had its beginning
in Alexandria on the Custis estate. It all began when the grandson of Martha
Custis Washington, George Parke Custis, fell in love with his grandmother's
slave maid, Arianna Carter. Arianna, herself a product of miscegenation
and the slave system, in time became the mother of Maria. George Washington Parke Custis and his sister Nelly had lived as children with George
and Martha Custis Washington at Mount Vernon, but when they died, the
Mount Vernon estate went to Washington's brother and his descendants.
George Washington Parke Custis and his family then returned to the estate which had been purchased originally by his father, John Parke Custis,
in 1778.

To one familiar with the approach to Washington National Airport,
the Custis-Lee mansion sits on the crest of the hill overlooking the graves of
the Kennedy brothers and within a stone's throw of Arlington National
Cemetery, once a part of the huge 1,100-acre estate. In 1857, the estate
went to the grandson of Custis, William Henry Fitzhugh Lee, the second

son of General Robert E. Lee. Hence, the property is commonly called Custis-Lee.

The great house was begun about 1802, but not completed until after the War of 1812. During that time, George Washington Parke Custis was adding to the substantial wealth which he had inherited by raising imported merino sheep. It was in the parlor of the great house that Charles Syphax, who worked in the dining room of the Custis home, and Maria Carter were married by an Episcopal minister. Their son, William, was born on April 4, 1825 on the Arlington estate in what was known as the Syphax quarters. Maria was freed with her first two children, Elinor and William, in 1826. Charles Syphax remained technically a slave until the death of Custis in 1855, although he had freedom to come and go at will. The laws of Virginia would have forced him as a free man to remain in D. C. or in Virginia. At the death of Custis, Maria Syphax received the seventeen acres of land which had been a word-of-mouth wedding gift over a quarter of a century before.

Around 1825, Charles Syphax, William Wormley, and John F. Cook paid one hundred dollars apiece to purchase a piece of land out in the country in which to bury the "free" persons of color. It was the beginning of the Harmony Society—a "society" because meetings for purposes neither religious nor fraternal were forbidden by the common council.

The Harmony Society was just one of the projects for which the Syphax, Wormley, and Cook families were to work together during the years ahead in Washington, D. C.

Colonization

For many slaves, hope for a reasonable solution had been abandoned, and the failure of the petitioners only made it more feasible to take drastic steps.

On August 30, 1800 in Henrico County, Virginia, a massive plan for insurrection by Gabriel, a slave on the Prosser estate, came within a hair's breadth of success. However, the day of the scheduled revolt, a furious storm swept away bridges, submerged roads, and made it impossible for the members of Gabriel's operation to get to their appointed place. Gabriel postponed the revolt, and the news of it leaked out to the plantation owners and slaveholders. Martial law was proclaimed, and every black who looked a white man in the eye was arrested on suspicion. Arrested one day, they were hanged the next in public view as a lesson to any other who may have gotten ideas about freedom and liberty.

One slave on his way to the gallows, when asked what he had to say, replied:

> "I have nothing more to offer than what General Washington would have had to offer had he been taken by the British officers and put to trial by them. I have ventured my life in endeavoring to obtain the liberty of my countrymen, and am a willing sacrifice to their cause, and I beg . . . that I may be immediately led to execution. I know that you have predetermined to shed my blood, why then all this mockery of a trial?"[1]

Gabriel was soon captured, tried, convicted, and on October 7, 1800 was hanged. He did not confess nor implicate any of his confederates who numbered from one to ten thousand slaves, depending upon the persuasion of the estimator. A brief era of seeming tranquility had ended.

The Virginia legislature in its next session took up the proposal to deport all slaves. After 1800, whites' attitudes toward blacks hardened perceptibly, and increased methods of repression against free Negroes and slaves caused many families who had lived in relative comfort, security, and hope for a better world to reconsider what their options might be.

Colonization was one of these, and Paul Cuffe, master mariner, merchant, ship builder, and philanthropist, was perhaps the first black colonizer.

Cuffe had been born free in 1759 on the island of Cuttyhunk, off the New Bedford coast. His mother was an Indian woman named Ruth Moses. His father, Cuffe Slocum, had purchased his freedom, married Ruth, acquired a farm on Martha's Vineyard, and raised a family of ten children. The children discarded the slave name Slocum two years after the Declaration of Independence and took Cuffe as their family name. At sixteen, Paul went to sea. Like James Forten, he spent three months as a prisoner of the British, although he was held on the mainland. He and his brother John later went to jail on the issue of equal rights for equal taxes.

In 1784, Cuffe married Alice Pequit, a Wanpanoag Indian, like his mother. He and his brother-in-law, Michael Wainer, also an experienced seaman, went into partnership in the fishing industry.

As Cuffe prospered and expanded, he became more community-minded, building a schoolhouse in Westport "on his own land and with his own money" and donating it "freely . . . to the use of the public."[2] In 1808, he joined the Friends. However, what he considered to be the unfulfilled concept of the revolution continued to disturb him.

He finally arrived at the conclusion that the only hope for black people in the Americas was to go back to Africa and build a new civilization. If whites refused to extend equality to blacks who had fought with them for the nation's freedom, then perhaps the Negro should seek to build a better life in the land that had been his ancestral home. It did not occur to Cuffe then that his idea would be adopted by the very people he disliked most— the slaveholders—and used to weed out the potential leadership in the free black community.

Between 1810 and 1815, he made three voyages. In 1815, he outfitted his ship and paid the expenses of some thirty out of a total of thirty-eight families, delivering them to Sierre Leone.

It is possible that Cuffe may have had second thoughts about the wisdom of the colonization plan after his second voyage to Sierre Leone. He, himself, had decided against immigration to Africa and wrote to a friend in 1812, "Paul Cuffe doth not at present go to Africa . . . but shall send such characters as confidence may be placed in. At present, it is thought that I may be as serviceable toward the promotion of the colony, as though I was to removed. However, as my wife is *not* willing to go, I do not feel at liberty to urge, but feel in duty bound to exert myself to the uttermost of my ability for the good cause of Africa."[3] He made one final trip to Africa in 1815, unaware that his colonization dream would be twisted out of context by the American Colonization Society whose chief sponsors, Henry Clay and Andrew Jackson, sought advice which Cuffe gave freely. His eyes were opened to their real motivation only when he received a letter from his friend, James Forten, which told him that,

> "The people of colour here was [sic] very much fritened [sic] at first. They were afrade [sic] that all the free people would be compelled to go, particularly in the Southern states. . . . Three thousand at least attended [the meeting] at Rev. R. Allen's church the other evening, [and] there was not one sole [sic] that was in favor of going to Africa. They think the slaveholders want to get rid of them so as to make their property more secure."[4]

Cuffe's death in October, 1817 left the question moot, but he was no longer available to be used by the Colonization Society.

Not surprisingly, the independent moves on the part of the free blacks, coupled with the revolutionary spirit that had been manifest in the defeat of France in the Haitian rebellion, created a sense of suspicion and alarm on the part of the white slave owners and industrial leaders.

The American Colonization Society was an organized response. They espoused the idea that Negroes could not assimilate with whites. They had no future in the country except as slaves. For those no longer slaves, the only solution was to have them carried back to Africa. Unstated, but implicit, was the idea that it would relieve the country of a class of people who, by their successful example, were a constant menace to the slave system. Thus, by ridding the slaves of a bad example—the free Negro—

and also diverting the attention of the North from abolition of slavery to the colonization of free blacks, the institution of slavery in the South would be more secure.

The idea of moving Negroes to some place outside the South, whether in or out of the country, was not new to the Virginia legislature. Thomas Jefferson, in his privately printed "Notes on Virginia" (1781), had suggested that the Northwest Territory (Ohio) might be a good place to set aside as a Negro colony. His suggestion was never acted upon, but following the Gabriel insurrection of 1800, the idea got renewed currency. The Virginia discussion had been held in secret. The resolution which came from that meeting requested that Governor McPherson correspond with President Monroe regarding the feasibility of purchasing land outside the limits of the then existing United States where persons who had fallen out of favor might be sent.

The primary purpose of this was to get rid of those blacks who might be considered to be "troublemakers." For many whites, the answer was simple: Colonization or Slavery.

On January 1, 1817, the American Society for Colonizing the Free People of Color of the United States met. The meeting was directed at the advantages to be gained by moving free blacks from the country. The membership was composed of Bushrod Washington, a Southerner, as president; twelve of the seventeen vice-presidents were Southerners, including Andrew Jackson; and all of the twelve managers were slaveholders.

The free black community immediately responded with almost universal distaste against the colonization plan, and called a meeting of free blacks in Philadelphia on January 7, 1817 at which James Forten presided.

The group met at Bethel Church. The resolutions which were adopted without a dissenting vote indicated that, though the African-Americans realized that they were in a "temporary" state of disfranchisement, America was their native land, and they had never wavered in their loyalty. Said Forten, "Here we were born and here we intend to die." And although they would never cease to work to remedy the injustices, Forten stated: ". . . [we] would never separate ourselves voluntarily from the slave population of this country; they are our brethren by the ties of consanguinity, of suffering and of wrong; and we feel that there is more virtue in suffering privations with them, than fancied advantages for a season."[5]

This resolution and the other were signed by Rev. Absalom Jones, Rev. Richard Allen, James Forten, Robert Douglass, Francis Perkins, Rev. John Gloucester, Robert Gordon, James Johnson, Quamoney Clarkson, John Summersett, Randall Shepherd, and Russell Parrott.

On January 14, 1817, the Honorable John Randolph of Roanoke presented a memorial from the American Colonization Society to the House of Representatives calling attention to the "low and hopeless condition" of the free Negroes and urging Congress to establish a colony in Africa in the interests of "moral justice" and "political foresight."

The issue of colonization was to be a divisive chord running through the community of free colored people until the eve of the Civil War.

James Forten had taken the leadership at the mass meeting at Reverend Allen's Bethel Church to protest the American Colonization Society's plans. In the absence of the venerable Absalom Jones, who was in declining health at the time of the meeting, Forten's chairmanship clearly indicates that he had moved in to fill the void left by Jones's absence and to insure the participation of the St. Thomas Episcopalians.

With the death of Absalom Jones on February 13, 1818, the second decade of the nineteenth century began to draw to a close. In Congress, the weary debate over the entrance of Missouri into statehood dragged on, deadlocked over the issue of slavery and its extension into territory which had been a part of the Louisiana Purchase. When an agreement was finally reached, it was really satisfactory to almost no one since it provided for the admission of Maine as a free state and Missouri as a slave state, prohibiting the extension of slavery north of a line west from Missouri's southern boundary of 36 degrees and 30 minutes. On August 10, 1821, Missouri became the twenty-first state of the United States, and the union was less united than ever before.

Intellectual Insurrectionist

Denmark Vesey, free black of Charleston, South Carolina, has been referred to as the first of the "intellectual insurrectionists."

It was in the atmosphere of colonization that the Vesey "business" occurred, threatening even more the precarious position of free blacks in the United States.

Until 1800, Vesey was the personal attendant to a sea captain on a ship operating between the Virgin Islands and Santo Domingo (Haiti). Winning a lottery, Vesey purchased his freedom from the captain whose name he had taken, and settled in Charleston, South Carolina. He worked as a carpenter, and developed a substantial following among blacks who respected his superior intelligence and ability and whites who respected his superior workmanship. Fluent in French and English and deeply philosophical, Vesey was greatly concerned about the organization of the American Colonization Society, and the implications of the Missouri Compromise for the extension of slavery were not lost upon him.

In 1822, Vesey settled on a plan that would result in the "liberation" of all blacks in the Charleston area and the annihilation of all whites.

Using the cell as a unit of organization (long before Karl Marx and Engels or Lenin developed the idea for the socialists), Vesey recruited his people and made his assignments. Only he and two trusted lieutenants, Peter Poyas and Mingo Harth, knew the entire scope of the plan and all of the details. The date was set for July 16, 1822. Arsenals, guardhouses, powder magazines, and naval stores were all to be captured.

Again, as in the case of Gabriel, Vesey was betrayed by an informant. Along with him, thirty-five others were executed. Forty-three suspected participants were banished from the United States, and the situation for free blacks became even more oppressive. But now, the great fear of white people had been realized—that a literate and intelligent free black would organize the slave population in a revolt.

Now, more than ever, free blacks were viewed as the crux of the problem. Many states required the prompt deportation of newly freed blacks, and in areas where there had been free colored settlements for generations, new restrictions were placed upon their mobility, and in some cases, they were forbidden to cross county lines.

Morris Brown, the man who was to succeed Richard Allen as AME bishop, barely escaped Charleston with his life. A white friend, General James Hamilton, hid the minister in his home until it could be arranged to get him safe passage to the North. Arriving in Philadelphia, the grateful Brown sent word back to his family to, "Thank the Lord." The following year, they joined him "up North."

The Charleston AME church was immediately forced to suspend operation as all gatherings of free or slave people were strictly forbidden in the wake of white fears of black uprisings.

Even the Brown Fellowship Society suspended meetings for a time, so agitated was the entire community.

The Issues Articulated

$\mathcal{T}$ he last part of the 1820s was filled with events that were to be significant in the developing history of the free person of color and the slave, as well. In 1827, slavery came to a legal end in New York State. And, as though that were the clarion call to free expression, another significant event took place.

With the preamble to their first editorial stating, "We wish to plead our own cause," two young black men in New York City, Samuel Cornish and John Russwurm, published the first black newspaper in the United States, *Freedom's Journal,* in 1827.

Though the words "advocacy journalism" were not used, certainly *Freedom's Journal* was born out of the desperate need for a vehicle with which to carry the message of the Negro and, at the same time, a mechanism for defense against the slander that was being published without fear of rebuttal by the anti-black forces in the South and North. Russwurm, a native of the West Indies, had been an honor graduate of Bowdoin College and the first black man to graduate from a college or university in the United States. Samuel E. Cornish, minister and intellectual, fearless and able, though without the formal credentials of Russwurm, left the editorial department to Russwurm and concentrated on selling the periodical. Within two years, the paper had become the voice of American Colonization Society, and Russwurm had made his decision to immigrate to Liberia. Cornish came back to edit and publish *Freedom's Journal,* shortly changing the name to *Rights of All* to indicate its new militant stance. The first issue of *Rights of All* was published May 29, 1829. Reverend Samuel Cornish later published the *Colored American.* In its initial impact and for setting a standard, *Freedom's Journal* had been an unqualified success.

In 1829, David Walker, son of a free mother and a slave father, published his *Appeal* in Boston. David Walker had been born in Wilmington, North Carolina on September 28, 1785. Leaving the South, he settled in Boston and opened a clothing store where he sold mostly used clothing. He became very active in Boston's Colored Association and was an active anti-slavery worker. He was an agent for *Freedom's Journal,* which printed the pamphlet containing his *Appeal.*

The *Appeal* was a series of four articles with a "Preamble to the Colored Citizens of the World, but in particular and very expressly, to those of the United States of America." It was the most articulate, angry, plain-spoken, and unflinching indictment of the treatment of blacks by whites to have been written and published up to that time. Walker did not mince words on his opinion of slaveholders and industrialists alike who got rich off of black labor. On colonization, Walker stated emphatically, "Here is a demonstrative proof of a plan got up by a 'gang of slave holders' to select the free people of color from among the slaves, that our most measurable brethren may be better secured in ignorance and wretchedness to work their farms and dig their mines and thus go on enriching the Christians with their blood and groans. What our brethren could have been thinking about, who have left their native land and gone away to Africa, I am unable to say. . . ."[1]

Blacks were no longer mute or without voice. But whites were still in control.

In response to Walker's *Appeal,* all free Negroes who had come into the state of Louisiana after 1825 were expelled immediately. In Virginia, the legislature took up a bill forbidding the circulation of such "sedition publications" and forbidding the education of free Negroes. The mayor of Savannah wrote the mayor of Boston demanding that Walker be punished. The mayor of Boston demurred on the grounds that Walker had done nothing that made him "amenable" to the laws. In 1830, all blacks were driven out of Portsmouth, Ohio. In Cincinnati, Ohio, where there was a large community of free Negroes, there were riots, and blacks were given sixty days to leave town. Over 1,000 left their homes.

And in Boston, whether by the hand of Providence or through foul play, the results were the same; within a year of the publication of the *Appeal,* Walker was dead of mysterious causes. His impassioned words lived on, however, and black men were emboldened to come together in their own behalf. His son, Edward Garrison Walker, grew up to be one of the first blacks to sit in the legislature of any state of the Union. He and Charles L. Mitchell were elected in 1866 to the Massachusetts House of Representatives from Boston.

Photographs

Benjamin Banneker (l.)
helped plan the New
Federal City, renamed
Washington, D.C. Maria
Syphax was the daugh-
ter of the grandson of
Martha Washington. John F. Cook, co-
founder of the Harmony Society, was
one of eighteen relatives whose
freedom was purchased by his aunt,
Alethia Browning Tanner.

M. Syphax

J. Cook

A. Tanner

54

Merchant, mariner, shipbuilder
Paul Cuffe (opposite) led
back-to-Africa movement in
early 1800s.
Nat Turner (above) plans 1831
slave uprising before capture
(left) and hanging in
November, 1831, as reported
by newspaper article of
the period.

55

FREEDOM'S JOURNAL.

" RIGHTEOUSNESS EXALTETH A NATION."

CORNISH & RUSSWURM, Editors & Proprietors.

NEW-YORK, FRIDAY, MARCH 30, 1827.

[VOL. I. No. 3.

MEMOIRS OF CAPT. PAUL CUFFEE.

Being now master of a small covered boat of about 12 tons burthen, he hired a person to assist as a seaman, and made many advantageous voyages to different parts of the state of Connecticut and when about 25 years old married a native of the country, a descendant of the tribe to which his mother belonged.—For some time after his marriage he attended chiefly to his agricultural concerns, but from an increase of family he at length deemed it necessary to pursue his commercial plans more extensively than he had before done.—He arranged his affairs for a new expedition and hired a small house on West-Port river to which he removed his family. A boat of 18 tons was now procured in which he sailed to the banks of St. George in quest of Cod-fish and returned home with a valuable cargo. This important adventure was the foundation of an extensive & profitable fishing establishment from Westport river, which continued for a considerable time and was the source of an honest and comfortable living to many of the inhabitants of that district.

At this period Paul formed a connexion with his brother-in law Michael Warner, who had several sons well qualified for the sea service, four of whom have since laudably filled responsible situations as Captains and first mates. A vessel of 25 tons was built, and in two voyages to the Straits of Belisle and Newfoundland he met with such success as enabled him, in conjunction with another person, to build another vessel of 41 tons burthen in which he made several profitable voyages. Paul had experienced too many disadvantages of his very limited education, and he resolved, as far as it was practicable, to relieve his children from similar embarrassments. The neighborhood had neither a tutor nor a school-house. Many of the citizens were desirous that a school-house should be erected. About 1797 Paul proposed a meeting of the inhabitants for the purpose of making such arrangements as should accomplish the desired object. The collision of opinion respecting mode and place occasioned the meeting to separate without coming to a conclusion; several meetings of the same nature were held, but all were unsuccessful in their issue. Perceiving that all efforts to procure a union of sentiment were fruitless, Paul set himself to work in earnest and had a suitable house built on his own ground, which he freely gave up to the use of the public, and the school was open to all who pleased to send their children. How gratifying to humanity is this anecdote! and who that justly appreciates the human character would not prefer Paul Cuffee, the offspring of an African slave, to the proudest statesman, that ever dealt out destruction among mankind?—About this time Paul proceeded on a whaling voyage to the straits of Belisle, where he found four other vessels completely equipped with boats and harpoons, for catching what Paul discovered that he had not made proper preparations for the business, having only ten hands on board and two boats one of which was old and almost useless. When the masters of the other vessels found his situation they withdrew from the customary practice of such voyages and refused to mate with his crew. In this emergency, Paul resolved to prosecute his undertaking alone till at length two other masters thought it most prudent to accede to the usual practices as they apprehended his crew, by their ignorance might alarm and drive the whales from their reach and thus defeat their voyages. During the season they took seven whales: the circumstances which had taken place roused the ambition of Paul, and his crew: they were diligent and enterprising and had the honor of killing six of the seven whales; two of these fell by Paul's own hands.

(To be Continued.)

PEOPLE OF COLOUR.

I have had three objects in view in thus going into the examination of the nature of slavery as a legal institution. In the first place I wish it to appear that the relation between the master and slave is a proper subject of legislation. It is a conventional right and depends entirely upon the laws.—as the laws create it, they may modify, enlarge restrain, or destroy it, without any other limitation than is imposed by the general good. It is not so much a right of property, as it is a legal relation; and it ought to be treated as such.

The second object was, to relieve slave-holders from a charge, or an apprehension of criminality, where in fact, there is no offence. There can be no palliation for the conduct of those who first brought the curse of slavery upon poor Africa, and poor America too.—But the body of the present generation are not liable to this charge. Posterity are not answerable for the sins of their fathers, unless they approve, their deeds. They found the blacks among them, in a degraded state, incapable either of appreciating or enjoying liberty. They have, therefore, nothing to answer for on this score, because they have no other alternative, *at present*, but to keep them in subjection. There is nothing so de- [illegible] by our principles, to the acknowledgment of guilt, in that which we at the same time believe to be absolutely unavoidable, and in which therefore, it is impossible really to feel self-reproach. Our southern brethren have high ideas of liberty.

There is nothing so calculated to make men restive under command, as a habit and love of commanding others. Upon their own principles, they have been forced to acknowledge even the existence of slavery, in any shape, as criminal. They have therefore concluded that as heavy a curse hung over the present generation for continuing slavery, even when it is plainly unavoidable, as over the last for introducing it. The consequence has been, that those who seriously bewailed the evil, have folded their arms in despair; and those who regarded only their own gratification, expecting to hear the curse at any rate, have taken the desperate resolution, "Let us eat and drink, for to-morrow we die." But the principle is preposterous, and the conclusion incorrect. A Christian *may* hold slaves, and exact their services, without any occasion to feel a pang of self-reproach *merely on account* of his holding slaves.

The third object aimed at, was to fasten the charge of criminality on the very spot where such a charge will be; and where it ought to be felt; and where alone reformation is practicable. There are no duties, without corresponding rights, and no rights without corresponding duties. While it is the duty of the slave to submit himself to his own master, so long as the laws of his country make him a slave, it is his right to be protected, *by the laws*, in the enjoyment of life, health, chastity, good name, and every blessing which he can enjoy consistently with the public welfare.—And on the other hand, masters and legislators should feel, that subjection itself, in the best circumstances, is a sufficient calamity; and that the yoke ought to be made as light as possible. Christianity enforces this dictate of sound reason.* "Thou shalt love thy neighbor as thyself," is as much the law between master and slave, as between any other members of the human family. This is so obvious, as to appear almost like a truism. And yet this is the very thing that has always been lost sight of, among slave-holders. It has been wholly disregarded, in our own nation. Here is the point to be debated, and settled. This is the ground for fastening the charge upon our whole nation. The law of God requires that all the provision should be made *by law* which the public welfare will admit, *for* the protection and improvement of colored subjects, as well as white subjects. *And this has not been done.* We cannot free ourselves from this charge, by pointing to the comfortable mud or even *brick* cabins, the warm jackets and shoes, and the abundance of corn and salt, with which the slaves are furnished.—We are travelling out of the record, by comparing their situation as regards food and lodging, labour and health, with that of the labouring peasantry in the old despotisms of Europe. We do not answer to this indictment, unless we either plead guilty, or show that our *laws*, our customs our modes of thinking and acting, recognize the humanity of the blacks. We must show that their rights are acknowledged, their protection secured, their welfare promoted; and that, in every particular, excepting that of involuntary servitude and its *necessary* attendants, they stand upon the same ground with their masters.—When this is done, we shall feel no guilt on the subject. We shall fear no divine vengeance. We may hope to enjoy the favor of our merciful heavenly Father. But this is not done. I think I may venture to assert, that most of the slave-holding states, neither the laws, nor public opinion, secure to the slaves any of the privileges of humanity. Nothing more is done for them, in *kind*, than is done for the domestic beasts; and nothing more in *degree*, except as they are a more valuable species of property, and are recognised, to some extent, as possessing rational faculties. Let the contrary be shown. I say that of all that kind of provision, which goes to purify and elevate the character, and to create in the subject affection and confidence towards the government, every trace and track is completely excluded. The culture of their minds, the preservation of their morals, their instruction in the only religion which can make them good servants, happy neighbors, and hopeful heirs of eternal life, every thing of the kind is guarded against, by the *laws* at least, even more studiously than the abuse of their persons, and the destruction of their lives. Whatever is attempted for their improvement, is done by individual effort, and in direct violation of the laws. Here is our guilt; our full, dark, unmitigated guilt. It is the guilt of our nation. We in the non-slave holding states, do not feel it as we ought. But we cannot wash our hands, until we can safely declare, that we have done every thing we can, by public and private efforts, to remove the injustice. We have not done this. Comparatively speaking nothing has been done. The Colonization Society has indeed made a beginning, and done as well as could be expected. But I ask how long it will probably be, before that institution can dispose of 30,000 blacks in a year, which is only the *present* annual increase? Until they can do this, the number must be continually increasing. Indeed, I do not believe our southern brethren, in general, intend to do any thing more than to provide a sort of *safety valve*, by this Society, to serve as an outlet for their free blacks and supernumeraries. In our country, acts of the legislature are to be taken as to the expression of the public feeling, on all great subjects.—Towards the blacks, the language of each successive legislature has been, "Our fathers made your yoke heavy, but we will add there to; our fathers chastised you with whips, but we will chastise you with scorpions." Something must be done, to avert the fearful consequences.

We cannot expect any efficient measures to be adopted spontaneously in the slave holding states. The natural effects of slavery, upon the morals, industry, population, strength, and elevation of character, of a state, are so destructive, and it produces so much vexation, trouble and danger; the necessity of it is so very questionable; and its advantages are so trifling, compared with its evils, that we should naturally expect that those who are embarrassed with it would be solicitous about nothing else, than how to be delivered from the curse. But it is not so. The people are so wedded to their habits, and so fond of exercising unlimited power, and so many of their comforts seem to depend upon slavery, that we cease to wonder, at not finding any thing done by them towards improvement. I quote the language of Mr. Clarkson, the great friend of the blacks. "Their *prejudices* against the slaves are too great to allow them to become either impartial or willing actors in the case. The term *slave* being synonimous according to their estimation and usage, with the term *brute*, they have fixed a stigma upon their blacks, such as we who live in Europe could not have conceived, unless we had irrefragable evidence upon the point.—What evils has not this cruel association of terms produced? The West Indian master looks down upon his slave with disdain. He hates the sight of his features, and of his color; nay, he marks with distinctive opprobrium the very blood in his veins, attaching different names, of more or less infamy to those who have it in them, according to the quantity which they have of it in consequence of their pedigree, or of their greater or less degree of consanguinity with the whites.—Hence the West Indian feels an unwillingness to elevate the condition of the black, or to do any thing for him as a human being. I have no doubt, that this prejudice has been one of the great causes why the improvement of our slave population *by law* has been so long retarded; and that the same prejudice will continue to have a similar operation, so long as it shall continue to exist. Not that there are wanting men of humanity among our West Indian legislators. Their humanity is discernable enough when it is to be applied to the *whites*; but such is the system of slavery, and the degradation attached to slavery, that their humanity seems to be lost or gone, when it is to be applied to the *blacks*. Not again that there are wanting men of sense among the same body. They are shrewd and clever enough in the affairs of life, where they maintain an intercourse with the *whites*; but in their intercourse with the *blacks* their sense appears to be shrivelled and not of its ordinary size. Look at the laws of their own making, as far as the blacks are concerned, and they are a collection of any thing but—wisdom."† If these remarks are not applicable to the slave laws of our own states, let the contrary be shown.

See Ep. vi. 5, 9. Col. iii. 22. iv. 1.

† "Thoughts on the necessity of improving the condition of the slaves, &c. with a view to their ultimate emancipation," p. 10, 11.

(To be Continued.)

CURE FOR DRUNKENNESS.

In speaking, on a former occasion, of the remedy for Intemperance proposed by Dr. Chambers of this city we expressed ourselves with a considerable degree of caution. As it is a subject of great importance to the community, and one on which they ought to be explicitly and accurately informed, we have within the past week spent more than one whole day in making a personal investigation into cases where the remedy has been applied, and into the nature of the medicine, in the hope of coming to a full and satisfactory conclusion. The result of our enquiries will be seen in the sequel.—*N. Y. Obs.*

The remedy is not the same with that proposed by Dr. Loiseau of New-Orleans: or if it is, the coincidence is unknown to Dr. Chambers. They have had no manner of intercourse on the subject, and are entire strangers to each other. Dr. C. has been in possession of the secret, in its essential principles, for a number of years.

The medicine is taken in liquor:—that of which the patient is most fond, is usually preferred. It is not unpleasant to the taste, as we have ascertained from those who have taken it, and still more accurately, from having tasted it ourselves.

In its operation it is powerful, but not dangerous. It usually operates as a cathartic, and also as an emetic; but not always in both respects. In all cases nausea is produced.

There are three modifications of the medicine; adapted to the peculiar habits of the patient and inveteracy of the disease. Of course it is important, in making application for persons at a distance, to state these particulars as definitely as possible. In the mildest form, we are told by Dr. C. that it fails of curing in about four cases out of twenty. Resort is then had to the other modifications.

In almost every instance, more than one dose is necessary. The greatest number of doses which have been taken in any case which we have examined, is seven or eight. The cure is generally complete in the course of a single week.

Before being mingled with the liquor in which it is to be taken, the medicine subsists in two forms—as a liquid and as a powder. The former is of a red color, the latter of a light brown, in this form it can be forwarded through the Post Office, in letters containing the proper directions.

Dr. C. has had the generosity to offer it to the poor *of this city* who are unable to make any compensation, gratis. To others the price is not extravagant considering the nature of the remedy, and is varied in some measure according to the circumstances of the individual.

It has already been applied in a large number of cases; in only two of which so far as known to Dr C. has it failed of effecting a cure, unless prematurely relinquished.

We have conversed with two respectable gentlemen, entirely disinterestedly, which have had opportunity to witness its effects on a large number of individuals, and it is their decided opinion that it is a real remedy.

Several persons of good standing in society

Freedom's Journal, the first black newspaper in the United States, was founded by John Russwurm and Samuel Cornish, who later published the Colored American.

John B. Russwurm (r.), co-founder and editor of Freedom's Journal, was the first black to graduate from a college or university in the United States.

Pioneer abolitionist and philanthropist James Forten was held prisoner on the ship "Jersey" during the Revolution. Pennsylvania Hall, built by and for abolitionists, was burned by opponents shortly after its erection in 1838.

Robert Purvis (l.), son-in-law of Forten, joined with William Lloyd Garrison (inset) to found the Anti-Slavery Society in Philadelphia. In above cartoon, Garrison, publisher of the Liberator, is being ridiculed by his opponents. William Whipper (r.) was also an active abolitionist.

59

60 *Henry "Box" Brown (above) mailed himself out of slavery.*

Maryland Frederick County town.

I hereby certify that the person to whom this is given a colored man named Stephen H. Ivery Key aged twenty one years five feet nine inches high has a scar on his left knee is a free born as appears by the affirmation of _____ Dwilling on file in my office.

In Testimony Whereof I hereunto set my hand and affix the Seal of Frederick County Court this 9th day of August 184.

Wm B F, Clk

Slaves from Virginia (opposite) arriving in Philadelphia in 1856 escaped to freedom as did William Craft (opposite, r.) and wife Ellen (above) who cleverly masqueraded as master and manservant.

Freed slaves, including those migrating (l.) into free territories, had to carry papers and wear tags (above) in order to identify themselves.

61

Sojourner Truth

Frederick Douglass

Harriet Tubman

62

The New Breed of activists — all
slaves who obtained their freedom
through escape. purchase, or emancipation — emerged during the mid-
1800s as leaders in the fight for
racial equality.

Samuel Ringgold Ward

Henry Highland Garnett

William Wells Brown

*Douglass and Truth spoke out for
the abolitionist cause. Tubman
rallied for the Underground Railroad, while Ward and Garnet were
the vanguard of the anti-slavery
political organization, and Brown
became the first American Negro
to publish a novel.*

63

Mifflin Gibbs (l.) went West in search of gold, but made his fortune by operating the only retail shoe and boot store in San Francisco. Restaurateur "Mammy" Pleasant was there before the rush, as was William A. Leidesdorff, who left an estate worth over a million dollars.

Leidesdorff

Pleasant

Barney Ford pioneered in Colorado where he owned the Inter Ocean Hotel. Slave Robert Harlan purchased his freedom from $45,000 he made in gold.

Ford

Harlan

While the rush for gold was on in the West, Henry Clay urged Congress to pass the Fugitive Slave Law (1850) and Dred Scott was denied his freedom suit (1857) because, as a slave, he was not considered a citizen of the U. S.

65

The 'We' and 'They'

*I*n the spring of 1830, Hezekiah Grice of Baltimore sent a letter to prominent Negroes in free states asking their opinion on the question of emigration. For many, the situation had become totally untenable. In August of the same year, he received an urgent message from Richard Allen to come at once to Philadelphia. Upon his arrival, Grice found already assembled a group discussing a circular that had been sent out by Rev. Peter Williams, the rector of St. Philips Protestant Episcopal Church in New York, and Thomas Jennings and Peter Vogelsang, also of New York. The circular approved the idea of a convention of free colored men.

A call then went out from Allen for a convention of Negroes of the United States to be held in Philadelphia, September 15, 1830 at Bethel AME Church. At the September meeting, Bishop Richard Allen was elected president; Dr. Belfast Burton of Philadelphia and Austin Steward of Rochester, N. Y., vice-presidents; Junius C. Morell of Pennsylvania, secretary; and Robert Cowley of Maryland, assistant secretary. While this meeting may well be considered the first Convention of Colored Men, the participants thought of it as a pre-convention, a planning meeting for the full-scale convention that was scheduled for the following year.

Unfortunately, by June, 1831, Richard Allen was dead, and Hezekiah Grice had apparently made up his own mind about emigration, because he left for Haiti later in 1831 where he became a prominent contractor.

The convention opened on the 6th of June, 1831 and continued through the 11th of June. John Bowers served as president; Abraham D. Shadd of Delaware and William Duncan of Virginia as vice-presidents; William Whipper of Philadelphia as secretary; and Thomas L. Jennings of New York as assistant-secretary. Five states were represented.

The agenda at the 1830 convention had focused on the questions of emigration outside the United States; migration to a more desirable location within the United States; and "adoption of a policy that would make life in the United States more endurable."

The 1831 meeting added the question of establishing "a collegiate school on the manual labor system," and New Haven, Connecticut was suggested as the place for the early Tuskegee.

They resolved to appoint a committee to investigate the condition of the free people of color throughout the United States, and recommended that the work of organizations interested in a settlement in Canada be continued and the free people of color be annually called to assemble by delegation.

They also submitted "the necessity of deliberate reflection on the dissolute, intemperate and ignorant condition of a large portion of the colored population of the United States."

Finally, they renewed their opposition to the "operations and misrepresentations of the American Colonization Society in these United States . . . and we would call upon Christians of every denomination firmly to resist it."[1]

The committee report was unanimously received and adopted by the convention. Circumstances outside their control had created conditions which caused the free class of black citizens to come together to work out methods and means of mutual protection and benefit. It was to provide the basis for a network of relationships, of formal and informal arrangements, that would continue to the present time. Little did those free gentlemen, acting with such moderation and quiet deliberation at their Philadelphia convention, realize the impact on their lives of another quietly deliberate act spawned in the brain of a slave who was convinced that his mission in life was to destroy the white enemy and to make possible the time when "the first should be last and the last should be first."

At least fifty-seven white people were murdered by Nat Turner and his followers on August 22, 1831 at Jerusalem in Southampton County, Virginia.

The massacre sent Virginia and all of the surrounding areas into a state of panic. In addition to those arrested and executed in connection with actual participation in the event, scores of innocent blacks were slaughtered without trial or reason. As Charity Bowery, who was interviewed by Colonel Thomas Wentworth Higginson, said, "The brightest and best was killed. . . . The whites always suspect such ones. . . . The patrols would tie up the free colored people, flog 'em and try to make them lie against one another, and often killed them before anybody could interfere."[2]

In the South, instruction of slaves was forbidden, black preachers were circumscribed, and the assembly of three or more blacks, slave or free, except under white supervision, was prohibited. Slave hiring was sharply limited, and the possession of drums, whistles, and musical instruments forbidden for fear that they could be used as signals or message carriers in an uprising. Slaves more than eight miles from their family plantation were assumed to be runaways unless they could prove otherwise.

A bill was introduced into the Pennsylvania legislature to require all free Negroes to carry passes and to exclude all others from the state.

Free people of color were likewise forbidden to migrate into Tennessee. Maryland passed a law which, even though it was found to be unenforceable, stated that all free Negroes must be colonized back to Africa. Andrew Jackson's administration was likewise strengthened in the effort to remove all Indians from the South to the West by force.

The resolution regarding the establishment of a manual training school for black youths at New Haven aroused such fear among the white population that a public meeting was called by the mayor on September 8, 1831, and the following resolution was adopted:

> "Resolved by the Mayor, Aldermen, Common Council and free men of the City of New Haven in city meeting assembled, that we will resist the establishment of the proposed college in this plan by any lawful means."

The abolitionists and free blacks were universally blamed for having somehow incited the Nat Turner insurrection, and Garrison's *Liberator* and its free black supporters were prime targets.

In January, 1832, James Forten called yet another meeting of Philadelphia's black community. The right to assemble was still theirs. He was joined at this meeting by William Whipper and his daughter Harriett's husband, Robert Purvis. They drafted a petition of protest to be presented to the Pennsylvania legislature. They asked, "Why is this distinction now to be proclaimed for the first time in the code of Pennsylvania? Why are her borders to be surrounded by a wall of iron against freemen whose complexions fall below the wavering and uncertain shades of white? . . . Is it not to be asked, is he brave? Is he honest? Is he just? Is he free from the stain of crime? But is he black? Is he brown? Is he yellow? Is he other than white? . . ."

Forten's petition emphasized that: "Equally unfounded is the charge that this population fills the almshouses with paupers and increases, in an undue proportion, the public burden. We appeal to the facts and documents . . . as giving abundant refutation to an error so injurious to our character."

These "facts and documents," which accompanied the petition, indicated that, far from being paupers, the free people of color who were residents in Pennsylvania paid more taxes on the property than the amount of money expended from tax funds on the black poor; that blacks in the city of Philadelphia owned over $100,000 in real estate value; that they had over fifty self-help organizations of their own; that those who could afford it sent their children to school at their own expense; and that they were constantly striving to move from the unskilled to the skilled labor group. The petition reminded the legislature that: "Despite the difficulty of getting places for our sons as apprentices to learn the mechanical trades, owing to the prejudices with which we have to contend, there are between four and five hundred people of color in the city and suburbs who follow mechanical employments."

While the masses of blacks were no different from the masses of whites, Forten states: ". . . We are liable to be drawn aside by temptation from the paths of rectitude. But we think that in the aggregate we will not suffer by a comparison with our white neighbors whose opportunities of improvement have been no greater than ours. By such a comparison, fairly and impartially made, we are willing to be judged."[3]

The repressive laws had not been passed at the time, but, as history states, the situation for blacks had not yet culminated in its severity and indeed would grow worse.

Repression in the South was causing migration to be stepped up, and as more and more blacks crowded into the city, there were frequent clashes between the increasing numbers of European immigrants who were fleeing Europe's wars and famine. Drunkenness and hooliganism were common in both groups. In August of 1832, when the steam seemed to come from between the narrow Philadelphia cobblestones, a group of blacks and whites clashed at an amusement park. Word spread that blacks had insulted the whites, and a group of whites armed with sticks and bricks descended upon the park to beat up the blacks. The amusement park was wrecked in the melee, and several blacks were injured. The next day, a larger white group gathered and invaded the section where the black homeowners were located, breaking windows, battering in doors, seizing furniture, and throwing it into the streets to be broken to bits or burned by their fellow hoodlums. Blacks were caught and beaten without mercy. For four days the rioting continued, with every Negro in danger of losing his life. The sheriff begged for and got troops, which were stationed in various sections of Philadelphia. The soldiers' presence brought a degree of sanity back to the mob. Investigations were launched and committees appointed to try to prevent the repetition of this kind of violence.

The mob spirit that erupted in Philadelphia spread like a virus to the other seaboard cities where groups of free black citizens were acquiring the outward symbols of success—education, property and refinement. The Snow Riot in Washington, D. C. was worse than the Philadelphia riot, and demonstrated the growing power of mob terror and violence against the struggling free class.

Benjamin Snow, a free colored man and owner of a restaurant on Pennsylvania Avenue and 6th Street, NW, was supposed to have made an "impertinent" remark about the wives of some white mechanics. As a result, these mechanics descended upon the restaurant, destroying it. Snow, with the help and warning of white friends, escaped. It was learned later that Snow did not stop until he had safely reached the Canadian border. The restaurant gone, the mob then turned to the homes of prominent blacks—the Wormleys, the Cooks, and others—plundering, destroying, setting fire, and demolishing furniture while ostensibly looking for anti-slavery documents and papers. John F. Cook, the distinguished minister and educator, had taken a horse from the stable of his friend, Elisha Haywood, and escaped to Pennsylvania, which fortunately by then was more hospitable than his own territory. William Wormley, also sought by the mob, escaped, but the ordeal ruined his health. The school run by John F. Cook, and the Mary Wormley School, as well as all of the other schools for colored children were destroyed. Only Louise Parke Costin's school escaped destruction. John F. Cook remained in Pennsylvania for nearly a year before returning to Washington and reopening his school.

The school run by Mary Wormley had been built in 1830 by her brother William near the corner of Vermont and I Street, where the hotel and restaurant owned by James was later located. Mary had been educated expressly for teaching at the Colored Female Seminary in Philadelphia run by Mrs. Sarah Douglass. William was operating the livery stable started by his father and was quite well off. The school was a matter of great family pride. The experience broke William and it was left to James Wormley to recoup the family fortune.

Rumor circulated that Louise Parke Costin's school up on Capitol Hill had been spared by the mob because of "who" she was.

Many of the colored people who had lived peacefully with their neighbors over the decades felt bitter that the influx of poor and jobless blacks, untrained and unsophisticated in the ways of city living, should bring such disaster to their environment. They opined that they were not like that . . . they were refined, they were educated . . . they spoke softly and had good manners. Why should they be categorized with the black migrants who could neither read nor write nor speak the English language with clarity and preciseness? Why? To James Forten and those like him, the answer lay in more education, temperance training, and, above all, respect for the rights of others, black or white. But the unity which had been wholeheartedly expressed by Forten and the other free blacks in Philadelphia back in 1817, when they vowed that they would never "separate ourselves voluntarily from the slave population of this country . . . they are our brethren, . . ." was being severely strained and tested.

A small book published in Philadelphia in 1841, entitled *Sketches of the Higher Classes of Colored Society in Philadelphia,* delineates some of the perceptions that were held of this increasingly stratified community: "The public, or at least the great body who have not been at pains to make an examination, have long been accustomed to regard the people of color as one consolidated mass all huddled together without any particular or general distinctions, social or otherwise. The sight of one colored man . . . whatever may be his apparent condition . . . is the sight of a community; and the errors and crimes of one is adjudged as the criterion of character of the whole body."

Continuing the analysis: "Taking the body of the colored population in the city of Philadelphia, they present in a gradual, moderate, and limited ratio almost every grade of character, wealth, and . . . education. They are to be seen in ease, comfort and the enjoyment of all the social blessings of this life; and, in contrast with this, they are to be found in the lowest depths of human degradation, misery and want."

It was this dichotomy, both real and unreal, this unity and disunity, the togetherness and the apartness, that created the dilemma which persists to this day. The more the general population lumped all people of color into one amorphous mass, the more those who *could* struggled to have the differences noted.

The Search for Lebensraum

$\mathscr{B}$ lacks were on the move as early as 1819 moving out of the South, toward the North and West, into new territory searching for their *lebensraum*. Many went only as far as necessary from their old homes and loved ones, stopping in Pennsylvania and Ohio.

In Columbia, Pennsylvania, the first blacks who came were manumitted slaves forced from their Virginia homes by the stringent laws which were being enacted against free blacks. Later, there were fugitive slaves, protected and cared for by the more settled and prosperous free settlers. Among these prosperous blacks in the middle 1820s were Stephen Smith and William Whipper, lumber and oyster merchants. William Whipper was the son of a black woman and her white master, and the boy grew up on his father's lumber farm, inheriting it before 1830. He had been quite well educated and was of a philosophic and reflective mind.

A committee of North Carolina Quakers had been appointed in 1822 to examine the laws of the so-called free states with an eye to recommending the ones which would be most hospitable to free black settlers. The committee had recommended that Illinois, Indiana, and Ohio be the target states. The yearly meeting then voted to assist in the removal of free blacks to those states as soon as possible, and agreed to underwrite the migration plan for $200 per family.

Indiana seemed to be the state most favored, and the migrants went in groups, accompanied by a Friend or a group of Friends (Quakers) equipped with the necessary legal documents to expedite the settling process. In the decade following the Vesey insurrection attempt, the exodus was perceptibly accelerated.

In 1833, my great-grandfather Farrow Powell and two of his brothers, Eaton and Wyatt Powell, left their home on the Neuse River in Raleigh

County, North Carolina. They were seeking a safe place to live and raise their families. Farrow Powell, from whom the Powells in South Bend descended, was born in 1809. His mother was a mulatto; his father was an Indian. Grandpa Powell was married to Elizabeth Waldere in 1827, and they were the parents of seven children. The oldest two were born in North Carolina. They were James Powell, born February 27, 1829, and Catherine Jackson Powell, born December 24, 1832. They traveled in a wagon train drawn by oxen with their wives, children, and household goods, stopping with friendly families, usually Quakers, or sometimes with free colored people who had ventured West earlier. Eaton and his family left the group in Ohio. Farrow and Wyatt pushed on through Indiana stopping finally at Terre Haute, a village of about a thousand people at that time. The arduous trip had taken about sixty days, and that was on the shortest route, the Kanawha Road.

After a year or so in Terre Haute, Grandpa Powell moved to Spencer, Indiana in Owen County, where he lived with his family for the next twenty years, moving in 1858 to South Bend. The other Powell children were born in Owen County, Spencer, Indiana where they settled, or in South Bend. Colonel was born in Owen County, October 26, 1834; Larkin, April 12, 1836; Winnie Ann, March 20, 1839; and Elijah and his twin sister, October 2, 1841. Elizabeth Waldere Powell died in 1841, probably in childbirth at the time the twins were born, since the little girl was not named. Grandpa Farrow Powell remarried in 1843. He and his second wife, Rebecca Maria Bass, had nine children. My grandfather, John Wesley Powell, was born January 16, 1851 in Owen County, Spencer, Indiana. The other children were Esquire, born July 26, 1845; Lucinda, February 29, 1847; Benjamin Franklin, August 22, 1849; Harrison Allen, June 16, 1853; Nancy Jane, March 18, 1857; Eli Greenbury, August 3, 1859; Abraham Lincoln, November 10, 1862; and Farrow Fincher, November 10, 1866. Eli, Abraham and Farrow were born after the family moved to South Bend, Indiana in 1858.

In the decade between 1820 and 1830, the colored population in Ohio had increased by 102%, in Indiana by 195%, and in Illinois by 250%. As a result, black laws almost identical in nature were put on the statute books of each state in the early 1830s. As bad as the black laws were, they were not as repressive as the laws and the atmosphere which pervaded the South.

After the 1835 Snow Riot in Washington, D. C., schools for colored children in the South, if they existed at all, were operated in secret. One such school operated, for a time, in the home of William and Eliza De-Baptiste in Fredericksburg, Virginia. But fear of discovery and the severity of punishment if discovered made it difficult to maintain, and conditions continued to worsen. A new law was put on the Virginia books in 1838 forbidding the return to Virginia of any free black person who left the state. In order to obey the law, blacks living in Alexandria, Fredericksburg, or Baltimore and working in Washington, D. C. could no longer earn a living. If their children attended a Washington, D. C. school, they could not come home. It was virtually impossible for free blacks to provide an education for the children, outside the District.

In Virginia, the DeBaptistes were contractors and builders, Lomax Cook was a barber, and the members of the other free families of Fredericksburg had skills with which they could earn a living in any new community. It was at this point that the entire Fredericksburg colony of free colored people left Virginia. The Lee, Moore, DeBaptiste, and Cook families packed up, bag and baggage, and made the long and dangerous journey to Detroit, Michigan. For a time they shuttled between Canada and Michigan, finally settling in Detroit and becoming leading members of that burgeoning community. Detroit was the last stop on the Underground Railroad before entering Canada and sure freedom. The traffic between the Detroit colony and the Chatham, Ontario, and Windsor communities was constant during those years preceding the Civil War. It accelerated immediately after the passage of the Fugitive Slave Bill in 1850, when thousands of refugees fled their homes rather than risk being picked up by a slave hunter and sold or given back into bondage.

Abolitionists, Black and White

As the chains of slavery grew stronger, more and more men, women, and children were slipping through them and finding their way to freedom.

In February, 1827, Secretary of State Henry Clay had, upon instructions from President John Quincy Adams, opened negotiations with Great Britain proposing an agreement between the two countries that would provide for "mutual surrender of all persons held to service or labor, under the laws of either party, who escaped into territory of the other."

Mr. Clay mentioned that a provision for the restoration of fugitive slaves had also been included in a treaty with the Mexican government. (The Mexican government did not ratify the treaty.) In September, 1827, the American Minister to Great Britain, Mr. Albert Gallatin, sent word to Mr. Clay that the British government had determined that, "It was utterly impossible for them to agree to a stipulation for the surrender of fugitive slaves." Thus, Canada and Mexico remained as havens for those fortunate enough to reach the border of either country.

The mood was changing in the white North and among some whites in the South. More and more, in isolated places, the thought was being articulated that slavery was wrong and there was no getting around it. Where the anti-slavery societies of Benjamin Franklin's day had talked of gradual manumission and compensation to the slave holder with the colonization for the freed black, the idea had been re-examined, and now emancipation was proposed without indemnification. After all, do you compensate a kidnapper for the freeing of his victim, unless you label it *ransom?*

William Lloyd Garrison did not think so. Born into a poor family in Newburyport, Massachusetts and apprenticed at thirteen to a printer, the self-taught lad had moved from the position of the anti-slavery people to that which demanded immediate abolition of slavery. Garrison had tried twice to start his newspaper, and both times he failed. Then in 1830, he went to Baltimore to help Benjamin Lundy on his anti-slavery paper, *The Genius of Universal Emancipation*. He was arrested and put in jail for a libel he had written in Lundy's paper, and without money for bail, he remained there for seven weeks. In this period, his plan for the *Liberator* crystallized.

Garrison was well aware that free blacks controlled a substantial amount of capital, and that those in Philadelphia had more money, more education, and more sense of civic responsibility than in most other places. At the top of his list of these people of substance was James Forten. He wrote and asked for his help in starting the newspaper which he planned to launch upon his release from jail.

Forten responded on December 15, 1830, writing to Garrison:

> "I am extremely happy to hear that you are about establish-
> ing a paper in Boston. I hope your efforts may not be in vain;
> and may the 'Liberator' be the means of exposing, more and
> more, the odious system of Slavery, and of raising up friends
> to the oppressed and degraded People of Colour throughout
> the Union. Whilst so much is doing in the world to amelio-
> rate the condition of mankind, and the spirit of Freedom is
> marching with rapid strides, and causing tyrants to tremble,
> may America awake from the apathy in which she has long
> slumbered."[1]

He enclosed the money to cover twenty-seven subscriptions to the new paper, which appeared January 1, 1831.

Freedom's Journal and *Rights of All* were out of business, and David Walker was dead, possibly murdered by poisoning. A new voice was needed to tell the world of the plight of the American of African descent, both enslaved and free. Forten, who was at ease in the company of whites, felt that maybe this young white man could do for the black cause what the black papers had been unable to do, and so he invited Garrison to bring his friends and come as his guest to the Convention of Free Colored Men in June of 1831.

William Lloyd Garrison, Benjamin Lundy, Reverend S. S. Jocelyn of New Haven, Connecticut, and Arthur Tappan of New York (Benjamin Franklin's grand-nephew, and the man who put up the money to bail Garrison out of the Baltimore jail) were present, and a full account of the proceedings was given in the *Liberator,* to Forten's delight. He decided then and there to back Garrison and to keep the *Liberator* coming out as long as it was necessary. Further, in the company of Garrison and his other New England associates, Forten felt that he and his were treated as equals, and not looked down upon. In fact, increasingly, Garrison and the others pointed out how little difference there was between men like themselves.

So, while the initial contribution to the *Liberator* was not large in terms of dollars, it was gigantic in terms of the commitment and the relationship that was established. As Garrison grew in influence and power, it became difficult to determine who was the benefactor and who the beneficiary. Garrison, not unmindful of Forten's affection for him and his influence in the free colored community, continued to come to him and the black community when faced with financial strain. Forten responded by sending money, writing letters, and calling meetings to endorse the paper. It survived.

Meanwhile, Garrison, who had been in favor of colonization, adopted the prevailing point of view in the colored community, i.e., anti-colonization. His black supporters expanded to include some of the leading citizens of the day. John B. Vashon in Pittsburgh carried the paper in his barbershop, and from time to time advanced money to Garrison, which, according to the records, was never repaid. In December, 1832 Vashon sent Garrison fifty dollars, which he considered a loan, and eleven months later, another sixty dollars, which Garrison considered ". . . an extension of the loan."

The 1833 National Convention of Free Colored Men had sixty delegates from eight states. They were attracting growing numbers of black supporters, and attracting increasing attention to their program. "Colored capitalists" were urged to invest their money in free-produce stores, thereby boycotting slave-produced merchandise and slave-grown food. The New York Phoenix Society was described as an educational model to which other large communities could look for guidance in organizing their own block-by-block groups. The convention voted to send Garrison to Europe as their representative.

By some strange coincidence, as the National Convention Movement was really beginning to flourish, Garrison made the decision to organize a national anti-slavery society ". . . in order that the abolitionists of the country know each other, devise some plans for cooperation and make their influence more manifest." He issued the call in September, and the organization meeting was set for December 4, 5, and 6, 1833.

Representing the National Convention, Garrison had gone to England to raise money for the proposed Manual Training School. Although he had been warmly received, the trip had not produced much money for the school. Garrison's expenses were paid by donations from Forten and the other members of his inner group; his son-in-law, Robert Purvis, who was always generous with his funds, Whipper, and Stephen Smith. Garrison received small donations as well, ranging from fifty cents to $5.00. In London, Nathaniel Paul, a black Baptist preacher, lent him $200, ". . . so that I could return home without begging," Garrison told Lewis Tappan.

In April, 1834, the *Liberator* was faced with yet another financial crisis. This time Garrison used the pages of the paper to place the responsibility squarely on the backs of the Negroes, and the tone was stern. In an editorial, Garrison stated that while the *Liberator* had 2,300 subscribers, only one-fourth were white.

> "The paper then belongs emphatically to the people of color —it is their organ. Let them remember that so strong are the prejudices of the whites against it, we cannot at present expect much support from them. And surely, by a very trifling combination of effort and means, the colored population might easily give vigor and stability to the paper. . . . True, they are poor and trodden down; but how can they arise without having a press to lift up its voice in their behalf? They are poor, but taking the paper will not make them poorer . . . it will add to their respectability, their intelligence and their means. It is for them, therefore, to decide the question SHALL THE *LIBERATOR* DIE?"[2]

The American Anti-Slavery Society, which brought together the various anti-slavery societies, met at Philadelphia's Adelphi Hall and, interestingly enough, James Forten was not present. His son-in-law, Robert

Purvis, was, as were James McCrummel, the Philadelphia dentist; John Vashon, the Pittsburgh barber who had been a financial supporter of the *Liberator* from its inception; and Abraham Shadd of Delaware, one of the early activists in the convention movement. After three days of deliberation, the group came out with a "Declaration of Sentiments." Robert Purvis and Dr. James McCrummel were signatories. Vashon, Shadd, James G. Barbadoes, and Peter Williams of New York were named to the Board of Managers. Now Garrison had his own platform, and it would no longer be necessary for him to speak as an invited guest from the platform of the free colored convention.

Following the organization of the American Anti-Slavery Society, a group of the delegates dined at the Forten residence at 92 Lombard Street. They were Garrison; Reverend S. J. May, Louisa May Alcott's godfather; Edward Abdy, a British politician studying the American penal system; Arthur and Lewis Tappan; James Miller McKim; and John Greenleaf Whittier, the American poet.

The Reverend May later wrote about the occasion:
"James Forten was evidently a man of commanding mind and well informed. . . . He had for many years carried on the largest private sailmaking establishment in that city, having at times forty men in his employ—most if not all of them white men. He had acquired wealth and he lived in as handsome a style as anyone should wish to live. I dined at his table with several members of the convention . . . We were entertained with as much ease and elegance as I could desire to see. . . . The conversation was, for the most part, on the anti-slavery conflict."

Reverend May continued:
"I can never forget Mr. Forten's scathing satire. Among other things, he said, '. . . I have lived and labored in useful employment. I have acquired property and paid useful taxes in this city. Here I have dwelt until I am nearly sixty years of age, and have brought up and educated a family, as you see. . . . Yet, some ingenious gentlemen have recently discovered that I am *still* an African; that a continent three thousand miles, and more, from the place where I was born is my native

country. And I am advised to go home. Well, it may be so. Perhaps, if I should only be set on the shores of that distant land, I should recognize all I might see there, and run at once to the old hut where my forefathers lived a hundred years ago.' His tone of voice, his whole manner sharpened the edge of his sarcasm . . . on every countenance was that ineffable contempt which he felt for the presence of the Colonization Society.

"At his table sat his excellent, motherly wife and his lovely, accomplished daughters—all, with himself, under the ban of that accursed American prejudice . . . I learned from him that their education, evidently of a superior kind, had cost him much more than it would have done, if they had not been denied admission into the best schools of the city."[3]

While this kind of social intercourse was looked upon by Forten and his inner circle as the way things should be, it was looked upon by many outsiders with disfavor. Some blacks felt that there was in it too much of an attitude of patronization on the part of whites, while at the same time, they were eating black people's food and taking their money.

Garrison now had a virtual monopoly on the purse strings of the people of color who had any means at all. His attitude, and the attitudes of those around him, was subtly indicative of the change in his position with regard to his colored patrons.

Photographs

84

The Second U.S. Colored Artillery was one of twelve black heavy artillery units in the Union Army. Many of the decisive battles of the War were fought with the assistance of black soldiers. Seventeen black soldiers and sailors were awarded Congressional Medals of Honor for their valor in battle.

Union warship (below) typifies the conditions during the Civil War where blacks and whites were quartered together in the Union navy in which 30,000 blacks served. James Forten's granddaughter, Charlotte Forten, taught the "contraband" in South Carolina during the war.

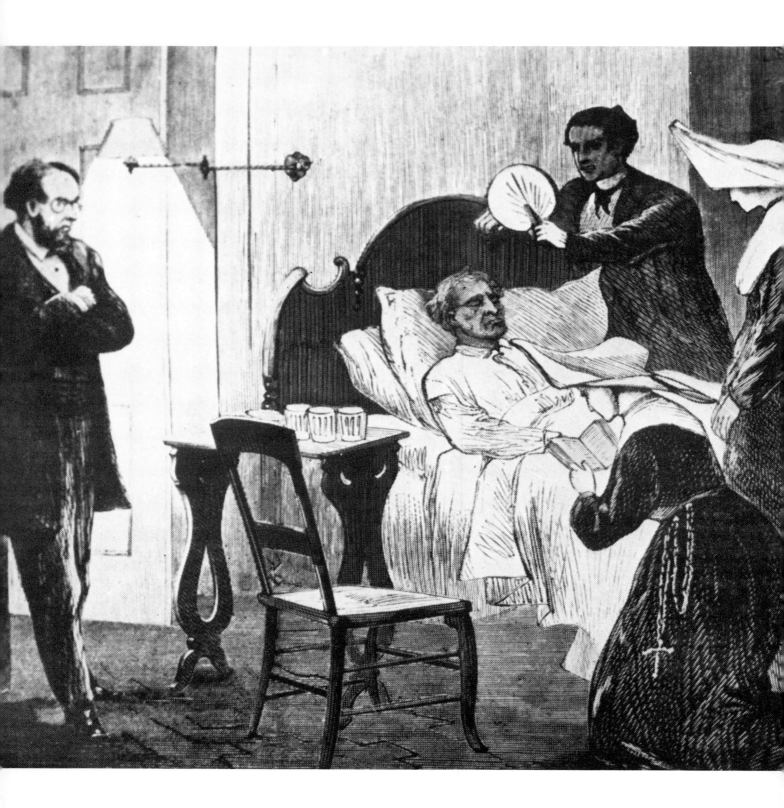

Man shown fanning
dying Lincoln in
1863 Harper's maga-
zine illustration is
alleged to be James
A. Wormley, close
friend of Lincoln.
Lt. Governor of
Louisiana during
Reconstruction was
Pickney B.S. Pinchback. Frederick Douglass
was president of Freedmens Bank at the time
of its closing in 1873.

Frederick Douglass   P. B. S. Pinchback

First leaders after War were primarily Oberlin trained. Examples were George F. Cook (top, l.), superintendent of colored schools in Washington, and John F. Cook 2nd (l.), D. C. tax collector for 25 years.

Howard University, at the time of its founding (below) in 1867, was the only black institution of higher professional education supported by congressional mandate. Hon. Mercer Langston (opposite, below, r.) was the first law school dean, and successor John H. Cook (top, r.) was in the first graduating class.

William Lyphax (above), Senator
Hiram Rhodes Revels (above right),
Rev. Patrick Healy (below, l.),
and Charles Purvis.

Prominent black citizens in Washington during Reconstruction were U. S. Senator (l.) Blanche K. Bruce and Rev. Benjamin T. Tanner (r.). The 42nd Congress was petitioned by a group of prominent blacks in behalf of civil rights.

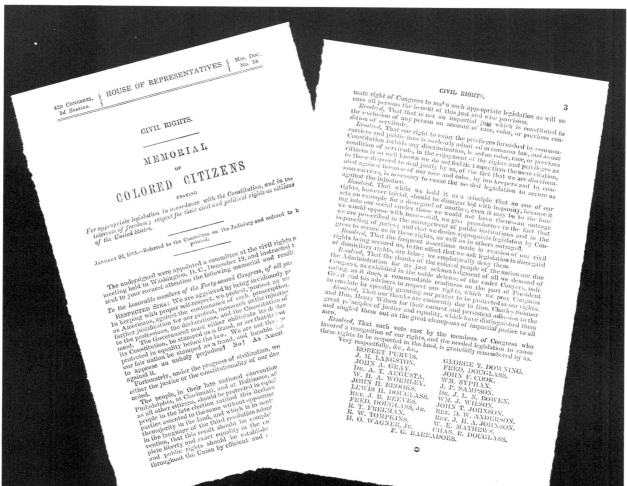

R. Elliott

F. Cardozo

W. Whipper

Francis L. Cardozo and Robert Elliott served in the predominantly black South Carolina legislature during Reconstruction. Another South Carolina lawmaker and judge was William Whipper, son of the abolitionist.

The White League, a group of terrorists, attacks police and militia in an abortive attempt to take over the Louisiana state government in 1874. During this period of reconstruction, Richard Cain served two terms in the South Carolina legislature, Richard Greener was a professor at the University of South Carolina, and T. J. Minton prospered as the first black lawyer in Philadelphia after completing law school in Columbia, S. C.

R. H. Cain   R. Greener   M. Minton   T. J. Minton

James Wormley

94

Mary Ann Shadd

Senator Charles Sumner

The National Colored Convention met in Washington, D.C., in 1869 during the Reconstruction when James Wormley's hotel was the most fashionable in Washington, and Senator Charles Sumner and Mary Ann Shadd were fighting for black civil rights.

Peter Weddick Moore

Mrs. Peter W. Moore

Bessie Moore Watt

Peter Moore became the first principal of the Elizabeth City State Normal School. The students wanted to improve basic skills. Also shown are Moore's wife (above c.), daughter (above r.) and mother (r.).

Annie J. Moore

Peter Moore's daughter, Bessie, married a druggist, Robert L. Watt, Sr. (below right). His father was Garland Watt (above) who was a drayman and one of the early black entrepreneurs. Bessie and Robert Watt's son, Garland Watt, is a Chicago judge.

Moore's students

Born in slavery, Rev. William H. McAlpine was founder and second president of Selma University. Below: His wife Emma at age 22 and 40, and their daughter, Ethel McAlpine Walker, who taught at Selma University.

(far right) Nathaniel D. Walker, age 5, with grandmother Mrs. Benjamin Walker and mother, Sophrinia. (top right) Dr. N. D. Walker and sons, Dr. William and Dr. Benjamin Walker. (bottom, l.) Helen Walker Williams with son Charles, is professor at Providence College, R.I., (bottom r.) Ethel and James McAlpine, sister and brother. Not shown is Eunice Walker Johnson, other daughter of N. D. and Ethel McAlpine Walker.

House Dividing

$\mathcal{O}$ut of the apparent unity of 1817 had come the national convention movement, but by 1837, less than a decade after Allen and Forten had called the first convention in Philadelphia, there was a perceptible crack in the body politic of the "free men of color." What had been a hairline crack developed into a major fissure. The crack had been present in 1794 when Absalom Jones and Forten had opted to stay within the framework of the Episcopal Church, while Richard Allen and his followers determined to separate from any superstructure under white domination and control.

By the latter part of the 1830s, the free black community had become increasingly divided between the "Garrisonians," like Forten, Purvis, Whipper, Smith, and Morris Brown, and the increasingly militant leadership of men like Samuel E. Cornish and his *Colored American* newspaper, which held that free Negroes, organized in their own groups and fighting for their immediate rights, could most effectively prove that blacks were men and Americans equally involved in the struggle for American freedom. Forten, Sr. and Jr., Purvis, and William Whipper were active in the organization of the American Moral Reform Society, which lent its prestige and financial assistance to the Garrison theories of "moral suasion," as opposed to mass demonstrations, militant actions, and separate black organizations. Under Garrison's influence, the 1835 convention had voted to abstain from celebrating the Fourth of July, which was their right as Americans, on the basis that to do so would be to avoid conflict and mob incitement and to "promote morality."

Cornish and his followers felt that the resolution went against the right of the people to demonstrate, and Samuel Hardenberger of New York accused "the upper class of Negroes" of going against the wishes of the vast majority of colored people.

An even more emotional issue was the business of what blacks were to call themselves. The *National Reformer* magazine, edited by William

Whipper, came out against the use of such terms as "Negro" and "colored," and sought to remove the terms "African" and "Afro" from the names of existing institutions. The magazine's platform was to fight for integration of the colored people into the life of America, to continue to stand firm against emigration and deportation, and to oppose the continuation of separate organizations. They declared their common cause with the American Anti-Slavery Society, and refused to recognize that they themselves really constituted a separate Negro organization. As a class, they were becoming farther and farther removed from the sufferings and hopes of the masses of black people.

Cornish (who had broken early with John Russwurm on the issue of colonization), in reprinting the proceedings of the Reform meeting, still attempted to preserve as far as possible the unity of the colored community. However, he felt that it was extremely important and necessary for him to give constructive criticism, and he felt that the Reform Society's articulated goals were "visionary in the extreme." He said, "We found a Purvis, a Whipper, and others (of whose Christian benevolence and cultivated intelligence we have so many and such strong evidences) vague, wild, indefinite and confused in their views. . . . They fought the wind and bayed at the moon for three days." He expressed his sympathy for James Forten, Sr., now aged and infirm, who tried his best to get the younger members of the group out of the fog of abstraction, but without success.

And although Garrison's Anti-Slavery Society gave a few prominent places in the organization to leaders like Robert Purvis and John Vashon, the rank and file still had to fight against the prejudices which existed within the group, and that factor continued to be a major source of distraction from the fundamental struggle.

The split became more real when the National Convention voted to broaden the base and to make it a real people's convention, more representative of the masses of colored people. A resolution was passed that, "Hereafter, delegates to our National Convention shall be elected by the people in general meeting assembled . . . that all delegates from larger centers be elected by the people, not arbitrarily chosen by a few of the more prominent Negro organizations," and that white friends and abolitionists be elected as "honorary members, or to represent communities unable to send Negro delegates."

Cornish, in the *Colored American,* expressed regret that the colored people had allowed themselves to get involved in the factional disputes of white abolitionists, saying the colored people should drop all factionalism. "If not, we shall have the unseemly sight of bodies of colored men arrayed against abolitionists, giving food to our enemies and pleasure to the devil."

Nonetheless, he brought down the wrath of the Garrisonians, who denounced him, and all those who dared to pronounce their opposition to Garrison's stand.

In fairness to Garrison and his followers, it was not difficult for them to remember that he had addressed the 1831 convention with the following admonition, "Support each other. . . . When I say 'support each other,' I mean sell to each other and buy of each other in preference to the whites. This is a duty: The whites do not trade with you; why should you give them your patronage? If one of your number opens a little shop, do not pass it by to give your money to a white shopkeeper. If any has a trade, employ him as often as possible. If any is a good teacher, send your children to him and be proud that he is one of your color. . . . Maintain your rights in all cases and at whatever expense. . . . Where you are allowed to vote, see that your names are put on the lists of voters, and go to the polls. If you are not strong enough to choose a man of your own color, give your votes to those who are friendly to your cause; but if possible, elect intelligent and respectable colored men."[1] Certainly, no thinking man could argue with this advice.

But before James Forten died in 1842, he saw that moderation, piety, and good citizenship were not necessarily reciprocated by the Commonwealth, because in 1838, the new Pennsylvania State Constitution reinterpreted the meaning of "freemen," and deemed that the "free men of color," who had been voting for nearly half a century, were no longer entitled to cast their ballots in the Commonwealth of Pennsylvania. Men like Robert Purvis, who had been voting and paying taxes for all of their adult lives, were sorely shaken by the backward drift where the rights of non-white people were concerned.

An era ended with the death of James Forten in Philadelphia on February 24, 1842. He was prepared. He had made his will some time before, and although he had suffered reverses as a result of the 1837 bank failure and the resulting financial panic, he was still reasonably well-off and able to provide for his loved ones. He figured that, conservatively, he was still worth something in the neighborhood of $300,000. He left his Lombard Street home to his wife, Charlotte, along with all of his personal property. He left his sister, Abigail Dunbar, whose husband had died earlier, the house and lot he had bought her and an adequate sum to pay the taxes and keep up the repairs. He left a bequest to the African Church of St. Thomas and a similar bequest to the Anti-Slavery Society of Philadelphia. His business, the still prosperous sail loft, he left to his widow and to his sons, Robert and James, Jr. The balance of the estate was to be shared with equal distribution by all eight of his children.

A Philadelphia newspaper, the *North American and Daily Advertiser,* wrote of Forten:

"We learn that James Forten, an old and highly respectable colored citizen, died yesterday morning. Mr. Forten has been for many years the leading sailmaker in this city. His strict integrity and great amenity of manners made him many friends among our best citizens. Mr. Forten, when a boy, was taken prisoner by the British whilst cruising in one of our vessels and confined in the celebrated Jersey prison ship during part of the Revolutionary War . . ."[1]

The *Philadelphia Public Ledger* reported that Forten's funeral,

". . . was one of the largest funeral processions we ever saw—numbering from three to five thousand persons, white and colored, male and female, about one-half white—to an extent never before witnessed in this city. . . . Among the white portion were seen some of our wealthiest merchants and shippers, captains of vessels and others. . . . The deceased had the reputation of being strictly honest, liberal to a fault, of unvarying kind and courteous demeanor."[2]

It was true that for the greater part of his life James Forten had been the man to whom the needy turned. It was not surprising that his estate had suffered accordingly. When the inventory was completed in the spring of 1842, James Forten was worth less than $70,000, but his place as a pacesetter was secure. He had been responsible and responsive, and he had never forgotten those who still "wore the yoke."

Forten's daughter's husband, Robert Purvis, had increasingly assumed the position of leadership which had been Forten's. There were other new voices being heard, and the country itself was still in the throes of becoming a nation. While Forten had maintained his residence in the heart of the city, Purvis preferred to remain at the country estate originally purchased by his father, the Englishman, William Purvis, at Byberry on the outskirts of Philadelphia.

A contemporary writer described his home:

> "The stage put us down at the gate, and we were warned to be ready to return in an hour and a half. His dwelling stands some distance back from the turnpike. It is approached by a broad lawn, and shaded with ancient trees. In the rear stands a fine series of barns. There are magnificent orchards connected with his farm, and his livestock is of the most approved breeds. We understand that he receives numbers of premiums [prizes] annually from agricultural societies. In this fine old mansion, Mr. Purvis has resided many years."

The writer continued,

> "We were ushered upon our visit into a pleasant dining room hung with a number of paintings. Upon one side of an old-fashioned mantel was a large portrait of a fine-looking white man; on the other side, a portrait of a swarthy negro . . . Mr. Purvis has written a number of anti-slavery pamphlets, and is regarded by rumor as the president of the Underground Railroad. He has figured in many slave-rescue cases, some of which he relates with graphic manner of description. He is the heaviest tax payer in the township and owns two very valuable farms . . ."[3]

Reverend Samuel May remembered his first meeting with Robert Purvis:

> "He was then [1835] an elegant, brilliant young gentleman, well educated and wealthy. He was so nearly white that he

was generally taken to be so. When I first saw him at *our*
[italics mine] anti-slavery convention in Philadelphia, I was
taken to him by his fervent eloquence, and was surprised at
the intimation which fell from his lips that he belonged to
the proscribed, disfranchised class. Away from the neighborhood of his birth, he might easily have passed as a white man.
Indeed, I was told that he had travelled much in stage-
coaches, and stopped days and weeks at Saratoga and other
fashionable resorts, and mingled without question among the
beaux and belles, regarded by the latter as one of the most
attractive of his sex. Robert Purvis might therefore have
removed to any part of our country far distant from Philadelphia and have lived as one of the self-styled superior race.
But rather than forsake his kindred or try to conceal the
secret of his birth, he *magnanimously* [italics mine] chose to
bear the unjust reproach, the cruel wrongs of the colored
people, although he has been more annoyed, chafed, exasper-
ated by *them* than anyone I have ever met with."[4]

Purvis was indeed the "president" of the Underground Railroad, and
was also the organizer and head of the Philadelphia Vigilance Committee,
which helped slaves escape through the city, providing them with money
and directions for the last leg of the journey. Their work became even
more crucial after the passage of the Fugitive Slave Act of 1850.

His close friend and associate in the work of the Vigilance Committee
and the Moral Reform Society was William Whipper.

According to William Still's account in *The Underground Railroad:*

"Columbia [Pennsylvania], where Mr. Whipper resided for
many years, was a place of much note as a station on the
Underground Railroad. The firm of Smith and Whipper
[lumber merchants] was likewise well-known throughout a
wide range of country. Who, indeed, amongst those familiar
with the history of public matters connected with the colored
people of this country, has not heard of William Whipper?
. . . as an able businessman, he hardly had a superior. As an
operator of a station on the Underground Railroad, Whipper

himself describes the route which brought the fugitives to his care: 'You are perfectly cognizant of the fact that after the decision in York, Pennsylvania, of the celebrated *Prigg* case,[5] Pennsylvania was regarded as free territory, which Canada afterwards proved to be, and that the Susquehanna River was the recognized northern boundary of the slaveholding empire. The borough of Columbia, situated on the eastern bank in the county of Lancaster, was the great depot where the fugitives from Virginia and Maryland first landed. The long bridge connecting Wrightsville with Columbia was the only safe outlet by which they could successfully escape their pursuers. When they had crossed this bridge, they could say to the slave powers: "Thus far shalt thou come, and no farther." . . . my house was at the end of the bridge, and as I kept the station, I was frequently called up in the night to take charge of the passengers.' "[6]

Whipper indicates that his desire to get the fugitives safely away was mainly one of *self-preservation*.

". . .'I knew that it had been asserted, far down in the slave region, that Smith and Whipper, the Negro lumber merchants, were engaged in secreting fugitive slaves. On two occasions attempts had been made to set fire to the yard for the purpose of punishing them for such illegal acts. I felt that if a collision took place, we should not only be made to suffer the penalty, but the most valuable property in the village be destroyed, besides a prodigal waste of human life be the consequence. In such an event I felt that I should not only lose all I had ever earned, but peril the hopes and property of others, so that I would have freely given one thousand dollars to have been insured against the consequences of such a riot. I then borrowed fourteen hundred dollars on my own individual account, and assisted many others to go to a land where the virgin soil was not polluted by the foot-prints of a slave.' "[7]

Whipper's young son, William, was taken in 1853 to Canada, and then remained in Detroit during the years of strife when so many free-born colored people were in such great danger from the kidnappers. Whipper purchased land in the vicinity of the Sydenham River " '. . . with the intention of making it [his] future home.' "

While Whipper was often accused of being overly abstract and too much a part of the Garrisonian "moral suasion" turn of mind, his own words make one think that perhaps that was a part of his protective covering when he stated:

> "It would have been fortunate for us if Columbia, being a port of entry for flying fugitives, had also been the seat of great great capitalists and freedom-loving inhabitants; but such was not the case. There was but little anti-slavery sentiment among the whites; yet there was many strong and valiant friends among them who contributed freely; the colored population were too poor to render much aid, except in feeding and secreting strangers. I was doing a prosperous business at that time and felt it my duty to contribute liberally out of my earnings. Much as I loved anti-slavery meetings, I did not feel that I could afford to attend them, as my immediate duty was to the flying fugitives."[8]

The Higher Classes

While it may be that the overriding concern of the free colored communities was at all times and in all places the abolition of slavery and the extension of civil and political and economic rights to *all* people, all work and no play was, even then, an unwise program. So, there were entertainments, musicales, weddings, funerals, debates, and meetings of the various literary societies and lyceums, where discussion of current events took place. That these activities took place within a rigidly circumscribed set of circumstances, which could not have been more circumspect, is clearly indicated in some of the observations in a chatty little volume called *Sketches of Higher Classes of Colored Society*. Published in 1841, the style and manner of this social activity is described. The values and standards of the "higher class" lady and gentleman of color is implicit in the following:

> "It will not, it is believed, be expected of the writer, in speaking of the ability of the higher classes of colored society to maintain social intercourse on terms of respectability and dignity, to give an elaborate statement or inventory of the furniture of their dwellings—its quality and cost—the size of their market baskets . . . and the usual character of their contents; it will not be necessary to say that their parlors are carpeted and furnished with sofas, sideboards, card tables, mirrors, etc, with, in many instances, the addition of the pianoforte. These, with other relative matters governed by no particular standard, the reader is left to form such an opinion of, as he may deem most correct! I will say, however, that usually, according to pecuniary ability, they fail not to gratify themselves in this wise to the extent and after the manner that gains observance among other people.

> "Visiting *sans ceremonie* does not obtain to a very great extent with the higher classes of colored society. Even among those who are otherwise intimate acquaintances, the order

of unceremonious visits is but limited. They are mostly by familiar or formal invitation, or in return for others previously received. This . . . observance is most rigidly adhered to by many. . . . The period of paying and receiving visits is mostly confined to the evening; among the gentlemen almost entirely so. Many circumstances combine to render this arrangement most convenient and agreeable to all parties. Their attendance upon the ladies is mostly confined to visiting them at their dwellings. . . . With the young ladies at home, they pass their evenings agreeably if so disposed. It is rarely that the visitor in the different families where there are two or three ladies will not find one or more of them competent to perform on the pianoforte, guitar, or some other appropriate musical instrument; and these, with singing and conversation on whatever suitable topics that may offer, constitute the amusements of their evenings at home.

"The observance of abstinence at the parties of the higher classes of colored society—total abstinence from all that has a tendency to intoxicate—is worthy of remark. So far as my observation has extended, the only drinks that are presented . . . may consist of lemonade, or some pleasant and wholesome syrup comingled with water. No wines of any description—not even the lightest and mildest—are ever brought forward. Whether this arises from a pure love of temperance or a disposition to avoid unnecessary expenditure, either of which is commendable, I shall not pause to inquire."[1]

Upward mobility could only come through education, and the severe lack of it caused blacks to seek ways for self-improvement within the scope of their means.

Because they were not permitted access to libraries and reading rooms, it was imperative that the colored community establish their own, and the Philadelphia Library Company of Colored Persons was established January 1, 1833. The nine members who organized the group were Frederick Hinton, James Needham, James Cornish, Robert C. Gordon, Jr., William

Whipper, John Dupee, J. C. Bowers, Charles Trulier, Robert Douglass, Jr., and James C. Matthews.

The members maintained a library which included books of every description, and their meetings were held in the basement of St. Thomas Protestant Episcopal Church. The group was incorporated in 1836, and there was a one dollar membership fee, and twenty-five cents monthly dues.

Those who were not included in the first group organized on March 1, 1837 the Rush Library Company and Debating Society. Their members were John L. Hart, William D. Barton, Littleton Hubert, Harrison R. Sylva, James Bird, and Charles Brister.

Two years later, on January 10, 1839, The Demosthenean Institute was organized at the home of John P. Burr, and included as its members David Gordon, Benjamin Stanley, William Jennings, G. W. Gibbons, Lewis B. Meade, E. Parkinson, and B. Hughes. This group had expanded their mission to include not only debating, but activities which would have been appropriate to a preparatory school, where the members were trained to fit themselves for appearances before public audiences by skill in parliamentary procedure and public speaking, as well as debating. The *Demosthenean Shield* was a publication of this group, and it was the only newspaper—excluding the pamphlet-type publication, the *National Reformer,* which William Whipper edited as the organ of the Moral Reform Society—coming out of Philadelphia during this period. This paper had a subscription list of 1,000 when it made its first appearance in 1841.

Women were not excluded from such social and cultural activities, and The Minerva Literary Association, which was organized in October, 1834, had thirty women as members. Readings and recitations of original and selected pieces were encouraged, with the emphasis being on "polite" literature.

The Edgeworth Literary Association had the same objectives, and only one, The Gilbert Lyceum, which was established in January, 1841, encouraged participation by both men and women. Its members were Mr. Robert Douglass, Sr., Mrs. Grace Douglass and Miss Sarah M. Douglass, Mr. Robert Purvis and Mrs. Harriett Purvis, Mr. Joseph Cossey and Mrs. Amy M. Cossey, Mrs. Hetty Burr, Miss Aurelia Bogle, Mr. John C. Bowers, and Mr. Jacob White. At The Gilbert Lyceum, education and polite literature were the items on the agenda, and the issues of the day were not discussed for the public record.

Our observer in *The Higher Classes of Colored Society* makes some telling points when he says:

> "No one, of course, expects unanimity in all matters of policy among any people. Differences are expected and will always arise. But it is expected that those differences will be marked by an open, manly and honorable course of procedure and not by low scheming and chicanery. . . . It is hardly necessary to add that those who merit reproach for indulgence in the last named practice are always the very first to pounce upon and impeach the motives of their heights. . . . It is certainly to be hoped that the young men—and there are many of them—who are just entering the stage of public action in behalf of their fellow men, will guard against the rocks and shoals upon which their senior contemporaries have nearly wrecked all hopes of ever being able to do any permanent, general good. Had they, instead of striving with and endeavoring to destroy each other, united their energies and labored for the mutual benefit of all, they might have presented a state of society which would have been an invincible argument against the tyrannical act [disfranchisement] . . . and perhaps secured for their posterity all of the 'rights, privileges and immunities' enjoyed by other citizens of the Commonwealth."[2]

It is likely that Purvis and Whipper and their fellow Garrisonians read those words. It is also very unlikely that the new breed, Henry Highland Garnet, Frederick Douglass, Martin Delany, and William Wells Brown read those words or took the time to ponder them.

The New Breed

Up to the end of the 1830s, the fight for abolition had primarily been waged by petition, convention, broadside, and the occasional insurrection. Those blacks identified with the anti-slavery movement were men of substance and standing in their communities. They argued against slavery because it was wrong, while pointing out as Forten had done that their fathers "had never worn the yoke."

But by 1840 there was a new breed on the scene. It was the man who had not had a kind master and been manumitted. It was a man who had not been permitted to "buy his time." It was a man who knew the auction block firsthand, and who had felt the lash of the overseer's whip. In short, it was an escaped slave. It was Frederick Douglass, William Wells Brown, Henry Highland Garnet, Martin Delany, and Samuel Ringgold Ward. It was the creativity involved in the daring escapes of William and Ellen Craft and Henry "Box" Brown. It was the intrepid Harriet Tubman, who fearlessly led from bondage hundreds of Maryland slaves.

Henry Highland Garnet was an outstanding example of this new kind of black man. He was born on a plantation on the eastern shore of Maryland, as were Frederick Douglass and Harriet Tubman. Garnet's father feared that the slave system would ultimately divide his family, so he boldly sought permission to attend the funeral of another slave some distance away from the home plantation. Permission granted, the trusted slave Garnet took his family and several other slaves in a covered wagon to Wilmington, Delaware where they were given shelter by a Quaker Underground Railroad operator, Thomas Garrett. From there the family was sent to Bucks County, Pennsylvania and on to New York City.

In New York, Henry Highland Garnet was sent to The African Free School, which had been established in 1787 and came under the New York Board of Education in 1834. Some of Garnet's classmates were Patrick Reason, an early black artist; Charles L. Reason, a poet and teacher; Ira

Aldridge, an actor; James McCune Smith, a physician; and Samuel Ringgold Ward. Garnet finished his education at Oneida Institute in upstate New York.

Garnet was inspired to enter the ministry, but he was too radical in his writing. His home was invaded by slave hunters, "blackbirders," looking for his father. He had his leg amputated as the result of an infection, and his health was never again robust. In 1843, his address to the slaves of America, at the National Convention of Colored Americans, in Buffalo, New York, was so inflammatory that the convention refused to permit him to address the gathering. He later had it printed. In it he said:

> ". . . Your brethren have been meeting at these conventions, sympathizing with each other and weeping over your unhappy condition. In these meetings, we have addressed all classes of the free, but we have never sent a word of consolation or advice to you. . . . Slavery has fixed a deep void between you and us. . . . It is sinful in the extreme to make voluntary submission. . . . The forlorn condition you are now in does not destroy your obligation to God. You are not certain of heaven because you allow yourselves to remain in a state of slavery. . . . Neither God nor angels nor just men command you to suffer for a single moment. . . .
>
> "It is in your power so to torment the God-cursed slave holders that they will be glad to let you go free. If the scale were turned and the black men were the masters and the white men the slaves, every destructive agent and element would be employed to lay the oppressor low. Danger and Death would hang over their head day and night. . . . Let your motto be Resistance! Resistance! Resistance! No oppressed people ever secured their liberty without resistance. What kind of resistance you had better make, you must decide by the circumstances that surround you, and according to the suggestion of expediency. . . . Remember you are four millions!"[1]

The counterpart of Purvis, Whipper, and Smith in Philadelphia was David Ruggles of New York. The New York Vigilance Committee had been organized on November 20, 1835, following an upsurge in the kidnapping of free blacks from New York.

David Ruggles was named director, and his close associates on the committee were Dr. James McCune Smith and Philip A. Bell, who operated an employment agency which provided escaped slaves with opportunities for work. It was these "colored brethren" whose financial and organizational cooperation largely made its work possible.

The committee had white members who helped with money and jobs, but the major risks were taken by blacks themselves in danger of being captured under the *pretext* of being fugitive slaves.

The primary jobs of vigilance committees were to help runaways establish themselves, keep a lookout for slave hunters and kidnappers, and provide transportation, clothing, shelter, food, and legal aid in cases where blacks were taken as runaways and tried in court.

Most often, runaways were not permitted to stay in New York City, but sent to Boston, Providence, Syracuse, Albany, or Rochester. If escape into Canada was necessary, it could be done more easily from Albany and Rochester, New York.

One of the fugitives handled by the vigilance committee was an escaped slave from the eastern shore of Maryland named Frederick Douglass.

Douglass declined to tell how he got to New York from Baltimore, but he said, "The flight was a bold and perilous one." However, once in New York City, Douglass found that:

> ". . . in the midst of thousands of my fellowmen, [I was] yet a perfect stranger. In the midst of human brothers, and yet more fearful of them than of hungry wolves! I was without home, without friends, without work, without money and without any definite knowledge of which way to go or where to look for succor."

Finally, at the end of his rope, Douglass decided he had to trust someone, and so he told his story to a sailor named Stewart who:

> ". . . listened with a brother's interest. He took me to his
> house and went in search of . . . David Ruggles. . . . Once in
> the hands of Mr. Ruggles, I was comparatively safe. I was
> hidden with Mr. Ruggles several days. In the meantime, my
> intended wife, Anna, came on from Baltimore . . . I had
> written informing her of my safe arrival . . . and in the pres-
> ence of Mrs. Mitchell and Mr. Ruggles, we were married
> by Reverend James W. C. Pennington."[2]

Douglass was sent with his bride to New Bedford, where it was hoped
he could get work at his trade of caulker in the shipyards. It was at New
Bedford that Frederick Augustus Washington Bailey became Frederick
Douglass, after a character in Scott's *Lady of the Lake.*

In less than six months after his arrival in New Bedford, Frederick
Douglass had been given a copy of the *Liberator,* and came into contact
with ". . . the mind of William Loyd Garrison." Douglass said, "His paper
took its place with me next to the Bible."

In 1841, still in New Bedford, Frederick Douglass went to his first
anti-slavery meeting. He was so moved that he felt bold enough to speak
to the group and to recount his personal experiences as a slave. His speech
was dynamic, the more so because it came from the heart. Parker Pillsbury,
a white abolitionist who attended the meeting, later recorded the events
and general mood of that evening:

> "When this young man closed late in the evening, though
> none seemed to know or care for the hour, Mr. Garrison rose
> to make the concluding address. I think he never before nor
> afterwards felt more profoundly the sacredness of his mis-
> sion . . . I surely never saw him more cleverly inspired. His
> last question was, 'Shall such a man ever be sent back to
> slavery from the soil of old Massachusetts?' . . . almost the
> whole assembly sprang with one accord to their feet, and the
> walls and roof of the Atheneum seemed to shudder with the
> 'No, No!' loud and long. . . ."[3]

Douglass was from that moment a member of the Garrison camp, but
the alliance lived only as long as Douglass was willing to be a follower. The

Photographs

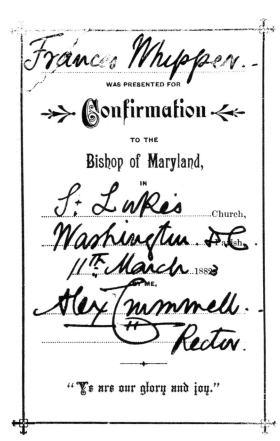

Frances Whipper

WAS PRESENTED FOR

Confirmation

TO THE

Bishop of Maryland,

IN

St Luke's .... Church,

Washington .... D.C. .... Parish.

11th March 1882

BY ME,

Alex Crummell .... Rector.

"Ye are our glory and joy."

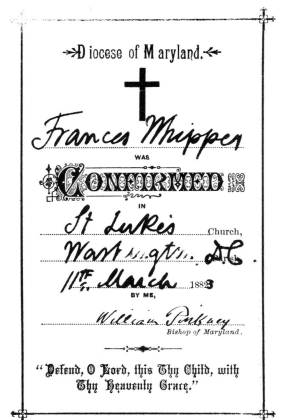

Diocese of Maryland.

✝

Frances Whipper

WAS

Confirmed

IN

St Luke's .... Church,

Washington .... D.C. .... Parish.

11th March 1882

BY ME,

William Pinkney

Bishop of Maryland.

"Defend, O Lord, this Thy Child, with Thy Heavenly Grace."

Francis Rollin Whipper, the wife of William J. Whipper, received her confirmation papers in 1882 from Alexander Crummell (r.) in Washington, D.C., where she became one of the first black women physicians in the United States.

The marriage certificate of Lawrence Faulkner and Hannah Doby was issued in South Carolina in 1883. They are the parents of Rev. William J. Faulkner who married Elizabeth Abele Cook.

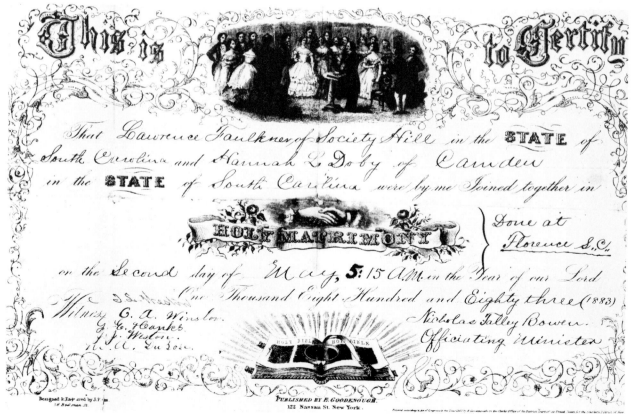

This is to Certify

That Lawrence Faulkner of Society Hill in the STATE of South Carolina and Hannah L. Doby of Camden in the STATE of South Carolina were by me Joined together in

HOLY MATRIMONY

Done at Florence S.C.

on the Second day of May, 5:15 A.M. in the Year of our Lord One Thousand Eight Hundred and Eighty three (1883)

Witness C. A. Winslow.
G. E. Hankes.
J. Winslow.
H. A. DuBose.

Nicholas Talley Bowen.
Officiating Minister

Designed & Engraved by J.F. Pin
16 Beekman St.

PUBLISHED BY F. GOODENOUGH.
122 Nassau St. New York.

Paul Laurence Dunbar
(bottom l.) made his
debut at the World's
Columbian Exposition,
reciting his poem,
"The Colored American," written for
Negro Jubilee Day. He later col-
laborated with Will Marion Cook
(above) on an operetta, Clorindy
The Origin of the Cakewalk, starring Cook's wife, Abbie Mitchell.

Aida Overton Walker, come-
dienne, dancer and wife of
George Walker (near r.),
was part of the act when
the team of Walker and
Bert Williams (far right)
was at its peak.

Noted actor Leigh Whipper, grandson of Underground Railroad operator William Whipper, in his many
roles, and (below l. to r.) sheet

music for The Entertainer by Scott
Joplin, opera singer Madam Sissie-
retta Jones, and composer/producers
Bob Cole and J. Rosamond Johnson.

Willis H. Cromwell, (l.) father of John W. Cromwell, (c.), gained freedom in 1851. Educated son at Institute for Colored Youth. John W. Cromwell, Jr. followed father's lead as historian and educator, as did daughter, Adelaide Cromwell Gulliver, director, Afro-American Studies, Boston University, and sister, lower left, Otelia Cromwell, author, educator and member of committee to develop Encyclopedia of the Negro (shown below).

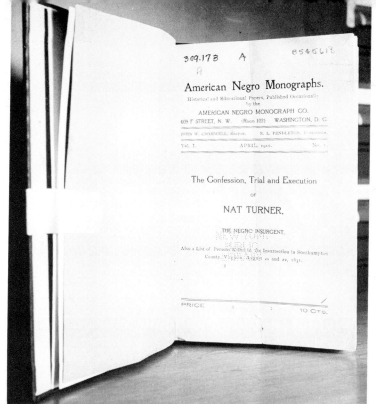

Intellectual activity
enhanced during the 90's by
presence of Charles W. Chesnutt, T. Thomas Fortune, and
brothers, Archibald (l.) and
Francis Grimke. A. Grimke,
and Chesnutt were Spingarn
medalists, 1919 and 1928.

121

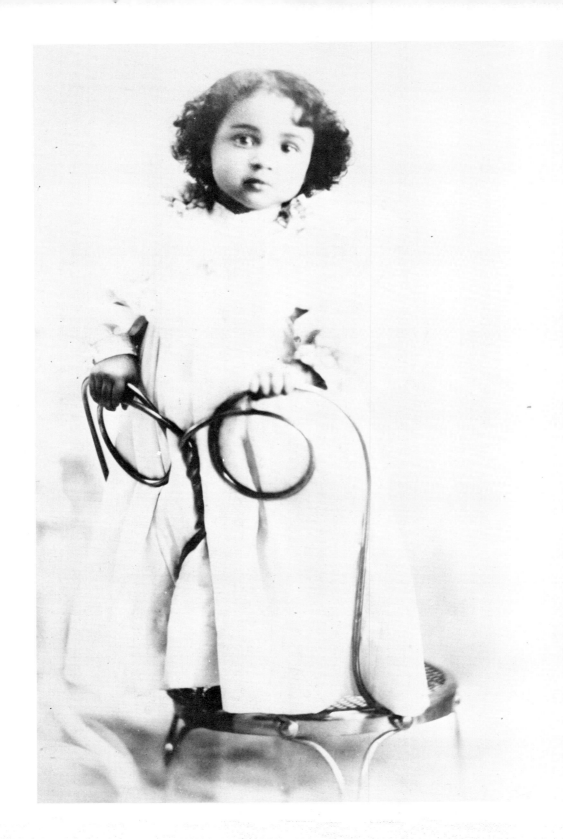

122

Two-year-old Gerri Hodges, her grandmother (top, left photo, center), her great aunt, Medora Powell, in 1883 Mishawaka graduating class, and two Powell family residences in South Bend.

123

A feud raged for many years between Provident Hospital's founder, Dr. Daniel Hale Williams, (bottom, right) and Dr. George Cleveland Hall, (top, left). (center) Theodosia Hall, bottom, Alice Williams. Dr. Williams was director of Freedman's Hospital, Washington, D. C. during which time, Drs. John Gilbert, Edward Williston, (seated) and John Mitchell, William Warfield, were staff.

Provident Hospital, established in 1891 by Dr. Daniel Hale Williams, was the first interracial hospital as well as the first Negro nurses' training school in the country.

125

Typical of the correct manner in which weddings and births were observed is the wedding invitation for the Abele-Cook wedding and the birth announcement for Lee Julian Purnell, son of Theodora Lee and William Whipper Purnell. Wedding above pictures Garrett Smith Wormley and wife Amelia Brent at daughter, Edith's marriage.

MRS. DR. PURNELL.

took place at 12 o'clock to-day at the residence of Mrs. John Jones, the bride's grandmother, 49 Ray street.

The Rev. Moses Jackson officiated. Miss Seales of Cleveland, O., was the bridesmaid, Miss Mabel Wheeler, a cousin of the bride, and Miss Helen Brown of Detroit, Mich., were the ladies of honor. Andrew Fraser Stevens, Jr. of Philadelphia acted as best man.

There were many guests from Washington, St. Louis, Detroit and Louisville.

The bride is a native of Chicago, being a member of one of the oldest and best-known colored families. She is a granddaughter of John Jones, who was for many years a substantial business man and a member of the first board of county commissioners. He was elected along with Carter Harrison and others, on what was known as "the fire-proof ticket," at the election held after the great fire in the fall of 1871.

Mr. Jones was an extensive property-holder and when he died some years ago left a substantial estate in real and personal property. During ante-bellum days his home was the western station of the abolitionists and was often graced with the presence of John Brown, Frederick Douglas, Owen Lovejoy and others.

Dr. Purnell is a practicing physician in the city of Washington. He is a graduate of Howard university and the medical school of the University of Pennsylvania. The young couple will reside in Washington.

Mrs. Theodore Lee Purnell became a mother last Sunday in Washington City her home, and mother and son are doing nicely. More than usual interest attaches to this child which is to be, if he lives, the heir of John Jones' wealth. The will is said to be so drawn that the child of Mr Jones' grandchild Theodora inherits the money left by Chicago's wealthiest colored man. In case she had no children, the money was to go to the city. Mrs. Purnell's grandmother, Mrs. John Jones has been in Washington for six weeks past and was present to welcome the newcomer.

Mr. and Mrs. John Jones

Dr. & Mrs. Wm. Whipper Purnell.

1516 New Jersey Ave. N.W.

Elizabeth Abele Cook.

Mrs. M. A. Abele requests your presence at the marriage of her daughter Elizabeth Rebecca to Mr. John F. Cook, Jr. Tuesday afternoon December fourth Eighteen hundred and ninety-four at half past four o'clock. Central Presbyterian Church Lombard Street below Ninth Philadelphia.

John Francis Cook

Wm. Whipper Purnell

127

Dr. Henry Minton
(above) was first
black pharmacist
in Philadelphia
before founding
Mercy Hospital
which eventually
merged and became
the Mercy-
Douglass Hospital
(opposite top). His
wife (left) was the
former Edith
Wormley. Minton was
one of the founders
of Sigma Pi Phi
(The Boule).

Founder of the Frederick Douglass Hospital in 1895 was Dr. Nathan F. Mossell. Mrs. Mossell (opposite, r.) was a contributing writer to many major publications.

129

Abolitionists intended for Douglass to speak but not to be "too learned" in his speech. The programmatics and strategy were to be left to the white abolitionists. He went to England in 1845 and there collected money to purchase his freedom and to start his paper.

In 1845, Douglass wrote the *Narrative,* and in 1847, he moved to Rochester and started his own paper, the *North Star,* with Martin Delany. He stated that he selected Rochester because it was outside of the territory where the *Liberator* had wide circulation, and so he could not be accused of competing with his former mentor. However, the white Garrisonians were angered. They finally split when Douglass affirmed that the Constitution of the United States was not, in itself, a pro-slavery document, and that black people should, wherever possible, engage actively in the political process in order to effect their civil rights and the abolition of slavery.

William Wells Brown replaced Frederick Douglass as the Garrisonians's drawing card on the anti-slavery lecture circuit. Brown was an excellent writer and a fair speaker, although he could not rival the spellbinding style of the great Douglass. While William Wells Brown could not substantiate it, he had been told that his father was a member of the Wickliffe family of Lexington, Kentucky, and his mother, a mulatto, was the daughter of Daniel Boone and a black woman. He was raised on a plantation, and until he was nine years old, he said, ". . . my life was such as falls to any young slave." But he was given the opportunity to become a companion for his master's nephew when he was nine and described the reason that it was important for him to get the job of companion to the young white boy:

> ". . . Whoever should gain the place was in the future to become a house servant; the ash-cake to be thrown aside, that unmentionable garment that buttons around the neck which we all wore and nothing else, was to give way to the whole suit of tow linen. Every one of us joined heartily in the contest, while old mistress sat on the piazza watching our every movement—some fifteen of us, each dressed in his own garments, some standing on our heads with feet in the air— the lady still looked on. With me it seemed a matter of life and death; for, being blood kin to the master, I felt I had

more at stake than my companions. At last the choice was made, and I was told to step aside as the 'lucky boy', which order I obeyed with an alacrity seldom surpassed. . . . I was the star of the plantation. My mother, one of the best mothers, placed her hands on my head, and with tears in her eyes said, 'I knowed you was born for good luck, for a fortune teller told me so when you was a baby layin' in your little sugar trough. Go up to de great house where you belong.' With this blessing I bade farewell to the log hut and dirt floor and started to the 'big house'."[4]

The family moved to St. Louis, and William was hired out to the *St. Louis Times,* edited by Elijah P. Lovejoy, the abolitionist. Lovejoy was eventually forced to leave his job in St. Louis after he openly decried the burning of a black man at the stake. He went across the river to Alton, Illinois where he began publication of an anti-slavery paper. He was killed by a mob, and his plant and building were burned to the ground.

In St. Louis young William began to ". . . feel more longings for liberty." But a short time later he was hired out to a slave trader named Walker. After a year, ". . . beholding scenes of cruelty that can be better imagined than described, I was once more taken home, and hired out as an under steward on the steamer *Patriot,* running to New Orleans. . . . Continued intercourse with educated persons, and meeting on the steamer so many travelers from the free states caused me to feel more keenly my degraded and unnatural situation." He made an unsuccessful attempt to escape with his mother, who by now had been sold to a St. Louis tailor. Finally, without his mother, he did escape and make his way into Ohio where, sick and cold and hungry, he was taken in by ". . . an old white-haired man, dressed in a suit of drab, with a broad-brimmed hat." He was the first person that the escaped slave had seen of ". . . the sect called Quakers, and his name was Wells Brown." He stayed with him until he had recovered his strength and been fitted out with clothes, shoes, and some money. He then went to Cleveland, Ohio where he became engaged in helping other escaped slaves to freedom. In one year, following his own escape, he estimated that he had assisted sixty fugitives into Canada.

He was invited by the officers of the Western New York Anti-Slavery Society to join and later to take the job of lecturer left vacant by Douglass, who had gone to Europe. From that time until June of 1849, he toured the New England states, Ohio, Illinois, and Indiana, lecturing and, in the latter months, exhibiting William and Ellen Craft. The Crafts had escaped from Macon, Georgia in 1848 in the disguise of a young white planter and his male body servant travelling to the North for the master's health. Mrs. Craft and her husband, after the passage of the 1850 Fugitive Slave Law, went to England where they remained until the end of the Civil War.

In July 1849, Brown accepted the invitation of influential English abolitionists and sailed for Liverpool on the royal mail steamship, *Canada*. He remained in England for more than five years writing, lecturing, and visiting on the Continent. He was a delegate to the Peace Congress at Paris on his first trip. In the autumn of 1854, he returned "home to America" to continue his work as an abolitionist, but like Douglass, he had taken the precaution of purchasing his freedom first.

The passage of the infamous 1850 act created a new climate of opinion among those colored people who had always been staunchly opposed to expatriation or colonization. Robert Purvis, at the end of his emotional rope, considered leaving the country and taking up residence abroad. He and Harriett had travelled in Europe as newlyweds in 1834, but it seemed to him that no progress had been made; if anything, conditions were worse than ever. Even he, as well-known and respected as it seemed he should be, had been insulted by the Philadelphia Chicken Fanciers who refused, in 1853, to permit him to exhibit any of his poultry, although Purvis had exhibited his fowl before and won first prize three times at the annual show.

In December of 1853, Purvis belligerently refused to pay taxes for the schools which his children were not permitted to attend. He wrote:

> ". . . You called yesterday for the tax upon my property in this Township, which I shall pay, excepting the 'School Tax.' I object to the payment of this tax, on the ground that my rights as a citizen, and my feelings as a man and a parent, have been grossly outraged in depriving me, in violation of law and justice, of the benefits of the school system which this tax was designed to sustain.
>
> "I am perfectly aware that all that makes up the char-acter and worth of the citizens of this township look upon the

proscription and exclusion of my children from the Public School as illegal, and an unjustifiable usurpation of my right. I have borne this outrage ever since the innovation upon the usual practice of admitting all the children of the Township into the Public Schools, and at considerable expense have been obliged to obtain the services of private teachers to instruct my children, while my school tax is *greater* [italics mine], with a single exception, than that of any other citizen of the township.

"It is true (and the outrage is made but the more glaring and insulting), I was informed by a pious Quaker director, with a sanctifying grace imparting, doubtless, an unctuous glow to his saintly prejudices, that a school in the village of Mechanicsville was appropriate for 'thine'. The miserable shanty . . . to which this benighted follower of George Fox alluded is, as you know, the most flimsy and ridiculous sham which any tool of a skin-hating aristocracy could have resorted to, to cover or protect his servility.

"To submit by voluntary payment of the demand is too great an outrage upon nature and, with a spirit, thank God, unshackled by this or any other wanton and cowardly act, I shall resist this tax which, before the unjust exclusion, had always afforded me the highest gratification in paying. With no other than the best feelings towards yourself, I am forced to this unpleasant position, in vindication of my rights and personal dignity against an encroachment upon them as contemptibly mean as it is infamously despotic."[5]

William Wells Brown noted that, ". . . by his influence the public schools of the township have been thrown open to colored children."

Martin Robinson Delany, a New Yorker, who had attended the African Free School, later attended the ill-fated Oneida Institute and Harvard University Medical School. He practiced medicine in Pittsburgh and was there during the cholera epidemic in 1854. He edited his own paper, the *Mystery,* and later wrote *The Condition, Elevation, Emigration and Destiny of the Colored People of the United States* (1852). From 1847 to

1850, he worked with Frederick Douglass as assistant editor on the *North Star*. They split on the subject of colonization because Delany felt there was no future for blacks in the United States. Immigrating to Canada West, he helped to organize an expedition to Nigeria in 1858 under the sponsorship of the National Emigration Society and the African Civilization Society. He negotiated treaties with chiefs of West African nations who granted land for prospective black American settlers. He organized a program for the development of the cotton export industry in Africa under black ownership, and set up plans for the importation of cotton gins. He went to England from Africa where he was lionized. He and Mary Ann Shadd Cary, the daughter of Abraham Shadd of Delaware, took issue with Douglass over the ability of the Abolitionists to bring about the necessary changes in the condition of colored people in the United States.

The entire Shadd family migrated to Canada following passage of the Fugitive Slave Act. Mary Ann Shadd, outspoken and articulate, had taught school in Pennsylvania and moved with her family to Chatham, Ontario when conditions in the United States reached their worst. She later opened a school in Windsor, and with the help of the American Missionary Association, continued the school until 1853 when support was withdrawn. In March of 1853, she was a member of the founding committee and acted as editor of the *Provincial Freeman*, a newspaper devoted to the problems and concerns of the refugees in Canada. The *Freeman* was published for four years, and Miss Shadd was probably the first woman on the American continent to establish and edit a weekly newspaper.

Frances Ellen Watkins Harper, while more involved in the literary world than the world of the abolitionist, was nonetheless a force in the publicizing of the plight of the slave and free Negro. Her poems were read from the time she was a very young woman on programs where the abolitionists were speaking, and her very presence refuted the stereotype of the dumb and illiterate black. Her first book, *Poems on Miscellaneous Subjects,* was published in 1854 when she was twenty-nine years old. She sold ten thousand copies simply in the course of her readings in the first five years of publication. It was reprinted three times.

Gold!

*B*etween 1850 and 1860, the black population in California quadrupled. There were 1,000 blacks in the 1850 census and 4,000 in the 1860 census. There were many reasons for the sudden migration, but the primary one and the one that accounted for new fortunes and some old ones lost was gold. It was discovered at Sutter's Fort in California near the American River in 1849.

The gold fever was indiscriminate in the people it attacked, and among those caught was James Wormley, the youngest son of Peter and Mary Wormley.

In 1841, James married Anna Thompson of Norfolk, Virginia. They were the parents of four children: William H. A., born in 1842; James Thompson, born in 1844; Garrett Smith, born in 1846; and Anna Matilda, born in 1850. These four children were the progenitors of the present Wormley clan.

James tried his hand at a number of things before really hitting his stride. He worked as a waiter and then as steward on both Potomac River and ocean-going ships, but he never quite made it. So in 1849, he went to California to seek his fortune. Once there, he found that for every man who struck it rich in the gold fields, at least a dozen lost everything they had. Before long, he worked his way back to Washington, wiser for the experience, but no richer. He and Anna then opened a small confectionery store which she operated while he went to work in Washington's Metro-politan Club as a steward. They expanded by fixing lunch pails on Capitol Hill, and they grew into a catering business. James opened his first hotel in 1856 on I Street between 15th and 16th.

Another young man who went West was Mifflin Wister Gibbs. Gibbs was the son of an industrious and frugal widow from Philadelphia, where he had been born free in April of 1828. His father, a Methodist minister, died when he was eight years old, but he managed to stay in school until he had acquired more than the bare essentials. He was apprenticed to a carpenter and builder, and as soon as he was able, he went into business on his own. He joined the Philomatheon Institute, the literary society for young men in which Purvis and Whipper were actively involved.

Because he was intelligent and had a fair education, it was not long before he had become a member of the Anti-Slavery Society and a worker with the Underground Railroad. Early in 1849, Frederick Douglass and Charles Lenox Remond invited him to join them on a lecture tour through New York, Ohio, and Pennsylvania. It was while he was touring in the western section of Ohio that gold was discovered in California. At the end of the lecture tour, instead of starting back with Douglass and Remond, Gibbs set out for the golden West, arriving in San Francisco in the latter part of 1850. He tried to get work as a carpenter or construction worker, but even in California, the whites who had preceded had established the ground rules of not working with blacks, thus making trades exclusive for white workers. Gibbs had to eat, so he got a job as a porter in the Union Hotel and opened up a shoe-shine stand out in front. While working in this menial capacity, he met a man named Nathan Pointer who went into the clothing business with him. They did well, but in 1852 Gibbs went into business with Peter Lester at 636 Clay Street where they operated the only retail shoe and boot store in San Francisco, importing fine boots and shoes from London, Paris, Philadelphia, and New York.

Gibbs's anti-slavery experiences were still fresh in his mind, and the racism and injustice that he saw being imported into California caused him to join in the Franchise League with Jonas H. Townsend, W. H. Newby, William Hall, and several other prominent colored men to draw up and publish in the *Alta California* a group of resolutions that clearly defined the rights of the American blacks and their determination to resist encroachments upon them.

The right to vote and the right to testify had been denied black men, and the entire situation came into focus when Gordon Chase, a black barber, was murdered by a white man. One of the witnesses who could testify against the white murderer was Robert Cowles. Physicians were called into the courtroom to examine Cowles's hair, and as a result, it was determined that he was one-sixteenth black and therefore his testimony was inadmissible in court.

While neither James Wormley nor Mifflin Gibbs made a fortune in gold, some blacks did. They included Moses Rodgers, who owned a group of mines at Hornitus; Robert Anthony, who owned the first quartz mill at Horncut; and a free colored man named "Dick," who discovered a vein of gold so valuable that he was able to sell several portions of it. He reputedly settled in Sacramento with capital in excess of $100,000. A group of free blacks, led by Albert Callis and Charles Wilkins and including five others, parcelled out the land at the fork of the Yerba River so that each could work his own section. There was so much gold on Callis's section that the town of Downieville, California sprang up around it. Some free blacks owned their own mining companies, among them the Rare Ripe Gold Company, the Sweet Vengeance Mine Company and the Silver Mining Company, which was incorporated in Marysville, California by President J. H. Gassoway, Secretary-Treasurer E. P. Duplex, G. W. Simms, and J. H. Johnson.

Other black people, notably Mary Ellen "Mammy" Pleasant, were making money in San Francisco. "Mammy" Pleasant was using the money she earned from a boarding house and a restaurant in the gold rush to help finance John Brown's fateful expedition. William Alexander Leidesdorff, an early California pioneer, died in 1848 leaving an estate of more than a million dollars in real property. His Mexican citizenship saved it from being expropriated by the state of California.

One man, an escaped slave, who started West but stopped half-way there, made a fortune, returned to the East and started West again, still in search of gold, was Barney Ford. Ford had escaped from his master and come to Chicago via the Underground Railroad where he was befriended by Henry O. Wagoner. Wagoner not only took the young refugee in but made him his assistant in the conducting of the refugees working along with John Jones, the leading black Chicagoan of the day and head of the Underground Railroad in Chicago. In time, Ford married Wagoner's sister, Julia.

In 1849, when gold was discovered, Ford had managed to save enough money to buy the passage of himself and his wife to California by way of Nicaragua. It was much too risky for an escaped slave to travel to

California overland through slave territory. Taking no chances, Ford took a ship. Changing political regimes in Nicaragua created such an interesting climate for investment and money-making that Ford decided to stay there and make the most of it. He opened the United States Hotel and Restaurant, and when the political scene changed again, he and his wife were able to get out, returning to the United States with several thousand dollars more than they had when they left.

The next time he went West, he went overland. This time, however, he was less fearful of discovery, because he had been abroad and felt that he had adequate credentials to cover himself in the event of trouble. He also had heard that his last owner was now dead. He staked several claims to prospective gold veins, but usually he and his companions were forced off the land. They were not permitted in Colorado to file claims in their names since the *Dred Scott* decision denied all blacks the right to sue in court. A white lawyer, who filed a claim for Ford in his own name, took the claim and had the sheriff force Barney Ford off the land. Thus, when the whites started to dig for the gold which they knew the black man had discovered and were unable to find any, they called the mountain where the claim was located "Nigger Hill," a name it retains to this day.

Another black fortune that came from California gold belonged to Robert Harlan of Cincinnati. He was a native of Mecklenburg County, Virginia, born December 12, 1816. Harlan had been taken to Kentucky as a small child where he was employed in the household of James Harlan, the father of John Marshall Harlan, the Supreme Court justice who gained fame with his noble dissent in the *Plessy* v. *Ferguson* case.

Although legally a slave, Robert Harlan was permitted the freedom to act as though he was a white man, coming and going almost at will and hiring his own time. He learned the barber's trade in Louisville and later opened a grocery store in Lexington, Kentucky. Going to California in 1848, he returned within three years with $45,000 in gold which he invested in Cincinnati real estate. Because of the necessity for papers attesting to his freedom following the 1850 act, Harlan purchased the necessary documents from the Harlan family for $500 and then went to England. He returned to Cincinnati where his wealth and experience made him a leading benefactor to the colored community. Racial tensions reached such a point in 1858 that he took his family back to England where they remained until 1868, at which time they returned to Cincinnati.

The Eve of Armageddon

Not since Nat Turner had thrown the fear of God into the white slave-holder, and the slaveholder, in swift retaliation, had thrown the fear of open revolt into blacks, did an event have such an impact upon the nation as the raid on the federal arsenal at Harpers Ferry, West Virginia on October 16, 1859. The perpetrator of the bold act was not a slave striking for his own freedom, but a zealot, a white man and his band of twenty-two followers, black and white, free and former slaves, who had decided that the act itself was more important than the danger involved in committing the act.

Among them, Shields Green, just twenty-three, and Dangerfield Newby, forty-four, had both been born slaves. Newby lost his life in the raid, and his wife and seven children remained in slavery until the Emancipation Proclamation. Lewis Sheridan Leary, father of an infant child and husband to a young wife, left both in Oberlin, Ohio and died in the raid. His nephew, John A. Copeland, Jr., born free in North Carolina and a student at Oberlin College, left school to join Brown's men. Osborne Perry Anderson escaped after the raid and lived to fight in the Civil War on the Union side. He later worked for the federal government in Washington, D. C. The Oberlin student, John A. Copeland, and Shields Green were both captured, tried, found guilty, and hanged with John Brown on December 2, 1859, the day known throughout the black community as Martyr Day.

Somewhat earlier, in September of 1858, an escaped slave named John Price who had been living in Oberlin, Ohio was seized by slave hunters and taken to Wellington, Ohio to be sent back South. At last fifty members of the Oberlin community, students and citizens, rushed to Wellington where they rescued Price. They got him safely out of Ohio and into Canada. Warrants were issued against thirty-seven of the participants in the "rescue," but only two of those indicted were brought to trial. The first, a white participant, was found guilty and served four months in jail.

The other defendant was Charles H. Langston, the half-brother of John Mercer Langston. The jury found him guilty, also, but he was permitted to make a statement before being sentenced.

His speech, which caused the spectators to break out in cheers and applause, charged that the judge, jury, and court-appointed legal counsel were prejudiced. He claimed that it was unrealistic for the law to say that taking away a man's liberty was within the bounds of the Constitution. He referred to his own father's service in the Revolutionary War and gave a logical and dramatic twist to the case. Langston emphasized that he in no way intended to break the law, but merely to free the man from unlawful seizure until such time as it was demonstrated that he was being legally held. The judge sentenced him to twenty days in jail, and gave him the minimum fine of one hundred dollars. Upon his release, Charles Langston and his brother Gideon were back, as active as ever, in the Ohio Anti-Slavery Society.

Oberlin College was founded in 1835 by anti-slavery leaders with a sense of dedication and a mission to educate all who came, regardless of sex or color. Oberlin admitted its first colored student in 1836 and granted George B. Vashon, the son of Pittsburgh abolitionist John B. Vashon, his B.A. degree in 1844. Vashon, a serious student, had spent a lot of his free time conducting a school in the surrounding community for colored children. He was well-known to Gideon and Charles Langston, and they secured him to tutor their young brother, John Mercer, who was preparing to enter Oberlin for his first formal studies. William Howard Day, anti-slavery lecturer who spent most of his time in England following his graduation, was an Oberlin graduate in the class of 1847. John Mercer Langston obtained his degree in 1849.

Before going to Rome to study sculpture, Edmonia Lewis of Boston was also a student at Oberlin. The child of an Indian mother and a free black father, she had been involved in a serious charge during her early days at Oberlin. Two white girls, both ostensibly friends of Edmonia, had been mysteriously poisoned. She was accused and tried for having perpetrated the evil deed, but the evidence was insufficient and she was exonerated. The lawyer who defended the young girl was John Mercer Langston. Befriended by white Bostonians, she left America and returned only once to exhibit some of her work at the Philadelphia Exposition in 1876. Frederick

Douglass and his second wife, Helen Pitts Douglass, ran into her in Rome in the 1880s, and they said she ". . . had almost forgotten how to speak English."

Many other young black men and women came to Oberlin in the years that followed, and for them the situation was not as traumatic as it had been for the young Edmonia Lewis. There is no way of knowing what her fate might have been had the Ohio bar felt differently about the amount of black versus white blood in John Mercer Langston's veins.

John Mercer Langston was the youngest son of Lucy Langston and a wealthy white planter, who had freed her and her children. Before his death, Langston's father established trust funds for them in Ohio under the guardianship of trusted white friends who saw to it that the estate was carried out to the letter. Young John Mercer was given the benefit of all the care and education that money could provide, although he was not without some knowledge of the value of money. After completing his studies at Oberlin, he applied for admission to several law schools in the area, but he was turned down. He finally took a theological course of study and then "read" law in the office of a friendly white lawyer, Philimon Bliss. He was admitted to the bar only after the examiners had decided that the issue was not whether a Negro or mulatto should be admitted, but that ". . . he had more white than Negro blood," and therefore the issue was moot.

There were other Oberlin graduates to come: George and John F. Cook, II, John Hartwell Cook, Mary Jane Patterson, and others. It was estimated that at the outbreak of the Civil War at least one-third of the Oberlin students were colored persons. For years, many uninformed people thought of Oberlin as a black institution simply because its black alumni were so prominent in political and civic endeavors.

Although the humor is open to question, Artimus Ward wrote in 1865:

> "I must mention the fact that on rainy days in Oberlin white people cannot find their way through the streets without the gas lit, there being such a numerosity of colored persons in town."[1]

But two other schools were making an impact on the educational lives of young black men and women. They were Lincoln University, which was established in Pennsylvania in 1854, and Wilberforce University, established in Ohio in 1856.

Founded by the Presbyterians at Oxford, Pennsylvania in 1854, Lincoln University was originally named Ashmun Institute. It was a preparatory school for blacks brought out of the South, who could be trained and then sent to Africa for colonization. They had earlier started a school at Parsippany, New Jersey, but it had failed, and so they bent their efforts to support Ashmun.

The Presbyterians had consistently been more liberal in their attitudes toward blacks than had the Episcopalians, and the doors of Princeton University had been opened to them for training. The Episcopalians had successfully muzzled both Peter Williams at St. Philips in New York and William Douglass, the rector of St. Thomas Church in Philadelphia. The Presbyterian ministry had been permitted to speak out for the emancipation of the race and the necessity of granting full citizenship to black people. Peter Williams, whose father had been such a rock in the building of the AME Zion Church, was emasculated by the Episcopal hierarchy. When he had taken an active role in the question of colonization and abolition, his bishop ordered that he should preach the gospel without any secular connotations, and that he should remain aloof from the social issues of the day. Although the Presbyterians were more liberal in their attitudes toward blacks, there were hardly more than 20,000 black Presbyterians in the entire nation on the eve of the Civil War.

Bishop Tanner commented upon the reason for the Presbyterian church's lack of appeal to the average black person seeking religious identification:

> "It strove to lift up without coming down and while the good Presbyterian parson was writing his discourses, rounding off sentences, the Methodist itinerant had travelled forty miles with his horse and saddle bags; while the parson was adjusting his spectacles to read his manuscript, the itinerant had given hell and damnation to his unrepentant hearers; while the disciple of Calvin was waiting to have his church completed, the disciple of Wesley took to the woods and made

them reecho with the voice of free grace, believing with Bryant, 'The groves were God's first temples'."[2]

Wilberforce University, on the other hand, had a different orientation at its beginning. Wilberforce was at one time a summer resort for Southern slaveholders and their female slaves. The hotel had some three hundred fifty rooms, extensive grounds, elaborate water works for fountains, and several cottages on either side of it. Because of the spring water, the hotel was known as Tawawa Springs. Following the economic depression of 1837, the place began to decline as a resort. Because of the increased activity of the Underground Railroad and the presence of multitudes of Quakers, who looked with stern disapproval at such flagrant wickedness, the patronage at the hotel fell off. It was finally sold for debt, and several planters banded together and bought the place turning it into a school for their Negro children.

From such a beginning, Wilberforce was more than ready for the administration of a man of the caliber of Bishop Daniel Payne of the African Methodist Episcopal church. Bishop Payne, one of the younger and more progressive members of the AME clergy and an educator by professional training, was offered an opportunity to purchase Wilberforce from the white Methodists who were then in control of the property. The matter had to be decided within a certain number of days, and there was no way for Bishop Payne to contact his colleagues to get a consensus on the purchase. Other interested parties were standing by ready to make the commitment when, as it is reported, Bishop Payne, without a dollar ". . . but with a firm faith in the omnipotent arm of the Jehovah, . . . stood in the presence of the person who was to sell. . . . Bishop Payne cried, 'In the name of God I purchase this property for the AME Church to be consecrated by them for the sacred cause of Christian education.' He lived to pay off every dollar of the debt which he incurred that day."[3]

By the end of the decade, it seemed as though God's dark children had indeed been forgotten. The 1850 act had decimated the ranks of outspoken blacks within the country. "The best and brightest" of this generation had not been hanged as they had in the Vesey and Turner times, but they had been driven into exile.

From 1850 to 1860 an estimated 20,000 colored people crossed the northern border into Canada. The entire Shadd family, Henry Bibb, J. W.

Loguen, Henry Highland Garnet, Alexander Crummel, Martin Delany, and William Wells Brown all left, although Brown returned when he had purchased the necessary papers to secure his freedom from recapture and re-enslavement.

Frederick Douglass wrote to the readers of his newspaper that, "The only way to make the Fugitive Slave Law a dead letter is to make half a dozen or more dead kidnappers."[4]

There had been a continuing debate on the issue of Negro rights to lands in the public domain, and some held, as did Congressman Augustus Porter of Michigan, that to specifically exclude Negroes from the public domain and territory within the federal land policy would be establishing a precedent which would ultimately affect the right of blacks to ". . . enjoy the protection of life, liberty and property," even though they could neither vote nor hold office in Michigan.

Others like David Wilmot, representative of Pennsylvania, proposed that slavery be excluded in territories acquired from Mexico, not because of "any squeamish sensitiveness upon the subject of slavery, nor marked sympathy for slave," but because he wanted the land—free states for free white men. "I would preserve to free white labor a fair country, a rich inheritance, where the sons of toil, of my own race and color, can live without the disgrace which association with negro slavery brings upon free labor."[5]

The *Dred Scott* decision dealt a stunning blow to the hopes and aspirations of the free as well as the slave black. It put into cold words a policy which had been haphazardly followed but not enunciated since 1820 when Secretary of State John Quincy Adams had protested a provision in the constitution of Missouri, which had not yet received statehood.

The provision entailed that the state legislature be permitted to pass any laws necessary ". . . to prevent free Negroes and mulattoes from coming to and settling in this state under any pretext whatsoever." Adams argued that such a provision was unconstitutional, and he stated that colored people ". . . already cursed by the mere color of their skin . . . already doomed by their complexion to drudge in the lowest offices of society, excluded by their color from all the refined enjoyments of life accessible to others, excluded from the benefits of a liberal education, from the bed, from the table, and from all the social comforts of domestic life, this barbarous article deprives them of the little remnant of right yet left them—their rights as citizens and as men."[6]

Now on 6 March 1857, Supreme Court Justice Roger Taney ruled against Dred Scott, a slave belonging to an Army surgeon, Mr. John Emerson. Justice Taney said that Scott was still a slave despite the fact that Mr. Emerson had taken Scott from Missouri, a slave state, into Illinois, a free state, through Minnesota, also a free state, and back to Missouri after two years. In 1846 Scott sued for his liberty claiming that his residence in free territory and a free state gave him freedom.

The question was whether Scott had the right, as a citizen of Missouri, to bring suit. A majority of the court held that Scott was *not* a citizen of Missouri and therefore could *not* sue in the federal courts. He also added that Negroes could not be citizens; that the Missouri Compromise, which had been repealed in 1854, was unconstitutional; and further that *Congress* had *no* power to restrict slavery in the territories.

Robert Purvis reacted at a mass meeting held at the Israel Church in Philadelphia on April 3, 1857, and he made one final point:

> "That we rejoice that the slave holding disposition lays its ruthless hand not only on the humble black man, but on the proud Northern white man; and our hope is that when our white fellow slaves in these so-called free states see that they are alike subject with us to the slave oligarchy, the difference in our servitude being only in degree, they will make common cause with us, and that throwing off the yoke and striking for impartial liberty they will join us in our efforts to recover the long lost boon of freedom."[7]

The die was cast; the pro-slavery and anti-slavery forces began to choose weapons in the duel that was more and more an inevitability.

Tensions mounted and finally erupted when Fort Sumter was fired on by Southern forces April 12, 1861. In this act, the blacks of the nation rejoiced, for now they might truly be free.

Photographs

Josephine Bruce   Mrs. John Francis   Josephine Ruffin   Mary C. Terrell

Black women, never silent, moved in
the 1890s to organize institutionally
by merging club groups, organizing
businesses, and taking to the public
forums and the press in the tradition
of Sojourner Truth, Harriet Tubman,
Mary Ann Shadd, and Francis Ellen
Watkins Harper. Their purpose was
to help those less fortunate. They
also went into the professions,
such as law (Ida Platt), medicine
(Ionia Whipper and her mother Francis
Rollin Whipper), and banking
(Maggie Lena Walker). Mary Jane
Patterson (below) was the first black
woman college graduate in the U.S.

Mrs. A. M. Curtis   Ida B. Wells

Ida Platt   Fannie B. Williams
Mary Jane
Patterson   Mrs. Booker T. Washington

148

Maggie Lena Walker (left) founded the
St. Luke's Penny Savings Bank in
Richmond, Va. in 1903 and became the
first black woman bank president in the
United States. Dr.
Ionia Whipper, the
daughter of William
and Francis Rollin
Whipper, founded
the Ionia Whipper
Home for Girls.   149

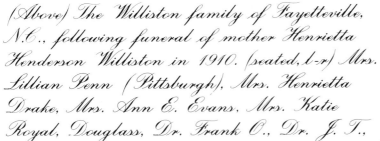

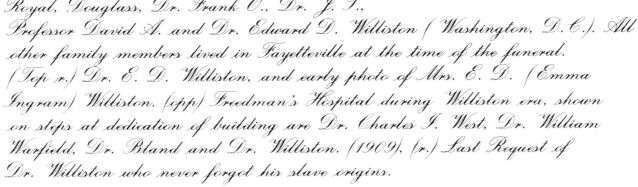

(Above) The Williston family of Fayetteville, N.C., following funeral of mother Henrietta Henderson Williston in 1910. (seated, l-r) Mrs. Lillian Penn (Pittsburgh), Mrs. Henrietta Drake, Mrs. Ann E. Evans, Mrs. Katie Royal, Douglass, Dr. Frank O., Dr. J.T., Professor David A. and Dr. Edward D. Williston (Washington, D.C.). All other family members lived in Fayetteville at the time of the funeral. (Top r.) Dr. E. D. Williston, and early photo of Mrs. E. D. (Emma Ingram) Williston. (opp) Freedman's Hospital during Williston era, shown on steps at dedication of building are Dr. Charles I. West, Dr. William Warfield, Dr. Bland and Dr. Williston. (1909). (r.) Last Request of Dr. Williston who never forgot his slave origins.

MY WISH AND REQUEST

I knew in the natural course of time, my end is approaching. I have no complaint—I am satisfied. I do not look upon death as an enemy, but as a friend. I have had my day—my opportunity. I've done the best I could with my limited knowledge and experience. If my life has been a failure, it is to be regretted. I did the best I could under the circumstances. Now when I pass the line, I wish to say that I am not a hypocrite; therefore I do not want any religious ceremonies. I never had a religious instinct, and to have a religious service it would classify me as a hypocrite. .

I am a product of human slavery. I am proscribed. Therefore I could not believe in the personality of a supreme, all-powerful being who controlled the destinies of mankind. I am simply a product of this earth. I wish a simple service by my friends—strictly non-religious. Afterwards my remains are to be cremated and my ashes buried in my mother's grave. I don't want any "flowers"—only an evergreen wreath (on the casket). I don't want any mourning nor any decorations. No "black" for me. I have absolutely no fear, and wish my friends to take a last look. I passed without malice or hatred—only sympathy for suffering humanity.

E. D. Williston

151

Colonel Denison was the highest-ranking black officer in U.S. Army during World War I.

Major Franklin A. Denison and wife Edna Rose (l.) at time of his service with 8th Illinois Regiment in Cuba.

152

Edna Denison (l.) with Dorothy, Denise, George, and Franklin in 1916. After death of Denison, she married Robert S. Abbott. Son George (l.) was ring-bearer at the Gerri Hodges-Dismond wedding.

Jacqueline, youngest child of Major and Mrs. Denison (r. and below r.), with husband Harvey Russell and family. Russell is a top executive with the Pepsico Corp.

Major Denison (above) with children. Dr. W.G. Dailey with Mrs. George Denison; Eleanor Dailey Cyrus, widow of Bindley Cyrus, founder of Victory Mutual Life Ins. and former consul to Barbados; and Eleanor Curtis Dailey, Dr. Austin M. Curtis's sister.

Labor Department's minority group consultant, Roberta Church, and father, Robert Church, Jr., a prominent Republican (below), resided in Church family home in Memphis.

Lecturer, teacher, civil rights activist Mary Church Terrell, daughter of Robert Church, Sr. and wife of Judge Robert Terrell (l.), during 1950s (above) and in 1904 (r.), the birth year of her daughter Phyllis.

Robert Jackson,

$5,726.00 was the price the Jackson family of Pittsburgh paid for freedom when they came out of Virginia in 1850's.
Robert Jackson (top) was head of contracting firm in Pittsburgh. Charles and Dan Jackson, were Chicago undertakers. Emmerline McKee (top-right) grand-father of Chicago Jackson's, whose mother was Emmeline McKee, niece of Colonel John McKee.

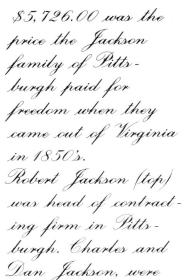

Bobby Jackson

Billy

Daughters and grandson of Thomas Coleman

Hadassah

Villa

Ralph

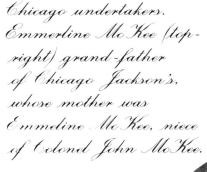

Emmerline McKee

Daniel McKee
Jackson

M'Liss

Robert Jackson
(brother of Dan
& Charles)

Charles L. Jackson
wife, Mattie

FOR OLD NEGROES

Home on Garfield Boulevard a Godsend to the Aged Infirm.

PLANS TO WIDEN ITS SCOPE.

Present Building Presented by Mrs. Bena Morrison Too Crowded Now —Contributions Desired.

One of the most worthy philanthropic institutions of the city, the home for aged and infirm colored people at 610 Garfield boulevard, is planning to enlarge its quarters and widen its field of usefulness. The broadening of the work will begin at once, as there are now many worthy applicants who cannot be accommodated. Major John C. Buckner, who was elected president of the institution a short time ago, is directing the movement to increase its facilities for doing good.

Through the philanthropy of Mrs. Bena Morrison the home now owns and occupies a pleasant two-story and attic frame house in a pretty location overlooking the West Fifty-fifth street driveway. Mrs. Morrison has been the good angel of the institution ever

MAJOR J. C. BUCKNER.
[President Home for Aged and Infirm Colored People.]

since she heard of its existence more than a year ago. On April 7, 1898, she deeded to the home the premises now occupied by it, and furnished the house nicely throughout. At the same time she also conveyed to the home the property at 620 Fifty-second street, from the rent of which the home has a monthly income of $14. This is the only source of income to the home in the way of an endowment. Mrs. Morrison has helped in many other ways, but with the exception of a few small contributions she is the only white person who has assisted.

Home Is Overcrowded.

The home presented by Mrs. Morrison at the time of sorest need is already overcrowded with its seventeen inmates, and the project is to build additions to the house, or if possible to erect a new and much larger building. The new building should be large

---

enough to have an amusement hall and a chapel for religious exercises in addition to improved dormitory arrangements which would permit of separate sleeping quarters.

MRS. JOE C. SNOWDEN.
[Secretary.]

A dispensary-room for aiding outside poor and other necessary features for such an institution are planned.

For the most part the home has been supported since its inauguration by contributions from the colored people of comfortable means, and no aid has been solicited directly from white people, although many well to do colored people have contributed regularly to several old people's homes from which negroes are barred because of their color. The Colored Woman's Aid Society, which was organized to help support the home, has contributed $12 each month and given much more in addition. The colored King's Daughters of the West Side, the Young Men's Charity Association and many other organizations have aided. Women from the various churches visit the home regularly to sew and help in other ways. All the colored

ED H. MORRIS.
[Auditor and Attorney.]

physicians of the city volunteer their services and the colored druggists and Provident Hospital donate medicines. A horse and wagon have just been presented to the home and will be used in calling for donations. It bears the name of the institution so that donations will reach the place intended. The wagon was given by Robert T. Motts, the horse by Mrs. Jerry Stewart and Mrs. E. H. Morris.

Contributions Will Be Welcomed.

It is now the intention of the officers of the institution to ask for contributions from the citizens of Chicago without regard to color or creed for the purpose of enlarging the home. The officers have the full confidence of the public, Major Buckner being a former member of the state legislature and Mr. Morris being a prominent attorney. The soliciting will be done by the officers, who will

---

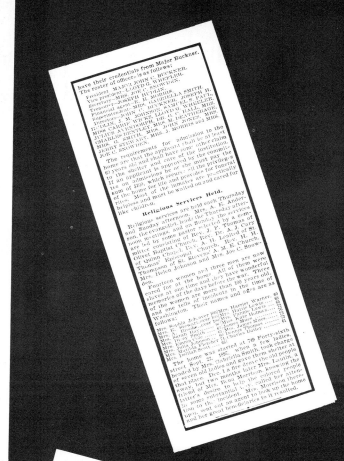

have their credentials from Major Buckner. The roster of officers is as follows:

President, MAJOR JOHN C. BUCKNER; vice president, LLOYD G. WHEELER; secretary, MRS. JOE C. SNOWDEN; treasurer, JOSEPH H. HOLLINS; financial agent, E. H. MORRIS. Superintendent, JOHN JOHNSON. Directors—MRS. NELLA SMITH DUDLIN, J. M. JOHNSON, JOSEPH H. MISS CARRIE WICKS, SAMUEL S. PAUL, JULIUS AVENDORPH, LLOYD G. WHEELER, CHARLES E. BENTLEY, DR. C. E. HALL, MRS. JERRY STEWART, MRS. M. DECAMERAGE, MRS. JOE C. SNOWDEN, MRS. E. SMITH, MRS. JONES, MRS. J. MORRIS and MRS.

The requirements for admission to the home are that the applicant shall be at least 65 years old and shall have some other claim to the shelter and care of the institution. If an applicant is approved by the committee on admissions he or she must pay the sum of $80, which must secure the privileges of the home for life and provide for funeral rites. Most of the inmates are practically helpless and must be waited on and cared for like children.

Religious Services Held.

Religious services are held each Thursday and Sunday afternoon. Mrs. A. E. Anderson, the evangelist, leads the Thursday afternoon meetings, and on Sunday the services are led by some pastor selected by a committee consisting of Rev. J. F. Thomas of Olivet Baptist Church, Rev. A. J. Carey of Quinn Chapel, Rev. A. H. Dr. A. Loved of St. Thomas Episcopal Church, Rev. H. H. Thomson of St. Stevens A. M. E. Church, Mrs. Helen Johnson and Mrs. Joe C. Snowden.

Fourteen women and three men are now cared for at the home. All of them were slaves at one time and they have wonderful memories of the days before the war. Three of the women are more than 100 years old, and one tells of incidents in the life of Washington. Their names and ages are as follows:

Mrs. Sophia Johnson	100	Mrs. Harriet Warner	68
Mrs. Stewart	99	Mrs. Hattie Lewis	76
Mrs. Brooks	90	Miss Fanny Holmes	75
Mrs. Sarah Rice	80	Mrs. Maud Jones	72
Mrs. Emma Smith	61	Mrs. Anna Smith	73
Mrs. Diana Chambers	65	Charles Thomas	62
Mrs. Matilda Fletcher	81	Charles Hatley	61
Mrs. Delilah Scott	61		

The home was started at 719 Forty-sixth street Sept. 22, 1897, when a few ladies, headed by Mrs. Gabriella Smith, took charge of seven old ladies and gave them shelter at that place. Dec. 1 a fire drove the old people away, but two months later Mrs. Fautin, a friend of Mrs. Bena Morrison, knowing the latter's desire to help the colored people in some substantial way, called her attention to the incident. Mrs. Morrison thereupon went out an agent to look up the home and her great beneficiaries to it resulted.

Chicago society, circa 1909, involved with good deeds and gracious living

Leaders were Edward Morris
& Mrs. John Jones
Dr. Charles Bentley
& the Dan Williams'

Peace on earth   Good will toward men

Christmas, 1909

The Register of the Treasury and
Mrs. William T. Vernon

420 T Street N. W.

Washington, D. C.

Dr Charles Edwin Bentley
sends
Christmas Greetings
and
All good wishes for
The New Year

HON. EDWARD H. MORRIS.

Mrs. E. H. MORRIS (nee) Montgomery

Jan 1st 1909

What you may wish
for your selves I wish for
you in the new year

With love
Mrs John Jones

Prominent Southern arbitrator Booker T. Washington
(1856-1915) advocated agricultural and manual
training for the achievement of civil rights and
economic self-sufficiency, a concept which he
nurtured through his founding of Tuskegee Institute.

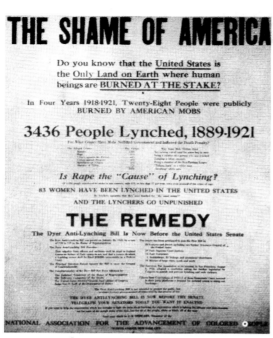

20th Century saw no decline in KKK rule and lynching.

W.E.B. DuBois (1868-1963) was one of the most vocal and powerful civil rights leaders of his day and a major opponent of Booker T. Washington. DuBois was the first black officer in the NAACP when he became editor of its official organ, The Crisis. Founder of the radical but influential Boston Guardian, William M. Trotter was totally unsympathetic with the conciliatory methods of protest, and his distrust of white liberals led to the eventual break from his friend DuBois.

161

War

At the outbreak of the Civil War, the first people to volunteer their services in behalf of the preservation of the Union were black people.

Mary Ann Shadd and Martin Delany immediately gave up on the emigration proposals that they had been urging; Shadd to Canada West, Delany to Africa or Central America. Frederick Douglass went to Washington to urge upon the president the wisdom of establishing units of black men serving under black officers. Hiram R. Revels, who had been preaching and teaching in Indiana, Illinois, Ohio, and Missouri, began to organize and recruit volunteers in Maryland.

Revels's family, like so many other free black families, had migrated west with Quaker assistance, from Fayetteville, North Carolina where he had been born September 27, 1827. He attended the Quaker Seminary in Union County, Indiana, and graduated from Knox College in Bloomington, Illinois. He converted, and in 1845 was ordained an AME minister following the encouragement of Bishop Paul Quinn. Bishop Quinn was at that time in charge of the Indiana Conference, where he organized and recruited churches and ministers with fanatic zeal. Revels then lectured throughout Indiana, Illinois, and Ohio until 1860 when he was transferred to Baltimore, Maryland. There, at the outbreak of the Civil War, he assisted in the organization of the first two colored regiments in Maryland. With the recruiting done, he served as chaplain of a colored regiment in Vicksburg in 1864.

One young Marylander who answered the call for volunteers was John Murphy, Sr., the founder of the *Afro-American* newspaper. Murphy, in a letter to his family written on his 80th birthday, December 25, 1920, but not to be opened until the centennial of his birth, wrote:

"Wars are for young people. All wars are fought for freedom and governments are wise. They promise citizens something in order to have them risk their lives freely for the home land, booty, adventure, comradeship, pensions, good pay, travel, uniforms, and brass bands, plus martial music that makes hearts beat faster. It doesn't take long to train soldiers. I enlisted March 18, 1864, and by summer was fighting with General Grant in the wilderness. By April, 1865, I was in North Carolina with General Sherman when he captured the rebel army of General Joe Johnstone. Ours was the 30th Regiment, U. S. Colored Maryland Volunteers. We entered this war with 151 men in our company and came out with 79. We lost 24 men by transfer to the navy, 24 were killed and 24 more got sick, lost or deserted.

"That was a real war for liberty. *I went in a slave and came out a freedman.* I went in chattel and came out a man with the blue uniform of my country as a guarantee of freedom, and a sergeant's stripes on my arms to prove that there is promotion for those who can earn it."[1]

Another who could not wait to get into uniform was Martin Delany. In 1856, he had left Pittsburgh and moved to Chatham, Canada, where he practiced medicine and argued with Shadd over the best place to go from the United States. In May of 1859, he sailed from New York on the *Mendi*, a ship owned by a group of black African merchants. Delany was the head of what was known as the Niger Valley Exploration Party, probably the first black men to ever leave the United States with exploration as the mission. After travelling in Africa for a year, Delany went to the Continent and to England, returning to the United States shortly before the war erupted. He determined that he must be involved in the fighting, and so he accepted the appointment of an assistant agent for recruiting and acting examining surgeon under Charles H. Langston and Charles Lenox Remond. Delany was assigned to Chicago, and it was not long before he sought and secured an audience with President Lincoln, where he also requested a black army under black commanding officers, except such whites as might volunteer. He was successful in the first aspect of his mission. Delany was commissioned as a medical officer and was made a major on April 5, 1865, and ordered to Charleston. There on April 14, standing on board the steamship *Planter* at the side of Robert Smalls, he witnessed the restoration of the flag on Fort Sumter.

Delany was not the first black man to be commissioned in the officer corps as a physician. Alexander T. Augusta had been born free on March 8, 1825 in Norfolk, Virginia and, like almost all of the Virginians of the dark period, had been taken to Canada. In 1856, he graduated from Trinity Medical College in Toronto, Canada with a degree in medicine. He moved to Washington, D. C. in 1862, and on October 2, 1863 was appointed Surgeon of the Seventh U. S. Colored Troops, which were part of the group sent to Beaufort, South Carolina. Later, he was in charge of a hospital at Savannah, Georgia, and on March 13, 1865, he was given the rank of lieutenant colonel, U. S. Volunteers. He remained in the service until October 13, 1866, when he returned to Washington and went on the faculty of Howard University's Department of Medicine.

Not all of the participation was by men, nor was all of the activity on the battlefield. Late in 1861, Union forces occupied a group of coastal islands, including Port Royal and St. Helena located between Charleston, South Carolina and Savannah, Georgia. Charlotte Forten went to St. Helena to teach freedmen.

The fleeing slaveowners had left behind thousands of illiterate and helpless slaves. These plantations were placed under the jurisdiction of the War Department, which named Northern superintendents to take charge of the "contraband of war." A program was established in the areas of health care, education, clothing, and shelter.

Charlotte Forten, the daughter of Robert and Mary Wood Forten and the granddaughter of James Forten, had lost her mother while she was still in her teens. But she had two aunts, Margaretta and Sarah, still at home in her grandfather's house. They were active in both women's rights and abolitionist movement activities, and so Charlotte was exposed at the most impressionable time of her life to the nobility of causes. She also spent time at the Purvis's Byberry estate with her aunt Harriett and her cousins. In 1854, she went to Salem, Massachusetts where she stayed in the home of a family friend, Charles Lenox Remond. She graduated from the Higginson School in February, 1855, and attended the State Normal School at Salem, where she completed the one-year course for teachers. In July, 1856, she was hired as a teacher at the Epes Grammar School in Salem becoming the first non-white woman to instruct white children. Ill health caused her to return to Philadelphia in 1858. She felt too unhappy to remain in Philadelphia after the war began, and she refused to go to Europe as some advised her to do. She felt that would be compromising her grand-father's ideals. Her father, Robert Forten, enlisted as a private in the Union army.

When the Union forces captured Port Royal Harbor off the South Carolina coast in the fall of 1861, the slaveholders fled, abandoning their property and the people they had held in bondage. The federal government decided to send aid to the "contraband," and the following spring teachers were sent from the North; fifty-three were in the first group, all white. They distributed clothing, helped the sick, and set up schools to teach read-ing, writing, and arithmetic. Six months after the first group arrived in the Sea Islands, the first Negro teacher arrived to join the group several months before black soldiers were permitted to enlist in the Union forces.

Charlotte Forten arrived on St. Helena in October, 1862, and began teaching in a small school which had been established a few months earlier. This was her first trip into the South and her first adventure into the real world unprotected by family and friends. In *The Journal of Charlotte Forten,* she recounts her inner turmoil, the tension, the suspicion with which she was confronted on the part of the local blacks, and her inhibitions which prohibited her involvement with a white man. When one paid her romantic attention, she confessed to her Journal, "Although he is very good and liberal, he is still an *American,* and w'ld of course never be so insane as to love one of the proscribed race."[2] Charlotte was in the Sea Islands on January 1, 1863 when the Emancipation Proclamation went into effect.

Black soldiers participated in both the navy and army, and performed heroically in several exchanges, notably Port Hudson, Louisiana; Milliken's Bend, Mississippi; The Battle of Fort Wagner; Petersburg; Chaffin's Farm; and others.

On the black troops at Petersburg, Secretary of War Stanton said, "The hardest fighting was done by the black troops. The forts they stormed were worst of all." Stanton reported that following Petersburg, ". . . they cannot be excelled as soldiers, and hereafter we better send them in a diffi-cult place as readily as white troops."[3]

The New Old Guard

Before the war ended, another Convention of Colored Men was held in Syracuse, New York, October 4–7, 1864. John Mercer Langston was the temporary chairman, Frederick Douglass, the president, and in attendance were such old familiar names as Henry Highland Garnet of Washington, James W. C. Pennington of New York, George L. Ruffin of Boston, and Ebenezer Don Carlos Bassett of Philadelphia. The names of a generation before had been supplanted and supplemented by the addition of men like John Jones from Chicago.

The war had brought to a head the festering sore which had been eating at the heart of America since the massive "All" in the Declaration of Independence had been accepted as the touchstone of American democracy. Horrible as it was, it was like a giant catharsis of the national body politic. There was a real chance that the country would now be able to be what it should have been from its beginning. To this end, the convention drafted An Address to the American People, with a Bill of Rights and Wrongs attached.

There were about four million colored people in the United States, and only a million of them were literate, so there was an enormous job to do in terms of education. There were thousands of men, women, and children homeless and without anything but the rags upon their backs for covering. So they had to be be housed and clothed and ministered to, physically and spiritually.

For the first time, the free Negro was in demand. The more so if he had education and training, because he knew how to function in a society without constraints. Also, since he had been fending for himself without the intercession of the master, he had experience in making decisions. The free person of color was needed to administer and teach in the schools, to tend to the sick, and to represent the freeman in the courts; and he was ready.

Because Washington, D. C. was the heart of the government and the place where all of the decisions were made, many like Frederick Douglass relocated. Douglass moved his home and his family from Rochester, N. Y. to Washington where he began publishing the *New National Era*. In 1874 he was named president of The Freedmen's Bank. For a long time after the war, Washington retained its magic as the "heartland" of black society.

George F. T. Cook, John Francis Cook's youngest son, wielded more power than most blacks because, as superintendent of colored schools, he was in charge of the hiring and firing of teachers, principals, and clerks in the entire colored school system. Because his standards were high, he had no qualms about moving a good person if a better one came along. He was very conscious of the prestige value of Harvard University, and although Mary Jane Patterson had been the first black woman to earn a degree in the United States when she graduated from Oberlin in 1862, it was not enough to give her job security when a Harvard man became available. Richard T. Greener had gone from Harvard to the Philadelphia Institute for Colored Youth, where he served as principal for a few months. In January of 1873, he came to Washington to take the principal's job at Sumner High School. Miss Patterson graciously stepped aside. Six months later, Greener was offered the chair of metaphysics and logic at the University of South Carolina, so he was off again. Mary Jane Patterson was back at Sumner, where she stayed until the end of the Reconstruction when she was again displaced; this time by Francis Cardozo.

There were, in the capital and on the hill, black men for the first time in positions other than the doorkeeper, elevator operator, and messenger, which had been the lot of the black federal employee before the war. There was progress. Grant appointed Frederick Douglass, John Gray, a Washington caterer, and Adolphus Hall to the eleven-man District of Columbia Committee. John Mercer Langston, who had been dean of the law school and vice-president of Howard University, was named legal counsel to the Washington Board of Health.

John Hartwell Cook, Oberlin 1864, had been recruited from Louisville, Kentucky to come to Washington where he served as chief clerk of the Freedmen's Bureau from 1867 to 1872. Meanwhile, he became a student in the evening classes at the fledgling Howard University Law

School where he received a degree in the first class on February 1, 1871. He was admitted to the bar in the District of Columbia the following day. In 1873, he was appointed to the Howard University Board of Trustees, and on July 14, 1875, was appointed professor of law. From 1876 to 1878, Cook served as dean of the Law Department succeeding John Mercer Langston. Cook died at the age of forty in 1878, leaving his widow, Marion Isabel Lewis Cook, and three young sons; John H., Jr., Will Mercer (Marion), and Hugh Oliver.

Charles B. Purvis, the son of Harriett Forten and Robert Purvis, had grown up with his seven brothers and sisters at Byberry, Pennsylvania. He was one of the children who were not permitted to go to the local school because of their race, creating the situation which caused his father to refuse to pay the portion of his property taxes allocated to the school system until the situation was corrected. In 1860, Purvis went to Oberlin, attending two years. He left in 1862 to enter the medical college of Western Reserve University where he graduated in 1865.

So great was the need for medical knowledge and trained physicians during the period of the war, the young graduate, without any real experience, was appointed as acting assistant surgeon with the rank of first lieutenant in the United States Army. He was assigned to duty in Washington, D. C. Two years later, the war now over, he was appointed assistant surgeon in the Freedmen's Hospital, which had just been opened. In 1868, he was named professor of materia medica and medical jurisprudence. He held that post for five years when he was transferred to the chair of obstetrics and diseases of women and children.

His cousin, Charlotte Forten, came to Washington to live with Purvis and his white wife and family. Her father, Robert, had just been promoted to sergeant major in the 43rd Regiment, Company C, U. S. Colored Troops, when he died while on duty in June, 1864. Charlotte, for a time, worked at Sumner School as a teacher, and later was hired by the Department of the Treasury as a clerk. Now a permanent resident of Washington, she joined the Fifteenth Street Presbyterian Church.

The Fifteenth Street Presbyterian Church had had its ups and downs following the death of its first pastor, John F. Cook, Sr. Bishop Daniel Payne of the AME church had given special dispensation to young Benjamin

Tucker Tanner, who had only been ordained into the AME discipline in 1860, to take over the work of the Fifteenth Street Church until a permanent minister was found to replace Reverend Cook. Tanner remained at the Fifteenth Street Church for eighteen months, during which time he organized the Sunday School for freedmen at the Navy yard. In April of 1862, he united with the Baltimore conference and was appointed to the Alexander Mission on E Street in Washington. In 1863, he was named the pastor of the Georgetown, D. C. church. However, by 1866 he had been moved again, this time to become principal of the Annual Methodist Conference School at Frederickstown, Maryland. The Freemen's Society also secured his services to help in organizing a grammar school. In 1868, he was named chief secretary of the AME church and also editor of the church organ, the *Christian Recorder*.

In 1878, Francis J. Grimke, who had studied law at Howard, returned to Washington with a theological degree from Princeton University and took up ministerial duties at the Fifteenth Street Presbyterian Church. On December 19, 1878, the Reverend Francis J. Grimke and Charlotte Forten were married. He remained as pastor of Fifteenth Street Presbyterian until 1885, when he was transferred to Jacksonville, Florida as minister of the Laurel Street Church.

Francis Grimke was the youngest of three sons of Nancy Weston and Henry Grimke, the other two being John and Archibald. Francis was born near Charleston, November 4, 1850, when his bride-to-be was already a girl of twelve years. On the death of Grimke's father, a plantation owner, his three slave children were willed to his brother, E. Montague Grimke, with the expressed wish that his sons be freed.

After the war, Archibald and Francis were sent to Lincoln University where they enrolled in 1866. They graduated in 1870 with Francis at the head of the class and his brother, Archibald, third in class rank. After graduation they both remained on the Lincoln University campus; Archibald working as an instructor and librarian, while Francis studied law and worked as an agent of the university.

In February of 1868, Angelina Grimke Weld, the sister of Henry Grimke, read in an anti-slavery journal that Francis Grimke was to speak to a group at Lincoln University. Knowing the name to be limited to those members of the family, she assumed that a former slave had adopted the name as his own. After several weeks of wondering about the connection, the white woman wrote to Francis Grimke, and he replied telling her that he and his brother were her nephews. She replied in a long letter saying:

> "I am glad you have taken the name of Grimke. It was once one of the noblest names of Carolina. You, my young friends, now bear this once honored name. I charge you most solemnly, by your upright conduct and your life-long devotion to the eternal principles of justice and humanity and religion, to lift this name out of the dust where it now lies, and set it once more among the princes of our land."[1]

From that point on, the colored Grimkes and the white Grimke-Weld family considered themselves as kinfolk in every sense of the word.

Shortly before the war, James Wormley had bought a house on I Street where he opened a hotel and catering establishment with his wife, Anna. His reputation for fine service and culinary art led him to be requested for the American Embassy in London during Reverdy Johnson's tenure as ambassador. During the time that he was in England, James Wormley acquired china, linen, and crystal for a first-class establishment, which he opened on 15th and H street in 1871.

Here his guests dined on Haviland and Limoges, drank from crystal, and cut their meat with sterling silver. Senator Charles Sumner took permanent rooms in the Wormley Hotel and moved his personal furnishings in. By now, James Wormley's three sons had taken their place in the business, and William H. A., James Thompson, and Garrett Smith all played important roles in the management and operation of the family business.

In a guide to Washington, D. C. published in 1884, the following description of the Wormley Hotel appears:

> "This standard and leading hotel ranks at the head of Washington's best establishments of that kind. Elegant in all its appointments and most efficiently managed, it has gradually won the reputation it holds at present. For years it has been patronized by our most eminent men, and it is the general

rendezvous for the foreign aristocracy visiting our country. All the late presidents, Mr. Hayes excepted, enjoyed the hospitality of its well-known proprietor."

The hotel could accommodate 150 guests and was "provided with all of the newest improvements as to elevators, telephone (the number was 13), and heating apparatuses, electric bells are introduced throughout the premises . . . Nowhere, neither the United States or abroad, can be found a better appointed hotel."[2]

James Wormley was indeed a friend of presidents and other influentials. He was depicted in an oil painting at the bedside of the dying Lincoln, and he was an honorary pallbearer at the Lincoln funeral. With Robert Purvis and Frederick Douglass, Wormley accompanied the body of Vice-President Henry Wilson to Natick, Massachusetts for burial following his death in 1875 in Washington, D. C. His friendship with Charles Sumner was well-known. He marched in the Negro honor guard with Frederick Douglass at Sumner's funeral, and it was Wormley who presented a portrait of Sumner to the State of Massachusetts to be hung in the Statehouse. At the time of his death, *The Washington Star* in a front-page story noted that . . . "Mr. Wormley was one of the most remarkable colored men in the country."

It had been the preponderance of white blood that swung the balance in the Ohio courts in favor of John Mercer Langston's admission to the bar of Ohio. It was the same consideration that was obtained in the case of Hiram Revels, when he came to be seated in the United States Senate. Revels, of mixed blood (an octoroon), was the first man of color to claim election to Congress. He had been elected from the state of Mississippi, and the seat he was to fill had been allocated to Jefferson Davis. The seating of Revels was contested on the grounds of the *Dred Scott* decision, which held that blacks were not citizens, and therefore could not be elected to Congress. Revels was able to prove to the satisfaction of the Senate that he had more white than black blood, and thus had been a citizen of the United States since birth. He was seated. Moreover, he was accepted by the colored elite.

But for pure blacks, like Robert Brown Elliott of South Carolina, it was different. The first black of unmixed lineage to be seated in Congress,

Elliott was sworn into the Forty-second Congress on March 4, 1871. Elliott's coal-blackness came as something of a shock, which accounted for his lukewarm reception in the Congress. There was, after all, a certain ambiguity about the light skins and aquiline features of the other Negro congressmen which made their presence bearable to the many Southerners and Negrophobes in the House. But Elliott's pure African blood, his wide nose, and thick lips no doubt assaulted their sensibilities and brought home the unpalatable truth that a member of what they considered the *inferior race* was now occupying a position equal to their own.

Even Frederick Douglass's *New National Era* used a faintly disparaging tone in describing Elliott, although it did acknowledge that among South Carolina politicians, he was generally considered the ablest man in the state delegation.

One of the white wives of an Ohio representative left the gallery reserved for the wives of members of the House when Elliott's wife, Grace, sat there in February, 1872. From that time on, Grace Elliott chose (or felt it the better part of wisdom) to sit in the regular ladies' gallery where there was no complaint lodged. After a time, she declined to come to Washington, remaining behind in Columbia where her social activities were not limited.[3]

The other colored men in the Forty-second Congress were Joseph Rainey, also of South Carolina, who was light-skinned as was Jefferson Franklin Long of Georgia. Although Long was a mulatto, he was darker skinned than Rainey and so considered more of a Negro than was Rainey. Benjamin S. Turner of Alabama, a mulatto, and Josiah Wall of Florida were also of mixed background. They fared better than Elliott when it came to accommodations and dining facilities. It is reported that Joseph Rainey felt so strongly about integrated public accommodations that he once refused to leave the dining room of a Virginia hotel until he was forcibly ejected from the premises.

But there was more serious business with which to contend than whether or not you were invited to one of the "old guard" parties. Robert B. Elliott was about that business. On March 10, 1871, the long-time friend and champion of the black cause, Charles Sumner, senator from Massachusetts, was removed as chairman of the Senate Foreign Relations Committee.

Sumner's bitterness over this rebuff by his colleagues deterred him from submitting any legislation dealing with the rise of Ku Klux Klan activities.

A bill was introduced into the House by Samuel Shellabarger of Ohio which gave the president the right to intercede with federal forces in cases of insurrection or obstruction of laws, *even if* such intervention was not requested by the state legislature or the chief executive. This bill was based on the powers inherent in the Fourteenth Amendment. Robert Brown Elliott, then only twenty-nine years old, spoke in behalf of the measure, which came to be known as the Enforcement Bill when it came to the floor. In his summary argument, he used the fall of Napoleon as an example for the United States. He said:

> "It is recorded that on the entry of Louis XVIII into Paris after the fall of the great Napoleon an old marshal of the empire who stood in the vast throng, unknown, was addressed by an ardent Bourbon who expiated on the gorgeous splendors that marked the scene, and exclaimed, 'Is this not grand? Is it not magnificent? What is there wanting to the occasion?' 'Nothing,' said the war worn veteran as his mind wandered over Lodi and Wagram and Austerlitz . . . 'nothing is wanting to the occasion but the presence of the brave men who died to prevent it.'
>
> "Such, sir, will be the bitter reflection of all loyal men in this nation, if the Democratic party shall triumph in the States of the South through armed violence."[4]

The prophetic quality of those comments is chilling. The bill did pass, and was signed into law on April 20, 1871, providing what seemed to be a security measure for the safety of Southern blacks.

Grant's intervention did not end with the Enforcement Act. Prior to that bill's passage, he had suspended the writ of habeas corpus in nine South Carolina counties. It was a drastic action, but the lawlessness that was becoming rampant in the South required drastic measures. The day that Grant suspended habeas corpus in South Carolina was October 12, and a letter of Robert Elliott to his wife dated October 13, which was a Friday, indicates that he felt that his life might be in danger. He wrote:

"Dear Wife,

I write this to inform you that I shall leave for home at 7 o'clock tonight, by the Richmond and Danville Railroad, and expect to reach home by the Charlotte and Columbia Railroad on Sunday morning before day. If anything should happen to me, I have a draft on the bank for $1800.00 [eighteen hundred dollars]. If it should be stolen, write immediately to Hon. N. G. Ordway, Sergeant-at-Arms of the House of Representatives and have him stop the payment on it, and send you a new draft. Mr. Ordway has also a life-insurance policy on my life for $10,000, which he will collect and after taking out what I owe him, the balance he will turn over to you. I do this, my dear, because life is uncertain.

I hereby constitute you my sole heir. All my property is yours. If anything happens send for [William] Whipper at once, and have him arrange your business for you.

Your affectionate husband,
Brown Elliott Robert"[5]

Siren Song of the South

During the last year of and immediately after the War of the Insurrection, many of those blacks who had been born and educated in the North or had migrated and/or escaped North went South to help their people and often themselves. The black leaders who became politicians were in many cases better educated and of higher intellect than those they replaced. Many, it's true, were poor and illiterate, but illiteracy has never been the same as stupidity.

Overall, three motives impelled these blacks to go South. Some found northern communities increasingly hostile and lacking in opportunity; many wanted to rejoin relatives from whom they had been separated when they had taken the "freedom train"; many more were accelerated by the excitement of a new challenge and a wide open arena in which to test their talents. This movement, together with that of migration to large urban communities, largely accounts for the depopulation and consequent decline of some black communities in the North after 1865.

An outstanding example was Blanche Kelso Bruce who had been born in slavery in Prince Edward County, Virginia in 1841. The son of a white father and a mulatto mother, he had been educated at Oberlin.

In 1869, he migrated further south than he had been in his life, to Mississippi. Being articulate, intelligent, and attractive, he made important friends quickly. Among them was Governor Alcorn who, after letting him work for a time as sergeant at arms in the Senate, dispatched him to Bolivar County as an assessor. Here, Bruce bought a one-thousand acre plantation, and in 1873 won election to a full term in the United States Senate. He began his term of office on March 5, 1875 in the Forty-fourth Congress.

Another was Theophilus Minton and his bride Martha Virginia McKee Minton. Martha McKee and T. J. Minton's marriage had united two Philadelphia families whose father's had come out of Virginia in the 1830's to make their fortunes in catering and real estate. They went to South

Carolina where T. J. could attend the law school of the University of South Carolina, now open to blacks. Their son, Henry McKee Minton, was born in Columbia, South Carolina on Christmas Day, 1870. When they returned to Philadelphia, Minton was the first black lawyer in the state.

Another young Pennsylvanian who became a "carpetbagger" was William J. Whipper, the son of William Whipper, the Philadelphia moral reformer and lumber merchant. He had served during the war in a volunteer company recruited in Michigan. He had remained in Detroit after the 1850 law had caused his father to consider leaving Pennsylvania and resettling in Canada. While there, Whipper had "read" law in the office of a friendly white lawyer. He was happy to volunteer to fight for freedom. When the war ended, he was in Charleston. Since he felt the opportunities were much greater in the new South than in Philadelphia or Detroit, he decided to remain. He had married Mary Elizabeth Byrd from New Haven, Connecticut. Their son, Cyrenius Byrd Whipper, was born in New Haven in 1864.

In 1866, Whipper opened a law office in the provost courthouse where he handled land deeds and all manner of legal work dealing with a city under military control. Martial law still prevailed and the city was patrolled day and night. The provost court had been established for trying most cases which the regular courts would normally have tried.

When Mary Elizabeth died in 1867, Whipper took young Cyrenius and a nurse with him to Columbia, South Carolina, where he became active in Republican Party politics. He left his adopted son, Demps Powell, in Beaufort with friends. After election to the South Carolina Constitutional Convention, he bent over backwards in attempting to view the entire process from a position of objectivity. This would have been strange for anyone other than a person of his background and breeding. He had been elected to represent *all* of the people, and this he intended to do to the dismay of some of his more militant and vengeful black colleagues. His objectivity did not mean, however, that he loved all whites or all blacks indiscriminately.

He was an aristocrat and he knew it. He scorned poor, illiterate whites and made no secret of his disdain for them. During a debate on the issue of public accommodations, Whipper denounced the suggestion that equality of access to public accommodations was in fact legislating social equality. He said,

> "Our race do not demand social equality . . . No law can compel me to put myself on an equality with some white men I know, but talk about equality and the member [of the legislature] imagines he must take you in his arms, as he probably would your sister, if she was good looking."[2]

Following the admission of his friend, Robert Brown Elliott, to the South Carolina bar in the summer of 1868, Whipper invited him to join him and Macon Allen in setting up a law firm. They opened it in Charleston at 91 Broad Street under the name Whipper, Elliott and Allen, establishing the first black law firm in the United States. (Macon Allen, older by several years than either Whipper or Elliott, had been admitted to the Massachusetts bar in 1845.) Whipper was appointed to a three-man committee to revise the South Carolina Legal Code, and the work his committee accomplished stood well the test of time. He was the single black in the group.

In September, 1868, Whipper married Miss Francis Ann Rollin in Charleston, and they had five children: Alicia, who died a few months after her birth in 1869; Winifred Rollin, born in Charleston; Ionia Rollin, born in Beaufort on September 8, 1872; Mary Elizabeth, born in Aiken, South Carolina in 1874; and Leigh Rollin Whipper, born in Charleston on October 29, 1876.

Francis Rollin Whipper's family was to Charleston, South Carolina what William J. Whipper's was to old-line Philadelphia—strictly top drawer. Well educated, well-to-do, and accomplished, the five "dazzlingly beautiful" daughters of a Frenchman and a mulatto woman were Francis, Katherine, Charlotte Marie, Louise, and Florence. They lived in a well-situated and graciously furnished home on a good street in Charleston. They were emancipated and liberated and came as close as any to being true *femmes fatale,* but they had brains along with their beauty.

Francis Rollin Whipper, under the pseudonym Frank A. Rollin, wrote *The Life and Public Services of Martin R. Delany* (Boston, Lee and Shep-

Photographs

HOW DID YOU SPEND YOUR VACATION?

L ONG, work-filled, irritating months in the office, the school-room, the factory or the shop in the dusty, noisy, grimy city cause the average tailor to look forward eagerly to the two or three weks or month allowed him each year for rest. The litle typist who pecks all day long on her machine in a hot office seventeen

floors up, dreams of long, lazy afternoons in the woods with only the latest novel and a two-pound box of chocolates for company, and moonlight evenings on the lake in the woods with the handsome young man from somewhere-or-other to row her boat. The

young school teacher sits at her desk on a hot June afternoon, and finds it hard to keep her mind on Johnny Jones, who just "can't get head or tail of grammar," when she longs for the murmur of the brook and the sound of the blue-jay and thrush.

(Continued on page 18)

A former municipal court judge, Anthony Overton began manufacturing cosmetics in 1898 and went on to organize the Douglass National Bank, Victory Life Insurance Company, and Half-Century magazine which featured fashion and travel articles.

180

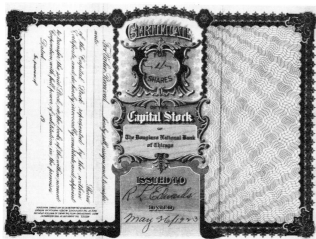

(Op. l.) Earl B. Dickerson,
Julian Lewis, and Dr. Midian
O. Bousfield join Overton in
saluting A.M.E. Bishop
Gregg. (center)

SMART AND PRACTICAL CLOTHES FOR AUTUMN

Black and white kumal-kumsn combines with black georgette to make this charmingly practical afternoon gown. It boasts of no trimming save self-covered Chinese buttons. Accordian pleated georgette give the sleeves the bell effect.

A midnight blue broadcloth suit is a splendid addition to any woman's wardrobe, especially when it has deep cuffs and a collar of chinchilla. Wide, black velvet hats are quite correct for afternoon wear.

A mink cape offers warmth and beauty to the woman who is fortunate enough to possess one. Dozens of brown mink tails add to its charm. The most correct silk skirt of the season is the one whose fullness is held in by means of a narrow band at the hem.

What They Are Wearing - - - By Mme. F. Madison

WITH the mercury hovering around 100 degrees, women, strange creatures that they are, seemingly have no thought save for furs and velour hats. And who shall say that they are not wise? There is a very brief period between the autumnal equinox and the falling of the first snow. Furriers tell us that pelts and hides of all kinds have advanced in price about two hundred per cent, so the furs for which you hesitated to pay fifty dollars last year will cost you about two hundred dollars this year, and in addition you will have to pay the government a luxury tax on them. But in spite of the extremely high prices furs are more popular than they have ever been. Fur chokers, big fur collars, deep fur cuffs and enveloping fur capes are seen in all the advance displays.

Fringe seems to hold its own, for some of the cloth is cut in half-inch wide strips that closely resemble fringe. One model of black silk jersey has a tunic of fringe extending from two inches below the waist line to the ankles.

Many of the skirts still show the narrow line at the hem but they are full above the hem. A number of designers are showing skirts that are hooped, some that are tucked to closely resemble the hooped skirt and skirts with a great deal of drapery.

Nearly all the models have a cut in look at the waist line. One can't have too many flounces this season, as many as eight are seen on some models. Paris is wearing her skirts a bit longer this fall but that doesn't mean that they are long by any means for Paris wore them fifteen and eighteen inches from the floor last season, or in other words they just covered the knee cap and the little length they

rather high pair of shoes.

Duvetyn, black satin, tricolette, chamois cloth and velvet are the smartest materials for the new fall costumes. Hats of duvetyn and velvet will be popular for afternoon wear and smart little tailored models of velours and felt will be worn in the mornings and for shopping. Hats are large or small just as preferred but to be ultra smart they must be very simple.

Laces and ribbons are popular as trimmings. Often a smart frock boasts of a lace bertha as its only trimming. Wide and narrow lace frills are used on gowns, especially organdies and georgette, which together with dainty flowered ribbons make the frock smart and appealing indeed. A reflection of other days is seen in the smart, perky, little bow perched jauntily upon either shoulder.

Madame C. J. Walker (shown above at age thirty) became a millionaire through her invention of a hair straightening method which she envisioned in a dream. Born in poverty in Delta, Louisiana (above right), she eventually owned a 30-room mansion in New York (opp.). Below with Booker T. Washington and in new car.

Madame Walker's daughter A'Lelia (above) in Wyoming (left).

Under A'Lelia Walker's leadership the Walker mansion became the social center for that era's black elite before her death in 1931.

Madame Walker's granddaughter, A'Lelia P. Bundles, was vice-president of the Madame C. J. Walker Beauty Colleges and was on the board of directors.

Family portrait: D. Arnett, George Gilbert (grandson, son of Nettie M. Gilbert) Martha Howard Murphy John H., Sr., Carl H. (at side), Francis L., Sue, George B., John H., Jr. (inset), Daniel, Rose, Lilly and Nettie.

Baltimore Afro-American founded by John Murphy, former slave, has grown into one of the most influential newspapers in black America. Progenitors of the Murphy clan are above, Susan Colby Murphy and Benjamin Murphy, Jr. Right, D. Arnett, Daniel, George B., John H., Jr., Carl H., Sr. (seated), John H., Sr.,

Bottom to top—
Mae M. Dyson,
Clementine
Murphy, Eliza-
beth Oliver
Abney, Ida M.
Smith Peters,
Rebecca M.
Young, Vashti
M. Matthews,
Carlita M.
Jones, Eugenia
M. Queen,
Genesta Gilbert
Lane, Betty M.
Moss, James H.,
Howard H.,
John Oliver,
Noah D. Thompson,
John H.

Lawrence Young (r.) presents
award to Judge Ernest Morial.
Below George B. Murphy Family
(l.-r.) Howard H., William H.,
Sister Constance, George B., Sr.,
Grace Hughes Murphy, James H.,
Rebecca M. Young and George B., Jr.

Founders — John Merrick, Dr. A. M. Moore, C. C. Spaulding

(r) J. M. Avery, early vice president-secretary, later became assistant manager; with wife Lula Aikens Avery and daughters, Janet and Vivian. (l) C. C. Spaulding, with sons, B. B. and C. C. Jr.

This six-story structure served as early home office. (Inset) W. J. Kennedy, Jr., chairman of the board; president (1952-1958). (Right) at merger of Unity Mutual with N. C. Mutual, officers: J. W. Goodloe, A. T. Spaulding, A. W. Williams and daughter, Mrs. Lillian W. Ward.

Staff shown at early home office in Durham (left). New $5 million building (r).

Above, officers, J. W. Goodloe, J. L. Stewart, L. R. Taylor, J. H. Wheeler and W. J. Kennedy, III. (Below) Retired president of North Carolina Mutual, Asa T. Spaulding (extreme right), receives award and congratulations from Mrs. O. H. Crosthwait, L. D. Jones, John F. Morning and George L. Harris.

Robert S. Abbott (l.) was the brother-in-law of Rosa Mae Sengstacke (above), mother of John Sengstacke Sr.

Home office for Sengstacke Publications is the Chicago Daily Defender founded by Robert Abbott.

Brothers Whittier and Frederick (not shown) and publisher John Sengstacke Sr. (far left with sons John, Robert, and Lewis) established the national newspaper chain.

President of National Newspaper Publishers Assn., Sengstacke gets plaque from Eisenhower as Thurgood Marshall and Myrtle Sengstacke look on.

189

Lt. Binga Dismond (above, right end) and officers of 8th Illinois.

Left to right: Col. C. Young, Col. F. Denison, Rev. W. Faulkner, C. Blackburn

Chicago lakefront crowd (above) surround returning "Fighting 8th." "Brown Skin Soldier Boys," a popular WW 1 song, appeared in 1919 issue of Half-Century magazine.

191

Marie and Hazel, daughters of Leonard Johnson
and Francis Powell. Their grandfather, Elijah
Powell served in the Civil War. Below (l.) Marie
J. Moore, a talented painter, who exhibits often.
(r.) Marie, with her husband, Judge Herman
E. Moore, was assigned to U.S. Virgin Islands
by President Franklin D. Roosevelt as one of
the first blacks named to the federal bench.

Dr. Farrow Raymond
Powell, above, his son
F. Raymond Jr. and wife,
Lillian Hancock (below inset).
Photo at far right shows
Dr. Powell, while a student
at Fisk University in
student play. Below (r.)
Gerri Hodges Dismond and
aunt Maude Lawrence,
during W W 1 training
program. Maude Powell
Lawrence (below). Mae and
Maude Powell and F.
Raymond Powell and Marie
Johnson Moore's mother,
Frances were all grand-
children of Farrow Powell,
by sons John Wesley and
Elijah.

ard, 1868). Then, after raising her and Whipper's children, she moved to Washington, D. C., where in the 1880s she became one of the first black women physicians in the United States, completing her studies at Howard University School of Medicine. Their daughter, Dr. Ionia Whipper of Washington, D. C., was a pioneer in providing health care services for ard, 1868). Then, after raising her and Whipper's children, she moved to young unwed black mothers, and the Ionia Whipper Home for Girls still operates in Washington, D. C.

The youngest son of Francis and William Whipper was Leigh Rollin Whipper, the distinguished actor, who died in July, 1975, only a year short of the centennial of his birth, in Reconstruction South Carolina.

More than any other, the name of Robert Brown Elliott is synonymous with the Reconstruction and South Carolina. The state of South Carolina sent more black congressmen to Washington than any other state—Rainey, Ransier, Smalls, Cain, De Large—but of them all, Elliott was easily the most noteworthy. Elliott, a Bostonian of West Indian extraction, was a gifted intellectual who found himself at the right place and at the right time. Educated in Jamaica and at the High Holborn Academy and Eton College in England, he returned to the United States where he worked initially as an editor on the *Missionary Record,* a paper published by AME Bishop Richard H. Cain in Charleston. Elliott was, by his unmixed heritage, able to give the lie to those who said only blacks whose blood was mixed were able to deal on the same intellectual plane as whites. It wasn't the blood as much as it was the opportunity and the exposure, as Elliott proved every time he opened his mouth. He spoke several languages, including German, read Latin and Greek, and maintained an excellent reference library for his and his friends' personal use. He served in Congress for two different sessions and each time returned to South Carolina where he was undoubtedly the biggest fish in the pond.

Elliott was appointed assistant adjutant general of South Carolina March 25, 1869, a post which he held until his election to the Forty-second Congress. He was commissioned August 1, 1870 as major general commanding the National Guard for the State of South Carolina. He sought and got an appropriation to hire Henry W. Purvis, a son of Robert Purvis. On January 31, 1872, Elliott requested that Purvis be commissioned adjutant and brigadier general with a view to appointing him his chief of staff.[3] William Whipper was also commissioned brigadier general in the Second Division of the South Carolina National Guard.

The white backlash against Reconstruction had been felt in other states before it reached South Carolina. Little by little, power in the former insurrectionist states had been restored to the hands of the white supremist Democrats. Tennessee had fallen in 1869, Virginia and North Carolina in 1870, Georgia in 1871, Arkansas, Alabama, and Texas in 1874, and Mississippi in 1875. Only three states remained in the hands of black men and their "liberal" white "friends."

South Carolina still had a firm black majority of 415,000 blacks against 289,000 whites in the state. There were twenty-seven black men in the legislature, and a substantial number of the members in Governor Daniel Chamberlain's cabinet were black. The adjutant general was black and Francis L. Cardozo, the state treasurer, was black. The chairman of the Republican State Committee was Speaker of the House Robert Brown Elliott, all the signs pointed to a move to recapture the state through a giant conspiracy. Once again the victims were the members of the black community; free and freed, they were all one now.

Terror reigned in the months leading up to the election. Throughout South Carolina, blacks were shot in the street and others were lynched. At Hamburg on July 8, 1876, a massacre took place. Governor Chamberlain, shocked and sickened, understood that the end had come for South Carolina as it had for the other states. "Such was the affair at Hamburg," he wrote to Senator T. J. Robertson in Washington. "If you can find the words to characterize its atrocity and barbarism, the triviality of the causes, the murderous and inhuman spirit which marked it in all its stages, your power of language exceeds mine. . . . What hope can we have when such a cruel, bloodthirsty spirit waits in our midst for its hour of gratification? Is our race so wantonly cruel?"[4]

Following Hamburg, Elliott called a meeting of all of the black politicians in the state to determine a course of action. Whites were excluded from this Convention of Colored People held on the 20th and 21st of July, 1876. Out of this meeting came his "Address to the People of the United States." In it he called upon the governor to ask the president for federal troops, and on July 2, 1876, Chamberlain wrote to the president asking that the federal government "exert itself vigorously to repress violence in the state during the present political campaign." He included a copy of Elliott's "Address to the People of the United States" in his correspondence. No action was taken.

The murders and terrorism continued, and by October, the governor declared that it was impractical to attempt to enforce the laws of the state by ordinary process of judicial proceedings.

The Northern blacks in particular found themselves in an extremely difficult and dangerous position. When the order regarding the troops came—and they knew that the federal government no longer supported their position nor offered them protection—they counselled Chamberlain to give up his fight. As the document drafted by Elliott and signed by his cabinet members indicates, ". . . We are agreed, therefore, in counselling you to discontinue the struggle for the occupancy of the gubernatorial chair, convinced as we are that in view of the disastrous odds to which its maintenance has been subjected by the action of the national administration, your retirement will involve no surrender of principle, nor its motive be misapprehended by the great body of that political party to which, in common with ourselves, you are attached."[5] The letter was received by Chamberlain the day the troops were withdrawn. Many of those who had come South prepared to return to the comparative safety of the North. Whipper and Elliott remained. Cardozo, Greener and Minton did not.

Elliott, who, with the other five state officers, had been duly elected as attorney general of the state, did not resign when the governor did. Although there had been only eleven years of freedom and nine of Reconstruction, it was back to normalcy. The prevailing mood during that time indicated the country was tired of Negroes and tired of their problems. White Americans wanted to get on with their own concerns and were willing to concede that the South probably knew better than the North how to handle "those people." Certainly, unless a large segment of the total population had agreed with the policy of "appeasement" implemented by Hayes, there could have been no Wormley Hotel Compromise, a series of meetings which ultimately resulted in the expiration of the civil rights of blacks.

To Teach The Freedmen

$\mathcal{T}$he preoccupation with education was almost universal among both the newly freed and those born free. The missionary spirit which had taken Charlotte Forten to Georgia during the war was exemplified by the hundreds of Northern whites and blacks who went South at the war's end to open school and to teach the freedmen so that they might eventually teach themselves.

The dismal lack of preparation and the prevailing state of ignorance among the freedmen demanded that education be the number one priority. In 1870 more than four million blacks in the South could neither read nor write, and if the citizenship and rights of suffrage which had been won and certified by constitutional amendment were to be anything but farcical, then the state of ignorance had to be eradicated.

Now, the war ended, the Freedmen's Bureau abandoned in 1872, and the North looking for accommodation with Southern interests, the cause of education for the black victims was left in large measure to the churches and philanthropists. The framework for education which had been formed under the Freedmen's Bureau provided the skeleton upon which most black educational institutions were built.

Between 1865 and 1900, at least seventy-five institutions for the higher education of black students were organized throughout the South. Although they took various names—academies, colleges, universities, normal and industrial schools, and theological seminaries—almost always their students came without even meager preparation. The standards of the majority of these institutions, therefore, were necessarily not higher than the reality permitted: If a high school equivalency was the result of the course at the normal or industrial institute, it was still a far cry from the vacuum it had filled, and it placed those who had completed the course that much closer to being educated and informed citizens.

While Howard University was unique in being a federal institution authorized specifically by act of Congress and the only one offering professional training, other institutions of higher education came into being as a result of the Freedmen's Act and the missionary efforts of the Protestant church. Lincoln, Wilberforce and Howard University aside, Atlanta University (1865), Fisk (1866), Talladega (1867), and Tougaloo (1869) were all organized under the auspices of the American Missionary Association. Hampton Institute (1868) was also organized by the American Missionary Association to train black farmers; its prototype, Tuskegee Institute, was established in 1881 by Hampton graduate Booker T. Washington.

At Fisk and Atlanta University, the emphasis was on classical education, while at Hampton, General Armstrong was putting into practice the theories of industrial education which had first been discussed in the 1831 Convention of Free Colored Men, but had actually been tried on Armstrong's home island of Maui with the native Hawaiian Islanders.

General Clinton B. Fisk, of the Tennessee Freedmen's Aid Bureau, along with the American Missionary Association and the Western Freedmen's Aid Commission of Cincinnati, formed the first consortium to pull together the school which was named Fisk University upon incorporation.

Housed in old army barracks with spelling books and bibles bought for the school with money raised from the sale of rusty old iron handcuffs and fetters from the Nashville slave pens, Fisk enrolled one thousand students in its first year following its opening in 1866. Some of its first students took ten years to complete the college curriculum because they first had to learn the basics—reading and writing. Five years after its founding, the new school was faced with the loss of government funding as the Freedmen's benefits were allowed to expire by a Congress now tired of the Negro problem. It was then that the school treasurer, George L. White, decided to take the Fisk choir on a tour to raise money for the school. He organized the Colored Christian Singers, later known as the Fisk Jubilee Singers, and in 1871, the seven women and four men began the tour that was to climax with a command performance at Buckingham Palace and the life-size painting of the group by Queen Victoria's official court painter, F. Havill. The group earned $150,000 in their two-year tour, and with it the present site of Fisk University was acquired and Jubilee Hall built.

While Fisk's first classes were held in the abandoned barracks, Atlanta University in 1865 began in a $310 railroad boxcar bought in Chattanooga, sidetracked, and cut into two units for classrooms. Its founder and first president was Edmund Asa Ware.

Morehouse College was started as a Baptist school in 1867 by Richard R. Coulter and William J. White, under the sponsorship of the American Baptist Home Missionary Society.

The Freedmen's Aid Society of the Methodist Episcopal church founded Clark College in 1870 with Reverend J. W. Lee and his wife. And two New England ladies, Miss Sophia Packard and Miss Harriett E. Giles, who determined that young colored ladies should have the benefit of a lady's education, opened Spelman College in 1881. The first classes were held in a church basement coal bin, where the girls wrapped their feet in burlap bags to keep warm. It was America's first college for black women. The college was named for Abby Spelman, the mother of John D. Rockefeller, after he became the school's benefactor by paying off the mortgage when it was faced with financial disaster.

Northern philanthropy in the establishment of funds for Southern Negro education was started by George Peabody in 1867-69. Three and a half million dollars was provided for teacher training, a portion of which was allocated for Negro use. Teachers came from the North from the class of poor but genteel to give their knowledge and principles to the freed people.

Without white patronage or control but through the efforts of the North Georgia and the Georgia Annual Conference of the AME church, Morris Brown College, a co-ed school, had as its first principal a woman, Mrs. Mary McCree.

Three other funds were exclusively for Negro use—the John F. Slater Fund of a million dollars in 1882, Daniel Hand's gift of one and a half million to the American Missionary Association in 1888, and the Anna T. Jeanes Fund. About half of the black children had no schools to attend in 1878, but by 1898, a million and a half were in school, at least for a period of each year.

Even while schools were being started all across the South under the auspices of religious and philanthropic groups, many still had no school of any kind, leaving a vast reservoir of knowledge-hungry black people. In many small communities, the colored families pooled their meager resources in order to pay a teacher for even a few weeks of every year between harvesting and planting time, and the teacher took room and board as part of his or her payment.

It is difficult to measure the impact of education upon these newly emancipated people. The history of black leadership in this period is full of examples of illiterate mothers and fathers who, holding no real hope of significantly bettering their own condition, nonetheless sacrificed beyond belief to make it possible for their children to get scraps of formal education. Booker T. Washington's autobiography, *Up From Slavery,* could have been written by countless other black educators who came out of a slave past and dedicated their lives to service and commitment by educating those who came along behind them.

Peter Weddick Moore of Elizabeth City, North Carolina and William H. McAlpine of Selma, Alabama were typical of these others who "let down their buckets where they were." Moore, born in 1858 in North Carolina of slave parents, was still very young when emancipation came. His father was a victim of the night-riders during the post-Reconstruction terrorism, and the education and training of the five Moore children, of which Peter was the eldest, was left to his mother. The first school which young Moore attended was operated by the Freedmen's Bureau, but when the Freedmen's Bureau pulled out, some resources came from the Peabody Fund.

Moore was inspired and encouraged by a young black teacher named Burke Marable, who had been trained at Lincoln University and returned to his North Carolina home after the war. He established his own school, which he called the Philosophian Academy. Marable taught all of the classes from the basic ABCs to Latin and higher mathematics. As soon as an older student was able, Marable put some of the younger students in his charge. Because most of the students had to work to help their families eke out an existence, the class terms were short. However, during the times when school was in session, the average class enrollment was approximately seventy-five students.

Motivated by Marable's example, Peter Moore devoted every free moment to reading and study, and by the time he was twenty, had attained a certificate to teach in a one-teacher school located near Clinton, North Carolina. Along with his teaching chores, he tenant-farmed a small plot where he managed to raise enough cotton for sale to help pay his tuition at Shaw University in Raleigh, North Carolina. Shaw had been founded in 1865 and was a Northern Baptist home missionary affiliate.

At Shaw, Moore came to the attention of the president, Dr. H. M. Tupper, and in much the same manner that General Armstrong at Hampton became Booker T. Washington's mentor, so Dr. Tupper took the aspiring young student-teacher under his wing. Moore received his A.B. degree in 1887, eight years after he entered as a student-teacher, but each year he returned to Clinton where he conducted classes. Upon his graduation from Shaw, he was hired as assistant to the principal of the state normal school in Plymouth, North Carolina.

In 1891 the North Carolina General Assembly voted to establish the Elizabeth City State Normal School for the Colored Race. Peter W. Moore was selected as principal of the new school, which opened in January, 1892 with sixty pupils, twenty of whom were already certified and licensed to teach. They, like Moore, who had taken his certificate and gone to Shaw, recognized their limitations and were bent upon improving their skills and broadening their own knowledge.

In Moore's reports to the trustees are some of the keys to the problems facing a nation of unschooled people trying to lift themselves by education out of their depressed state. Said Moore in 1897, "Much of the work done consisted of real class work in the common branches because the students were deficient in these things. A student cannot be taught very well the methods of teaching arithmetic until he learns how to work arithmetic."

William H. McAlpine was born in slavery in Buckingham County near Farmersville, Virginia in June, 1847. He was a young man nearly grown by the time of emancipation and had been sold twice before the war ended the traffic in human beings. He was eight years old when, in order to settle an estate, he, his mother, and a younger brother were separated. Taken to Talladega County, Alabama, where he remained in the same family until the war's end, McAlpine was given the job as companion and servant for the young children of the household. As such, he was permitted to mingle only with slaves who had access to the house as he did, but it was in this context that he learned to read and to write, and gained a knowledge of mathematics, grammar, and geography.

The year before the war ended, young McAlpine became a Christian convert and joined a white Baptist church in Talladega, Alabama. Meanwhile, he had learned the carpenter's trade, and this was the skill he employed to earn a living at war's end. When Talladega College opened in 1869 under the auspices of the Congregational church, McAlpine enrolled as a student and sustained himself by working as a hired hand. He quit six months short of completing the course in order to accept a call to pastor a Baptist church for colored people in Talladega. But even as a full-time minister, he did not abandon education, teaching classes even as he ministered to the spiritual needs of his rural Alabama constituency. By resolution and influencing public opinion, from 1873 on, Reverend McAlpine pushed the proposition that a Baptist institution for the higher education of colored youth should be established in Selma, Alabama.

In the fall of 1877, the Colored Baptist Convention voted to establish the school in Selma. With one thousand dollars for a down payment—much of which had been raised by William McAlpine as he canvassed the state preaching, praying, and talking about the proposed school—the Selma, Alabama Fair Grounds was purchased, the total cost amounting to three thousand dollars.

In 1881, Reverend William H. McAlpine was elected president of the Alabama Baptist Normal and Theological School (later called Selma University), a position which he held for two years, until a man with what Dr. McAlpine considered more acceptable educational credentials could be hired. When the right man was found, McAlpine resigned and returned to the active Baptist ministry.

The man who succeeded Reverend McAlpine was Reverend Edward M. Brawley, the free-born Charleston, South Carolina father of the eminent Benjamin G. Brawley, author and educator. Edward Brawley had been sent to Philadelphia as a child, where he attended the Institute for Colored Youth under Ebenezer Don Carlos Bassett, but following the war, had returned to Charleston where he was apprenticed to a shoemaker. While in Philadelphia, he had joined the Shiloh Baptist Church and become active in Sunday school work. In the fall of 1870, Edward M. Brawley became the first student enrolled in the theological school at Howard University, but because the school was suffering such growing pains, he only remained there three months, transferring to Bucknell University at Lewisburg, Pennsylvania. At the close of his sophomore year, he was licensed to preach by the white Baptist church at Lewisburg and was ordained upon his graduation from Bucknell in 1875. Sent by the American Baptist Publication Society as a missionary to South Carolina, his home state, he began at once to organize Sunday schools in the existing churches and to organize the churches into associations. He then formed all of these groups into a state convention. When he left South Carolina after eight years, the state was well organized as far as the colored Baptist church was concerned.

It was the wisdom of Reverend McAlpine and his lack of personal self-seeking that recognized the necessity for a man of Brawley's attainments at Selma if the institution was to achieve the academic recognition that he sought for it.

Across the South in those years following the war, the story could be told over and over, only changing names and incidents, of the self-sacrificing and dedicated men and women who were determined to bring the light of knowledge to those so long denied.

The Quality of Education

*T*he sacrifices which the poverty stricken and uneducated freedmen made to secure for their children the educational fundamentals were awesome.

The same will and determination to secure *the best education* was evident in the zeal and dedication with which the upper class in Washington, D. C. attacked the problem of gaining superior elementary and secondary educational facilities for their young people.

After the loss of the fight for integrated schools in the District, which had been led by Senator Charles Sumner, the trustees were insistent in their demands for equal standards and proportional representation for the two separate systems.

The Wormleys and Cooks and Syphaxes had been involved in the school situation from the earliest days of the Federal City, so that it was not surprising that public education of colored children fell to their control. To this group, Oberlin-trained for the most part, first-class status and acceptance into the mainstream of America's economic and civic life could only come through using the same avenues that the white leadership class used. Decision makers rarely met for the first time at the board table; more often they had attended the same prep schools, summer camps, and colleges.

The Preparatory High School for Colored Youth was the answer, or at least the first phase of it. From its inception in November, 1870, the primary and overriding purpose was the preparation of youth for leadership and the development of each student's utmost potential.

In the best days of this unique school, the faculty and staff were single-minded in the achievement of this goal, often using their personal funds to help an excellent student make it over the hump. Each year

205

the school produced graduates who would go to the Ivy League schools and the Seven Sisters to get acclimated to the rarefied atmosphere which American leaders have breathed since the country's founding.

The Preparatory High School's first home was the basement of the Fifteenth Street Presbyterian Church, under the pastorship of J. Sella Martin and for so long John F. Cook's church. The founders were William Syphax, the president and treasurer, and William H. A. Wormley, secretary of the Board of Trustees of Colored Schools of Washington and Georgetown. A. E. Newton, the superintendent, and Miss Emma J. Hutchins, the first teacher, were New England whites in the abolitionist tradition. George F. T. Cook was appointed superintendent in 1871 and served until 1899. Other superintendents were W. Scott Montgomery (1900-1907); Roscoe C. Bruce, son of Senator Blanche K. Bruce (1907-1921); Garnet Wilkinson (1921-1951); and Harold H. Haynes (1951-1954), who served until the year of the Supreme Court decision, *Brown* v. *Board of Education of Topeka, Kansas.*

The school moved from the basement of the Fifteenth Street Presbyterian Church to the Thaddeus Stevens School for one year (1871-1872) and from there to the Charles Sumner School, where it remained until 1877. The school relocated to the Myrtilla Miner School until 1891, when it was moved to the school on M Street between First and New Jersey Avenue, NW. The M Street School became the Paul Laurence Dunbar High School in 1916. In each of these locations, the spirit undergirding this school since its inception was maintained and fostered until it became institutionalized as tradition. The high standards were recognized to the extent that for many years college entrance examinations were not required of Dunbar graduates.

During the thirty-five years that George F. T. Cook was superintendent of the separate colored school system in the District, the school was developed which alone accounts for more of the contemporary black leadership class than any other group of preparatory schools or educational institutions in the United States. Among the thousands of men and women who count themselves as alumni of the school under any of its names, many have gone on to become living examples of the viability of the founding philosophy.

Dr. W. Montague Cobb[1] (Dunbar, 1921), the noted anatomist, and Mary Gibson Hundley[2] surveyed Dunbar graduates in separate studies. One of these indicated that between 1892 and 1954, Amherst College admitted thirty-four Dunbar graduates, of which twenty-five graduated; seven of those earned Phi Beta Kappa keys and three were awarded honorary degrees for achievement in later life.

Combined data from the Cobb and Hundley studies recorded the names of some of the school's graduates, making a list which sounds much like a "Who's Who" of colored America.

Amherst College—Percy Barnes, Laurence Burwell Jr., W. Montague Cobb, Mercer Cook Jr. and Sr., Francis Dent, Thurman Dodson, Charles Drew, Harold Haizlip, William Hastie, Charles Houston, James Hunter, Chauncey Larry, Harold Leves, John Pinkett, David Utz, Clarence White, George Williams.

Antioch College—Bessie Cobb, Anne Pratt, Joyce Samuels, Adrienne Walton.

Barnard College—Enid Tucker.

Bates College—Cornelius Alexander, John P. Davis, Roscoe McKinney, Theodore Pinckney.

Bowdoin College—David Harris, McDougall Holmes, Lincoln Johnson, David Lane, Arthur Payne.

Brown University—Samuel Compton, George Hayes, Roscoe Lewis, Lancess McKnight.

Bryn Mawr—Enid Cook.

Boston University—Wenonah Bond, Jesse Chase, Joan Hill, Martha Ann Lofton, Doris G. Morris, Gwendolyn Preston.

California Institute of Technology—Charles Weir.

Case School of Applied Science—Francis Gregory.

Catholic University—Harold Freeman.

Chicago University—William Brown, Clifton Hardy, Jennie Taylor, Charles Weir Sr.

Colby College—Russell Dixon, Jacqueline Taylor.

Colgate College—Robert Bowser Jr., Henry Robinson Sr.

Columbia University—Milton R. Edelin, Marjorie E. Garnett, Richard Tyler.

Connecticut College for Women—Barbara Pinchback.

Cornell University—Adelaide Cook, Jane Datcher, Talley Holmes Jr., Robert Ogle, Irene Trigg.

Curtis Institute—George Walker.

Dartmouth College—Samuel Bullock, Lenoir Cook, Thomas Ellerbe, Richard Fairley, Wendell Freeman, Bruce Gabriel, Norbert Gillem, Orlando Hobbs, Talley Holmes Sr., Peter Johnson, Stephen Lewis, Grant Lucas Jr., Robert McGuire Jr., Wilder Montgomery Jr. and Sr., Howard Payne, John Payne, Jr., John Phillips, Charles Pinderhughes, Henry Robinson Jr., Charles Wilder Sr. and Jr., Henri Williams, Thornton Wood, Lowell Wormley.

Elmira College—Katherine Harden.

Hamilton College—Maurice Clifford Jr., Joseph Jenkins, Morteza Sprague.

Harvard College—Joseph Carpenter, Eugene Davidson, Howard Fitzhugh, Nathaniel Geary, Herbert Hughes, Harry Keelan, Sheridan Perry, Ulysses Shelton, Robert Terrell, French Tyson, Robert Weaver, Nolan Williams.

Michigan University—Frances Cardozo, Joyce Collins, Beryl Claytor, Albertus Conn, Marie Corbin, Mary Cromwell, Frank Johnson, Leon Langhorne, Armstead Pride, Othello Thompson, Vivian Wilson.

Mount Holyoke College—Carolyn Cobb, Betty Hunter, Laura Lee, Charlotte Pinkett, Constance Quarles, Louise Russell, Ruth Smith.

College of New Rochelle—Janie Crawford, Harriet Gillem.

Northwestern University—Ernest Anderson, William Branch.

Notre Dame University—Elbur Hawkins.

Oberlin College—Rosabelle Lane, Evelyn Lawlah, Josephine Lawson, Edna Mayer, Kermit Mehlinger, Hortense Pace, Elsie Robinson, Clara Shippen, Charles Thomas, Gladys Thomas, Frances E. Walker, Garnet Wilkinson, Gladys Wilkinson, Audrey Wright.

Ohio State—Mary V. Ransome.

Ohio Wesleyan—Wendell M. Holloway.

Pembroke College—Suzanne Payne, Charlotte West.

University of Pennsylvania—Esther Butler, Dorothy Craft, Herbert Harris, William McNeill, Sadie Mossell, Barbara Stewart, Albert Tompkins.

Pennsylvania State University—Julian Cook Jr., Louis Ivy.

University of Pittsburgh—Charles Fisher, Harold Haynes, William Haynes, Robert Taylor, Granville Woodson.

Radcliffe College—Mary Bunton, Louise Cook, Ophelia Davidson, Nancy Durant, Mary Gibson, Dorothy Houston, Jean Jason, Antoinette Simmons, Letitia Young.

Rensselaer Polytechnic Institute—Clarence Banton, Lincoln Hawkins, Blanchard Lloyd, Edward Morton, Francis Steele.

Rutgers University—Louyco W. Holmes, Edward Lawson Jr., Reuben McDaniel.

Sarah Lawrence College—Lois Baldwin, Norma Edelin, Carol Graham.

Skidmore College—Willie Logan.

Simmons College—Ellen Robinson.

Smith College—Louise Arrington, Beatrice Black, Evelyn Boyd, Doris Collins, Adelaide Cromwell and her aunt Otelia Cromwell, Marjorie Felton, Annette Hawkins, Euphemia Lofton, Odessa McKenzie, Naomi Nimmo, Laura Phillips, Grace Ridgeley, Frances Yvonne White.

Springfield College—Roscoe Brown Jr., John Pinderhughes, Percy Pitts.

Stanford University—Clarence Gardiner.

Swarthmore College—Betty Hunter, Sarita Smith.

Syracuse University—Janet Avery, Daniel Edmonds, Frederick Hundley, Thomas Posey, Lorraine Redmond, Adela Rinen, James Saunders, Joseph Trigg, William Wilkinson Jr.

U. S. Military Academy—Ernest J. Davis, Henry Minton Francis, John M. Hamilton, Edward Howard, Bernard Hughes, Hugh G. Robinson, William Woodson.

U. S. Naval Academy—Wesley A. Brown, Lawrence Chambers.

Vassar College—Camille Cottrell, Ruth M. Smith.

University of Vermont—Barbara Boyd, John C. Leak, Peggy Lucas, Jean Westmoreland, Patricia Williams.

Wellesley College—Elizabeth Carter, Dorothy Danish, Jean Jennifer, Patricia Kelly, Elizabeth Neill, Ruth Savoy, Barbara Scott, Esther Toms, Lillian Washington, Elizabeth West.

Wesleyan College—Ellis Kendall.

Western Reserve—LaVerne Gregory.

Williams College—Sterling Brown, Eugene Clark Sr., Allison Davis, John A. Davis, James Henry, Rupert Lloyd, Sterling Lloyd, Rayford Logan, Clyde McDuffie (three years), Willis Menard, Bruce Robinson, Ralph Scott, Mortimer Weaver.

Wilson College (Pa.)—Nannie Miller.

University of Wisconsin—Mary Burke, Jeanne Hyde.

Yale University—Joseph Quander, Cyrus Shippen, Fred Syphax Sr., Carol Thomas, Sterling Tignor.

Ph.D.s:
    Fannie Belcher, Yale University
    Evelyn Boyd, Yale University
    Ruth A. Brown, Catholic University
    George H. Butcher, University of Pennsylvania
    Marion Elizabeth Carter, Catholic University
    W. Montague Cobb, Western Reserve University
    William Curtis, Georgetown University
    Annette Hawkins Eaton, Catholic University
    Euphemia Lofton Haynes, Catholic University
    James M. Henderson, University of Wisconsin
    Adelaide Cromwell Hill, Radcliffe College
    Benjamin Hunton, American University
    Dorothy Campbell Johnson, Columbia University
    John C. Leak, University of Illinois
    Ulysses G. Lee Jr., University of Chicago
    Harold O. Lewis, American University

Photographs

Critic Alain Locke was a leading campaigner for Renaissance writers...

Carter Woodson

Charles S. Johnson

Jean Toomer

Countee Cullen

The black literary movement of the 1920s
known as the "Harlem Renaissance" produced
such prolific writers as James Weldon
Johnson (r.), Arna Bontemps (below, l.),
Jessie Fauset (inset) and Langston Hughes
whose writings projected a racial pride and
self-awareness in a quantity never before seen.

213

Author Gerri Major and first
husband, Binga Dismond,
shortly after moving to
New York during 1920s
where Mrs. Dismond wrote
society column for the
Pittsburgh Courier.   Binga's
father, Dr. Samuel Henry
Dismond, was director of
Virginia Building Loan and
Trust. His maternal uncle,
214 Jesse Binga, was a Chicago
banker and real estate broker.

Williston family wedding (below) was typical of the social events which Gerri Dismond featured in her New York society column.

215

Frank Gillespie founded Liberty
Life Ins. Co. Harry Pace organized
Northwestern Life of Newark. T. K.
Gibson, Sr., helped organize
Supreme Life of Ohio. The three
merged in 1929 becoming Chicago's

Supreme Life. Earl Dickerson, past
president, T. K. Gibson, Sr.,
Jefferson Ish, T. K., Jr., and
William Dawson attend business
luncheon. John H. Johnson (below r.)
is chairman of board of directors.

Supreme Life's John H. Johnson (r.) with current president, Ray Irby, and members of the board (front row, l. to r.) Charles Carr, William Walker, Ray Irby, Johnson, Earl Dickerson, Loyd Wheeler, Dr. J. C. Wiggins, (back row, l. to r.) Elmer Henderson, Dr. Edward Beasley, Harry H. C. Gibson, D. C. Chandler, L. Benton Robinson, John F. Morning and A. P. Bentley.

Congressman, minister
and protest leader
Adam Clayton Powell, Jr.
with father (l.) whom
he succeeded as pastor
of Harlem's Abyssinian
Baptist Church. Powell,
at age three months,
(above) with father,
mother and sister, Blanche.
Powell, who was elected
to Congress in 1945,
with son (l.) Adam 3rd
and second wife, pianist
Hazel Scott.

Adam Powell 3rd at his wedding and (below) with family at father's funeral in 1972. Powell (above) with (l. to r.) Congressmen Diggs, Nix, Hawkins, and Dawson during the 88th Congress, which was only time since Reconstruction that there were five blacks in Congress.

Mary McLeod
Bethune was
National Youth
Association advisor
during the 1930s
New Deal Era, but
unofficially she
was advisor to
President Roosevelt
and personal friend
of Eleanor
Roosevelt.

Many blacks were relatively unaffected by the events of the 1930s, as evidenced by the advent of many young women's social clubs. The Chicagoans pictured were members of The Amigas and the Tri-Phis.

*Above (l.-r.) William H. A. Wormley,
Henry P. Cheatham, Dr. Lowell C. Wormley,
Dr. Stanton Wormley, Hugh M. Browne,
Marion P. Shadd and (right), Dr. Margaret
Just Butler. Members of the Wormley-
Shadd-Cheatham-Just families have made
distinguished contributions to the fields of
politics, medicine, science and education.*

222

Dr. William J. Faulkner, minister emeritus, Park Manor Congregational Church (Chicago), former chaplain, Fisk University, outstanding folklorist and author. Above, with wife Elizabeth Abele Cook (descendant of Absalom Jones), children, William Jr., who lost life in WWII and Josephine. (R.) Dr. and Mrs. Faulkner (rear), Mrs. Ralph (Vivian) Cook, daughter, Marie F. Brown and Josephine F. Webster. Front, John O. Brown, Jr., wife, Gail and son, John O. III.

Mr. and Mrs. William T. Syphax (above), Syphax family in Virginia (r.), and Dr. Burke Syphax (bottom photo, l.) are descendants of William T. Syphax.

Mr. and Mrs. William Custis Syphax (above) and Mrs.
Mary Gibson Hundley, the only direct descendant of
William T. Syphax, all reside in Washington, D.C.

Williston Lofton, American University
John W. Mangigault, University of Rome
Carroll L. Miller, Columbia University
Sadie Mossell, University of Pennsylvania
Marjorie Holloman Parker, University of Chicago
Enid Cook Rodaniche
Charles W. Thomas, American University
Bennetta Bullock Washington, Catholic University

Rosenwald Fellows:

W. Montague Cobb
Esther Victoria Cooper
Joseph Henry Douglass
Adelaide Cromwell Hill
Rayford W. Logan
Thomas E. Posey
Elizabeth Catlett White
Evelyn Boyd

Alumni Achievements:

George Bruce Robinson—appointed Assistant Attorney General of the Commonwealth of Massachusetts; later appointed Assistant Corporation Counsel of Boston.

Judge William Hastie—Spingarn Medalist; first black governor of the U. S. Virgin Islands; Federal judge.

Charles R. Drew—Spingarn Medalist; developed blood plasma bank during World War II.

Samuel Z. Westerfield—Ambassador to Liberia.

Francis Ellis Rivers—New York City judge.

Mrs. Sarah Pelham Speaks—New York City attorney.

Hilyard Robinson—architect; designed building for Liberian centenary.

Edward Brooke—U. S. Senator from Massachusetts; Attorney General for the Commonwealth of Massachusetts.

Dr. Charles I. West Jr.—Chief of Medical Services, Public Health Mission, Liberia.

Major Granville Woodson—Chief, Engineering Services, Public Health Mission, Liberia.

Colonel Campbell C. Johnson—U. S. Commendation for work in veterans' reorientation and re-employment program.

Sterling A. Brown—appointed to faculty of Vassar College as Visiting Professor of English.

Adelaide Cromwell Hill Ctulliver—Director, Afro-American Studies, Boston University.

Enid Cook Rodaniche—Director, Division of Epidemiology and Bacteriology of the Department of Health and Public Works, Panama City, Republic of Panama.

Dr. Robert C. Weaver—first black cabinet member, Department of Housing and Urban Development, under President Lyndon B. Johnson.

Thurgood Marshall—first black U. S. Solicitor General; first black U. S. Supreme Court Justice.

William C. Syphax—Veteran's Employment Representative, D. C.

Attorney Oliver W. Hill—elected to Richmond, Virginia City Council.

Charles S. Lofton—Principal of Dunbar High School.

Lieutenant Willard Savoy—author, *Alien Land,* a novel.

Dr. Margaret Just Butcher—visiting professor at Lyon and Grenoble, France under Fulbright Act; later member of D. C. Board of Education.

Edward H. Lawson Jr.—member of United Nations Secretariat.

Dr. Otelia Cromwell—honorary Doctor of Laws, Smith College.

Julian Mayfield—actor, *Lost in the Stars.*

George Olden—Art Director, CBS, New York City.

David Harris—pastor, St. James Episcopal Cathedral, Chicago.

Dr. Roy A. Anduze—Health Commissioner, U. S. Virgin Islands.

John A. Davis—Associate Professor, Political Science, New York City College.

Sylvia Olden Lee—Accompanist/Coach for Metropolitan Opera Staff.

Attorneys Francis M. Dent, George E. C. Hayes, Frank Reeves, and James Washington participated in the cases on segregated schools before the U. S. Supreme Court.

Dr. W. Montague Cobb—Elected first black president of NAACP.

Many of the early graduates of the Colored Preparatory High School returned there as teachers or administrators. The first class of 1870 had as students Caroline E. Parke and John C. Nalle, both of whom served later as teachers, Nalle becoming a principal in the school system. In many families, successive generations were proud to trace their academic roots back to this shining example of educational excellence.

In her concise history of Dunbar High School, Mary Gibson Hundley, a direct descendant of William Syphax, points out the families that "came out" of Dunbar or its distinguished predecessors.[3] Among them were members of the Brooke, Bruce, Bullock, Cardozo, Cook, Craig, Cromwell, Evans, Francis, Hollomon, Savoy, Shadd, Shippen, Syphax, Waring, Webb, West, Wilkinson, Wormley and Wright clans.

Hardly any of the students were in a position to attend the best of the Eastern colleges without financial aid, and it is to the credit of those early educators that they became an unsung task force seeking admission and assistance in the form of scholarships and grants for their worthy students.

H. Minton Francis, deputy secretary of defense and a fifth generation Dunbar graduate, the son of Alice Wormley and Dr. John Francis, Jr., said of Dunbar: "It was a source of brain power; it has contributed to the history and lifeblood of this city. And Dunbar wasn't a school for the elite. Students from all economic classes went there. Brains were recognized, not money."

Interfacing Families

B y the 1880s, the families which were to form the foundation of black society had begun to interface, but the interlocking family structures had their beginnings in the earliest days of the nation. To examine a few will give a microcosmic view of the whole.

In Washington, the first John Francis Cook had married Jane Mann, the daughter of the Honorable John Randolph of Roanoke, a slave holder, whose pious words on the condition of the free colored in the Memorial to Congress back in 1817 must have been cause for some grim humor among those who knew about his part-Negro, part-Indian child by Rachel Mann, who was part Algonquin and part black. Jane Mann and John Francis Cook were the parents of Victoria, Rachel, Joseph, James, John Francis, Jr., and George F. T. Cook.

After returning from his year in Pennsylvania, where he had gone during the Snow Riot, Cook was deeply concerned with manners and morals as a result of his exposure to the philosophy of William Whipper and Robert Purvis. A fundamentalist in his religious training, Cook added the ministry to his teaching duties, and by 1843 was appointed pastor of the colored Presbyterian church which had been started on Fifteenth Street in 1841. A delegate to the 1835 Convention of Free Colored Men, he also took an active part in the Moral Reform Society after it got underway. Following the death of his first wife, he married Jane LeCount of Philadelphia.

So, while Cook, Sr. devoted most of his time to the Presbyterian church, his sons, John Francis, Jr. and George F. T., took up his work at the school and became well established. At his death in 1855, John Francis Cook was the first of the three to be buried in the Harmony Cemetery.

John F. Cook, Jr. had been born in Washington, D. C. on September 21, 1833. Before settling down, he had taught school briefly in New Orleans, returning to take up his father's work as a teacher and community leader. He was married to Helen Elizabeth Appo of Philadelphia. Being an astute businessman and very active in the Republican Party, he was made a clerk in the office of Collector of Taxes for the District by President Grant and held the position through the Hayes, Garfield, and Arthur administrations. He was grand master of the Free and Accepted Masons for ten terms and trustee of Howard University for thirty-five years. Cook, Jr. died in 1910.

Three of Cook's children, Elizabeth, Ralph, and Charles C., all became educators. However, his son John Francis, III, unwilling to remain in the District, accepted a federal appointment as postmaster of Bonner's Ferry, Idaho. Here he took his young wife, Elizabeth Abele Cook, and their daughter, Elizabeth Abele, who was called Bessabel. The rustic life in a rural lumber town held little appeal for Mrs. Cook whose cultured and refined Philadelphia upbringing had ill-prepared her for Bonner's Ferry. She prevailed upon her husband to build a house in Spokane, the closest metropolitan community. When he agreed, she asked her brother, Julian Abele, the Philadelphia architect, to oversee the building of her home. For the next ten years, she lived in Spokane, and John Francis ("Frank") lived in Bonner's Ferry commuting the distance of a hundred miles or more to see his wife and growing family whenever his duties permitted.

By the time Bessabel approached adolescence, the practical and socially conscious Elizabeth Cook decided that all of her children—Bessabel, Mary Louise, John F., IV, and Julian Abele—had to have the cultural and educational advantages which could only be gained by returning to the East. Frank was determined to remain in Bonner's Ferry where he had owned the only electrical power plant in the area, had once served as mayor, and was still a leading businessman.

Elizabeth Cook sold her Spokane house and returned to Philadelphia where she and her children moved into her brother Julian's house, who was still unmarried. Even though they remained husband and wife, Frank retained his Bonner's Ferry residence. Bessabel met and married William J. Faulkner, a young Congregational minister and YMCA worker from Society Hill, North Carolina.

The marriage of Elizabeth and John Francis, III in 1894 had brought together the families of Absalom Jones of Philadelphia, the first black

Episcopal priest who had purchased his freedom from slavery before the turn of the century, and John Francis Cook, the school teacher/minister whose resourceful aunt, Alethia Browning Tanner, had purchased his freedom and that of his family with money earned selling produce.

Absalom's son Robert had married Elizabeth Durham, the daughter of Clayton Durham, who assisted Jones and Richard Allen in the organization of the Free African Society. One of their daughters, Mary Adelaide, married Charles S. Abele in 1864, and it was their eldest daughter, Elizabeth Rebecca Abele, who married John F. Cook, III.

Another equally expansive family lineage originated with James Wormley. His descendants are still contributing to the educational and cultural life of the nation. His oldest son, William H. A. Wormley, was married three times, and produced from his second marriage a bumper crop of ten children; most of whom were in the public service, either as teachers or in the medical or dental professions. One son, James Thompson Wormley, was the first graduate of the Howard University Pharmaceutical School in 1870 and opened the first colored drugstore in the District of Columbia.

Dr. Stanton L. Wormley, a grandson of William H. A., served as professor and chairman of the German Department at Howard University, acting dean of the graduate school, first academic vice-president, and acting president during the 1965–66 school year when President Nabrit was on leave to serve in the United States delegation to the United Nations. Stanton Wormley's first marriage was to Margaret Just, the brilliant daughter of a Spingarn medalist and marine biologist, Dr. Ernest Everett Just. The marriage was short-lived, but they were the parents of a daughter, Sheryl Everett Wormley. Margaret Just Wormley's second marriage in 1949 was to Professor James Butcher. They were divorced in 1959 with no children.

Stanton Wormley's present wife is the former Freida Hare of Amherst, New Hampshire. They have one son, Stanton L., Jr., a student at Howard University.

Garrett Smith Wormley, the middle son of James Wormley, also has several notable descendants. His son, G. Smith Wormley, married Mamie

Cheatham, a daughter of Congressman Henry P. Cheatham. A native of Henderson, North Carolina, Henry was the child of a house slave who had been permitted an education and whose favored position allowed her some advantages in educating her child. He was born in 1857 near the end of the slavery period. Cheatham graduated from Shaw University and was elected to the Fifty-first and Fifty-second Congress after having served as principal of the state normal school for colored students at Plymouth, North Carolina and as registrar of deeds for Vance County. He was characterized as a man who "always identified himself with the better class of white people."[3] He tried, during his service in Congress, to get legislation approved which would make some restitution to the depositors of the Freedmen's Bank who had lost their money when the bank failed. He was not successful but it did serve to focus attention once again on the inequitable treatment of black citizens by their government.

George White, a cousin of Mamie Cheatham Wormley, was the last of the so-called Reconstruction Congressmen. White, who served in Congress from 1897 to 1901, was born a slave, but succeeded in graduating from Howard University in 1877. Returning to North Carolina, he read law and by 1879 was licensed to practice in all of the state courts. He served as a member of the North Carolina legislature from 1880 to 1884, and was solicitor for the state's second judicial district.

White's famous parting speech at the end of his second term is probably better known to black school children than the Gettysburg Address or Washington's farewell to his troops. It held the sense of prophesy and hope that was vital during the nadir of 1901–1929. White said:

> "This, Mr. Chairman, marks the Negro's temporary exit from the American Congress, but let me say, Phoenix-like he will rise up some day and come again. These words are in behalf of an outraged, heart-broken, bruised and bleeding but God-fearing people, faithful, industrial, loyal people, rising people, full of potential force. . . . The Negro has been maligned. . . . The only apology that I have to make for the earnestness with which I have spoken is that I am pleading for the life, the liberty, the future happiness and manhood suffrage for one-eighth of the entire population of the United States."[4]

Before he left Congress, White succeeded in securing the transfer of $100,000 in unclaimed moneys owed to black soldiers, which was used for a home for aged and infirm Negroes in Washington, D. C. He also sought unsuccessfully to pass a bill making lynching a federal crime with all of those aiding and abetting to be judged guilty of treason. He stated publicly that only fifteen percent of the lynchings were caused by the rape of white women, and "there are many more outrages against colored women by white men than there are by colored men against white women." These remarks caused the *North Carolina News and Observer* to apoplectically charge that "White is typical of his kind, venomous, forward, slanderous of the whites, appealing to the worst passions of his own race. He emphasizes anew the need of making an end of him and his kind."[5] A man with the courage of George White was not quickly forgotten in the black community, and as black as he was, Mamie Cheatham Wormley was proud to call him a kinsman.

Mamie Cheatham and G. Smith Wormley were the parents of three children: Dr. Lowell Cheatham Wormley of Phoenix, Arizona; Edith Wormley, a pioneer in the field of American Indian education; and Mavis Wormley, the wife of Dr. John A. Davis, economist, long-time professor at Lincoln University and City College of New York, and one of the founders of the American Society of African Culture. Dr. Davis and his distinguished brother, Dr. Allison Davis, are both native Washingtonians and alumni of Williams University, where John is a member of the Board of Trustees. Dr. Allison Davis, co-author of several studies in social anthropology dealing with caste and class, was the first John Dewey Distinguished Service Professor of Education at the University of Chicago. He was married to the late Elizabeth Stubbs of Philadelphia. Their sons, Allison Stubbs Davis and Gordon Jamison Davis, are both lawyers.

G. Smith Wormley's parents, Garrett Smith and Amelia Brent Wormley, also had two daughters, Edith and Alice. Edith married Henry McKee Minton of Philadelphia. Alice married John R. Francis, Jr. of Washington, the son of Dr. John R. Francis, a member of one of Washington's old and respected colored families. The elder Dr. Francis had served the Washington community with skill and patience during some of its most trying times. He was a member of the school board and, for a period in the early 1890s, was acting head of Freedmen's Hospital, between the Purvis and Williams administrations.

As a school board member, Dr. Francis was instrumental in recruiting young Mary Church to Washington to teach in the colored high school after her graduation from Oberlin in 1888. While she had taught for two years at Wilberforce, the colored high school in Washington had already gained a national reputation for turning out black scholars able to compete on a parity basis with the graduates of the best Eastern prep schools. When Mary Church first came to Washington, she was a guest in the Francis home and later took room and board with Mrs. Cox, the mother of Betty Cox Francis. It was in their home that she met Robert Herbertson Terrell, the Harvard graduate and young Latin professor whom she was hired to assist.

Last in the Cook-Wormley-Syphax triumvirate was William Syphax. He was a quiet, private man, active in the affairs of the colored community in the District, but there is no record to show that he ever extended his influence beyond his immediate circle. He worked as a clerk in the Department of Interior where he had served as doorkeeper, and acquired the autographs of many influential men.

In 1864, during the Civil War, when Virginia was in a state of insurrection, the entire Custis-Lee estate was seized for unpaid taxes with the title going to the federal government. The Syphax rights were contested. Through his influential friends in the Congress, a "special act for the relief of Maria Syphax and her heirs" was passed insuring their right and title to the Arlington, Virginia property in perpetuity. It was signed by President Andrew Johnson in 1866. This property remained in Syphax hands until the New Deal administration of Franklin D. Roosevelt when it was acquired by the federal government to extend Arlington National Cemetery. Other Arlington properties were given in exchange. Today, the William T. Syphax Construction Company of Arlington, Virginia, one of the outstanding black businesses in the country, can thank William Syphax, the doorkeeper, for his role in recovering the Syphax land.

The Minton family of Philadelphia, into which Edith Wormley married, traces its roots back to the first Henry Minton who, with Henry Jones and Thomas J. Dorsey, comprised the famous triumvirate of Philadelphia caterers. Between 1845 and 1875, they ruled the profession and made an undeniable contribution to the economic well-being of many migrant black workers coming into Philadelphia from the South, new and unskilled in city ways. Minton had come from Nansemond County, Virginia in 1830 at the age of nineteen. After serving as an apprentice to a shoemaker, he went to work as a hotel waiter and later acquired moderate wealth from a restaurant which he opened at Fourth and Chestnut Streets. Minton married Catherine Galier, of the French mulatto colony in Philadelphia. They were the parents of three sons and one daughter—Theophilus, Henry, William, and Jenny.

Theophilus married Colonel John McKee's daughter, Martha Virginia (called Jennie). They had one son. Henry married and had two children, Ethel and Aubrey. William married Carrie Thompson, also from a Philadelphia family, and they were the parents of three boys—Herbert, Russell, and Henry. Jenny Minton married and had a daughter, Camilla Johnson.

Colonel John McKee was born in Alexandria, Virginia in 1822, probably a slave, although he may have been a free man. He had at least one younger brother, Emerline. John was apprenticed to a brickmason by his uncle, where he worked until he was twenty-one years old. When he arrived in Philadelphia around 1843, his first job was in a livery stable, but he soon got a job in the employ of a black man who owned an oyster house. His name has been lost, as well as that of his daughter. McKee was hard working and thrifty and, according to legend, so impressed his employer that it was not long before he was accepted as his daughter's suitor. As in all good romances, they were married and had two daughters; Abbie and Martha Virginia. When his father-in-law gave up his active role in the restaurant business, the energetic McKee continued to operate the restaurant and became involved in real estate.

At the outbreak of the Civil War, John McKee enlisted in the Thirteenth Pennsylvania Regiment, serving until the end of the conflict. He may have enlisted as a white man, because he is not listed on the colored records, and he was known as Colonel McKee following the war. In 1866, he gave up the restaurant and concentrated solely on the real estate business which he operated from the same basement office at 1030 Lombard Street where he had started.

While it is not known when his wife died, Colonel McKee never remarried and devoted the balance of his life to making money and acquiring property. One McKee daughter, Martha Virginia, was married to Theophilus Minton. The other McKee daughter, Abbie, married Douglass

Syphax of the Alexandria Syphax clan. They had several children—William McKee Syphax, Abbie Syphax Jones, Lillie Syphax Jackson, Bismark Syphax, Alma Syphax Scurlock, and Theophilus John Syphax. Douglass served in the union army, and he and Abbie are buried in Arlington Cemetery.

At the time of Colonel McKee's death in 1902, his estate, consisting mainly of real estate in New Jersey, Philadelphia, West Virginia, and Kentucky, was estimated in excess of four million dollars. His bequest created quite a stir, because the bulk of the estate was left to the Roman Catholic church to found a school for black and white orphaned boys. He willed his surviving daughter, Abbie McKee Syphax, who had taken care of him in his declining years, the pitiful sum of $300 a year. To his grandsons he left $50 a year for their lifetime. The estate was to be dissolved after the last grandson's death.

It was thought for years that Dr. Henry McKee Minton of Philadelphia was the last surviving grandson of Colonel McKee. However, when Minton died in December of 1946, Wall Street lawyer T. Vincent McKee revealed that he had been passing for white since 1904 when, as a student at Yale University, he had legally changed his name from Theophilus John Syphax to T. Vincent McKee. He had been married and divorced from a white woman by whom he had two sons, and was currently married to another white woman who was unaware of his racial heritage. A graduate of Columbia University Law School, McKee asked that the will be set aside and that he be declared the last legal heir. Camilla Johnson, Dr. Minton's cousin, testified in court that she had known Theophilus John Syphax. As a result, the Orphan's Court in Philadelphia declared that T. Vincent McKee and Syphax were one and the same, and that, indeed, he was the last living grandson of Colonel John McKee. Fate was unkind, however, and seven months after he revealed his true identity, McKee/Syphax was dead of complications following surgery. The estate was settled among the surviving heirs, the Catholic church hierarchy having determined the amount of the estate insufficient at that time to establish an institution of the kind Colonel McKee had requested.

Colonel McKee's brother, Emerline, who remained in Alexandria, had a daughter, Emmaline, who married Emanuel Jackson of Pittsburgh. The

Jackson parents had purchased the freedom of their entire family in 1858 for $5,726 before migrating from the Shenandoah Valley near Winchester, Virginia into Pittsburgh. The Jackson brothers started in the grocery business, but by 1867 Emanuel had branched out into the undertaking business, which grew to be the largest and best known in Pittsburgh.

Emanuel Jackson and his sons, Daniel McKee Jackson and Charles S. Jackson, came to Chicago in the early 1890s where they soon became the leading black undertakers. Emanuel's son Robert, II remained in Pittsburgh operating the funeral home. For decades, Daniel, Charles, and Robert were the funeral directors for the elite of Chicago and Pittsburgh. In 1967, the business observed its centennial of providing first-class funerals to the dear departed of the black upper class.

Meanwhile, Emanuel Jackson's brother, Robert, not to be confused with his son Robert, married Cornelia Moles in Pittsburgh in June, 1875. Cornelia was the daughter of a prominent Pittsburgh family of free colored background, and she and Robert were the parents of eight beautiful children. Tragically, the only one who survived to marry and have children was the eldest, Hadassah, who was married first to Isaac Jennings and later to Dr. William Coleman by whom she had one son, Thomas. Thomas is married to the former Alice Connors, and through their children the Jackson line continues. Hadassah's father, Robert Jackson, continued in the grocery business for several years, finally selling out and going into the contracting business, where he remained until his death in 1910.

Robert Jackson's company handled the contract for hauling the pipe for the Philadelphia Company, and also all of the rails, stone, and sand that were used for laying the first traction line of Carson and Smithfield Streets in Pittsburgh. The firm, which was known as the McKee Glass Company, also hauled all of the stone that was used in building the first glass house on Pittsburgh's south side.

Even though the old adage, "All Negroes who can read and write know each other, and more often than not, are kin-folks," is but a comical remark today, certainly that same aphorism must have been painfully unrefuted while such families as the Syphaxes, Cooks, Mintons, and Wormleys were molding black society.

After the Ball Was Over

*R*easonable men of good will, such as James Wormley, William Syphax, John Francis Cook, and his brother, George F. T. Cook, could not believe that there was a serpent in their Garden of Eden. Surely, the passage of the Civil Rights Act by Congress and the ratification of the Fourteenth and Fifteenth Amendments by the states offered them the protection and security that they had been seeking all of their lives.

James T. Wormley was a charter member of the Board of Trade; John F. Cook, Jr., District Tax Collector; George F. T. Cook was the superintendent of the colored schools, and had been since 1870. True, the masses of blacks who had descended on Washington during and following the war had made things more difficult. It seemed that many were irresponsible and would rather steal than work, but as soon as they were educated, given jobs and decent housing, they would develop the proper standards; at least this was the prevailing point of view of the educated blacks.

Meanwhile, the Organic Act, which had been temporarily enacted in 1873 when the District of Columbia faced bankruptcy for the third time in history, became law in 1878. Under its provisions, all residents of the District of Columbia were disfranchised in terms of local government. The District was to be operated under a Congressional committee and its appointees in exchange for federal guarantees of District obligations. Washington blacks could now play politics only at the national level.

One of the most active in this area was Frederick Douglass, who had been stung badly by the Freedmen's Bank episode and expected something to compensate for having been taken aboard a sinking ship after the crew had already deserted. One of the first appointments made by Rutherford B. Hayes, after he authorized the removal of troops from the South, was the March, 1877 commission of Frederick Douglass as marshall of the District of Columbia.

Another Hayes appointment, which helped to silence an otherwise vocal critic, was John Mercer Langston's as minister resident and consul general to Haiti in 1877.

The opening of the diplomatic service to blacks, which came about after Abraham Lincoln had recognized Liberia and Haiti, provided a convenient catch-all for articulate and perceptive blacks who might prove embarrassing to the Republican administration, unless they were personally obligated to refrain from overt criticism.

At the end of his term as senator from Mississippi, Blanche K. Bruce was appointed by President Garfield as register of the Treasury, a position which came to be looked upon as a Negro job, because for a period of thirty-two years, until the administration of Woodrow Wilson, it was held by black men.

The Garfield election was particularly exciting after the Hayes-Tilden tragedy. After compromising Hayes into one of the shabbiest deals in history, the Republican Party then denied him the nomination for a second term of office. Acting much like a man who lures a woman into premarital sex and then marries the nice girl next door because his paramour is a fallen woman, the Republican Party abandoned Rutherford B. Hayes after he had permitted himself to be so scandalously used in the Wormley Hotel deal. Denying the nomination to Hayes, the Republicans nominated James A. Garfield of Ohio for the presidency in 1880.

Garfield, a veteran of the Union forces in the Civil War, had been raised in Ohio and followed the tradition of the Western abolitionists. A graduate of Williams College in Boston, his first four months in office gave promise of better days to come for black folks.

It was said that more blacks than whites bought tickets for Garfield's inaugural ball. Colored men marched in the inaugural parade, and Garfield paid his political debts by patronage appointments to prominent blacks. John Mercer Langston was reappointed minister to Haiti and consul general to the Dominican Republic. Henry Highland Garnet was appointed minister to Liberia. Blanche K. Bruce was register of the Treasury, and Frederick Douglass, recorder of deeds.

In his inaugural address, Garfield made two significant points, namely that:

"Under our institutions there was no middle ground for the Negro between slavery and equal citizenship. There can be no permanent disfranchised peasantry in the United States."

He added that since the nation was responsible for the extension of suffrage to a large mass of illiterates, all of the constitutional power of the nation and of the states and all of the volunteer forces of the people should be used to provide for universal education to insure an informed electorate.

On July 2, 1881, a man described as "a disgruntled office-seeker" shot Garfield at the Baltimore and Potomac train station in Washington, D. C. Garfield lingered on for nine weeks before blood poisoning from the wound killed him, September 19, 1881.

His successor, Chester A. Arthur, was the second man in the New York State Republican organization, run by Roscoe Conkling. Conkling, as senator from New York, had escorted Blanche K. Bruce to his seat when no one else rose to do the incoming senator the traditional courtesy. Therefore, in the eyes of the colored people, Roscoe Conkling was a friend of the race—so much so that at least two mothers named their sons after him. His namesakes were Roscoe Conkling Bruce, Blanche K. Bruce's son, and Roscoe Conkling Simmons, the Republican orator and nephew of Booker T. Washington.

Because Arthur had conducted the office of the presidency without paying obeisance to the South, he too was denied renomination by the party stalwarts who controlled the votes. James G. Blaine was nominated, and it was this final treachery that caused James Monroe Trotter to turn his back on the Republicans. In his opinion, they had abandoned their black supporters and were merely using the black vote to retain power without duly responding to the needs of the black community.

James M. Trotter was a man of unwavering principle and deep commitment to absolute equality. He had been born in Grand Gulf, Mississippi, February 2, 1842 of a slave mother and a white father. He was taken to Ohio as a child and educated in Cincinnati at the Gilmore School where

John Mercer Langston had received his pre-Oberlin College training. Trotter had an overwhelming interest in music and as soon as he was able, began to study music and art seriously. After completing his studies with Mr. Gilmore, he began teaching, still concentrating on music when he wasn't paying court to Virginia Isaacs, the daughter of one of the Monticello Hemmings-Fossett daughters and Tucker Isaacs.

Trotter went to Boston to enlist in the Fifty-fifth Massachusetts Volunteer Regiment, working his way up from private to commissioned officer. Still uncompromising, he encouraged his fellow soldiers to refuse to accept the half-pay offered by the government until they were given their just due as United States soldiers. He was commissioned second-lieutenant on July 1, 1863 and wounded at the battle of Henry Hill, South Carolina, November 30, 1864.

Following the war, he married Miss Isaacs and returned to Boston where he established his home and where his three children, William Monroe, Maude, and Bessie were born. By 1883, Trotter was superintendent in the registered letter section of the United States Postal Service. He was, by now, an eighteen-year veteran, but beginning with Hayes-Tilden and culminating in the rejection of Arthur by the party, Trotter decided to resign his appointed position and publicly denounce the Republican Party. Joining the Democrats, Trotter campaigned for Grover Cleveland, and when Cleveland was successful, he showed his appreciation by appointing Trotter to the recorder of deeds spot in the District of Columbia. Never losing his musical interest, Trotter wrote a valuable book entitled *Music and Some Highly Musical People,* published in Boston in 1881.

Even though the Reconstruction had ended and erosion had already begun, Washington, D. C. at the end of the '70s and '80s was at the height of its brilliance for the *crème de la crème* of black society. There was no other single place in the nation where so many upper-class colored people were congregated. They were at the vortex of a life which they had watched from the outer edges for so many years, and it must have been a little giddy. Mary Church Terrell, in her autobiography, *A Colored Woman in a White World,* recalled her introduction to this world of top-drawer black society. It occurred during her freshman year at Oberlin College when Senator and Mrs. Blanche K. Bruce invited her to visit them during

Photographs

Old, established New Orleans families have been active in civic and social affairs and have been involved in banking, publishing, education and pharmaceuticals. Mathieu and Etnah Boutte operate a New Orleans pharmacy. She is the daughter of Victor Rochon, Creole Senator from Louisiana. Prudhomme and June De Joie (top r.) are of the prominent De Joie clan. C. C. De Joie, Jr., is the editor of the Louisiana Weekly newspaper.

Other New Orleans notables are Mr. and Mrs. Albert W. Dent (above). He is the former president of Dillard University. Alvin Boutte (far left) is president of Independence Bank of Chicago. He is shown here with Houston Astros's outfielder, Jim "Baseball" Wynn, at the American Airlines Golf Classic in San Juan, Puerto Rico. His daughter, Jeannett (near right), is employed at the bank.

245

The Walter Cohens, granddaughter Yolande and husband Dr. Marshall Cheatham

Distinguished New Orleans residents C. C. Weil and Dr. C. Haydell of Flint Goodridge Hospital in front of Dr. Rivers Frederick's portrait. Chicagoan Mrs. Selma LeCerne Barber with escort returns annually for Mardi Gras as do many other native sons and daughters.

246

Daughter of civil rights lawyer Alexander Tureaud (above, l.), Sylvia, at her wedding to Theodore Patterson. Prominent Alphas are Dr. Lionel H. Newsom, A. Maceo Smith, Ernest Morial, Dr. Charles Wesley and Atty. Belford V. Lawson.

Louisiana Court of Appeals Judge Ernest N. Morial (l.), the highest ranking black judicial officer in the South, with wife, Sybil, and children, Julie, Cheri, Monique, Jacques and Marc.

247

Philadelphia lawyers Raymond Pace and Sadie Alexander practiced law together for 32 years before he received judgeship in 1959. They are shown (l.) with daughters, son-in-law, and grandchildren.

248

The first black woman Ph.D. in the U.S. and the first woman to practice law in Pennsylvania, Sadie Tanner Mossell Alexander is the niece of famed artist Henry O. Tanner.

249

Dr. Midian O. Bousfield (l) and wife, Maudelle Tanner Brown were leaders in Chicago educational and civic life. Mrs. Bousfield was first black High School Principal. Bousfield was medical director of Supreme Life Insurance Company.

Maudelle B. Bousfield Evans

W. Leonard Evans (c) publisher of Tuesday, is shown with Chicago business-men, Anderson Schweich, president of Chicago Metropolitan Mutual Assurance and Garland Guice, head of Chicago Economic Development Corp.

Camilla Johnson daughter of Jenny Minton Johnson

Ainsley C. Minton

Dr. Russell F. and Marian Roland Minton

Dr. Russell F. Minton, Jr. Betty McKnight Minton

Rodney R. Minton

Raymonde M. Stevens

Paul, Monique, Michael Stevens

Descendents of Edward de Roland, the Haitian musician and Henry Minton, the caterer are joined in the Russell F. Minton family of Philadelphia.

251

THE FUTURE BELONGS TO THOSE WHO PREPARE FOR IT ,,

Dr. J. E. Walker (far l.), founder of Universal Life Insurance Company in Memphis. His son, A. Maceo Walker (l.), head of Universal and Tri-State Bank, served as ambassador to Mali in 1964. Board members of Universal (below) gather during its early years.

Family party given by Dr. Julian Kelso, former medical director of Universal Life, and Mrs. Johnetta Kelso, sister of A. Maceo Walker. Mrs. Kelso, with Walker and his family. Wife is the former Harriet Ish of Little Rock.

Claude Barnett and wife Etta Moten Barnett. Barnett's were early Africanists and travelled widely on the Continent. Barnett was founder of The Associated Negro Press and during lifetime, one of the men who had ear of Republican and Democratic Administrations. Etta Moten's work on concert stage and screen evolved into lecture circuit, on colleges campuses, and work with cultural organizations.

Spearheads of the Ish family of Little Rock were Dr. Stanley Ish and brother Jefferson G. Ish. (left) (Above) Dr. Stanley Ish, Harriett Ish Walker, Lucille Ish and Sue Barnett Ish.

The Barnett home in Chicago has been the gathering place for distinguished Africans since end of second World War. (l.) Mrs. Barnett with Nigerian guests, above daughters, Mrs. Sue Barnett Ish and Mrs. Etta Vee Traylor.

(Above) Mrs. Barnett with Blaise Senghor (2nd from l.) and Dr. and Mrs. G. S. Ish, E. Tinnin, and (r.) Dr. Clifton Johnson of Amistad Research Archives examines Claude Barnett's papers.

W. E. Mollison   Perry W. Howard   Dr. W. A. Attaway   E. H. McKissack

(l.) W. E. Mollison, Byron C. Minor, age 4, (below), Tougaloo College Faculty, Willye E. Mollison Minor, 2nd (l) front, (r) Walter G. Irwin C. and Welbourne, with wives, Louise Lanier, Patrisa Cowan. Mrs. J. C. Mollison (Alice Rucker) not shown. Mollison was first black Federal judge in Continental U. S. (1945)

Lydia M. DePriest   Welbourne Mollison, 3rd

Mississippi offered un-usual opportunity to blacks following Civil War. Business, politics and professions beckoned. Mollison, son-in-law, C. B. Minor were bankers. (r)

Irvin C. Mollison

Group (l-r) at dedication of Irvin C. Mollison School, Chicago. Courtney and Frank Willis Minor; Frances Anderson Minor, Patrisa Mollison, Harriett Minor, Ethel Minor, William E. Scott, Diane Minor, Mrs. Wendell E. Green, Walter Mollison, Byron C. Minor, Louise Mollison, Ann Mollison Payne, Welbourne A. Mollison.

the inaugural of President Garfield in 1881. Her father, Robert R. Church, Sr., and Bruce had been friends for many years. Mrs. Terrell said:

> "The Senator had a large plantation in Mississippi not far from Memphis, and Father used to purchase mules and supplies for him. . . . For many years, it was Senator Bruce's custom to stop with Father as he passed through Memphis on his way to and from his plantation.
>
> "Mrs. Bruce was a tall, beautiful, graceful woman, so fair that no one would suspect that she had a drop of African blood in her veins. She lived in what seemed to me a veritable mansion in what was considered a most desirable residential section of the capital. She had a horse and carriage, plus a coachman, Meekins, by name. . . . My mother had sent me some beautiful clothes from New York. . . . With Mrs. Bruce I attended dances and receptions galore, both large and small. Naturally, Senator and Mrs. Bruce took me to the Inaugural Ball, which was the biggest event of all. . . . For many years some women began to plan, as soon as one inauguration was over, what they would wear to the next one four years off."

The world of balls and musicales, afternoon visits, and evening entertainment was far away from the mounting violence and pressure on the white South to put the *nigger* back in his place. Even as James Forten and Robert Purvis had discovered in Philadelphia in 1838, refinement, gentility, soft speech, and good manners do not insure the destruction of prejudice against those who have a drop of black blood. Patience and good will were useless weapons against such a foe.

So the colored people who were like Langston, "more white than black," moved more and more in a circle of their own where they could move with a degree of freedom in and out of concert halls, theatres, museums, and restaurants without fear of challenge and subsequent embarrassment.

"Passing," whether consciously or unconsciously, was a device for maximizing one's opportunities within the system. The study of foreign languages was an essential ingredient in this life-style, because it was often necessary to lapse into French or Spanish if challenged by a store clerk, a waiter, or a theatre usher.

There were circumstances where social activities were broadened to include the mulattoes who had definite Negroid characteristics, but these occasions were limited to those times and places where skin color would not be a source of inconvenience.

Outsiders were not apt to be as patient as the fair-skinned members of Washington's black society. A Washington restaurant was sued in 1883 for refusing service to a Negro guest. The owner was sued under the criminal section of the Civil Rights Act, which guaranteed equal access to public accommodations. The judge found for the plaintiff, who was awarded $500 in damages. However, two months after the decision, in August, 1883, the blow fell that these responsible, long-suffering, patient people of color feared. The United States Supreme Court declared the Civil Rights Act unconstitutional in the states while binding in the federal jurisdictions, such as Washington, D. C. and the territories. It was another break in the armor of black unity.

The upper-class had not yet learned that acquiescence in the deprivation of rights to the lowly would mean the ultimate abrogation of rights to the "genteel and refined," as well.

The cleavage in the black community surfaced in the 1880s, and was brought into the open by a vocal black press. In Washington, the editor who took on the black establishment was Calvin Chase, whose writing in the *Washington Bee* attacked what he perceived as snobbery: "The Monday Night Literary is a cast[e] organization."

The German-American *Sentinel* reported that:

"The color line is rigidly drawn in what is known as society. Wealth, learning, official place, give no colored family the right or privilege of entering the best or the commonest white society in terms of equality or endurance."

According to the *Sentinel* in 1883:

". . . there were 700 octoroons and 1,100 quadroons who had, in addition to light color, the qualifications of antiquity of family, money, education and honorable occupations."

Honorable occupations were defined as including the professions, political positions of more than clerical nature, banking, real estate, and business, which were not identified with service occupations.

The *Bee* and Calvin Chase called this group of less than one-hundred families the "Negro Four Hundred." While Mr. Chase was constantly critical of this group, he nonetheless took it upon himself to warn them in the pages of his paper of the dangers inherent in permitting "unsuitable marriages" to take place between the members of old guard families and those "upstarts who have wormed their way into the social circle by joining a *tony* church, by enrolling in one of Howard University's professional schools, or by making a show of wealth."

By the 1890s, elements of black society in Washington were to be found throughout the entire nation. Those who were in it had already been identified. From this point forward, no new members were desired or required to perpetuate the group, and eligibility would be determined on the merits of each individual case.

Moreover, the black upper class was caught on the horns of a dilemma. The increasing pressure from the Ku Klux Klan, whose lynchings, burnings, and other anti-black violence proceeded without check from the 1870s well past the turn of the century, had created a situation requiring some response from the leadership.

On a national level, the Republican Party continued to use colored men, such as Frederick Douglass, John R. Lynch, Blanche K. Bruce, John Mercer Langston, and John Dewey, as window-dressing, giving some of the most prominent such appointments as Registrar of the Treasury, Recorder of Deeds, and Auditor of the Navy and sending them to Africa, the Caribbean, and Central America as diplomatic appointees. For these few political appointments, the most prominent men fought like dogs for a bare bone.

The Federal government's complete abdication of responsibility for the safety and protection of its black citizens had been followed in due course by the legal abrogation of those rights of suffrage which had been guaranteed by constitutional amendment. In 1890 Mississippi disenfranchised the black voter, and within a score of years all of the remaining states in the old confederacy, except Texas and Florida, had followed suit.

Douglass, in his declining years, had determined that assimilation was the only solution to the problem of race. It is possible that his marriage to Helen Pitts in the late 1880s had some bearing on this attitudinal shift. Miss Pitts was white, and to the numerous critics of his interracial marriage, Douglass responded that he had "paid his respects to his mother with his first marriage and to his father with his second."

Finally, weary of being manipulated, on July 1, 1891 Frederick Douglass resigned as Minister Resident and Consul General to Haiti. He returned to the United States and with Mary Church Terrell urged President Harrison to take executive action to stem the tide of lynchings. Harrison did nothing. Patronage and disunity went hand in hand.

Another one to speak out on lynching, although from a different point of view, was Charles Purvis, the son of abolitionist Robert Purvis and the long-time head of Freedmen's Hospital:

> "Negroes have been lynched ever since Reconstruction days. First they were lynched because they were uprising; second they were lynched because they wanted to be supreme in the South; and when all these charges proved untrue then they were lynched because they rape white women. The Negro is a victim of a condition from which he cannot eradicate himself. Both the raper and the lyncher are against society; they deserve the full punishment of the law. We are contending with a social disease. It must be exterminated, else our country is unsafe."

The national administration changed, and lynching continued.

When the Haitian pavilion was opened at the World's Fair and Columbian Exposition in Chicago, Douglass was named commissioner in charge of the exhibit. During that summer at the fair, Douglass gave what was to be the last great public address of his long career. It was on "Jubilee Day" or what was later called Colored American Day, the 25th of August, 1893. The black community was divided on the propriety and advisability of having a day set aside for the Negro. Many of Chicago's leading black citizens were against anything that would set them apart from the mainstream, and a day devoted to showing the progress of the Negro in the twenty-seven years since emancipation was not to their liking. Of the thirty thousand blacks in Chicago, fewer than one thousand attended the fair on Colored American Day. But those who came to hear Douglass never forgot his words:

> "Men talk of the Negro problem. There is no Negro problem. The problem is whether the American people have honesty enough, loyalty enough, honor enough, patriotism enough to live up to their own Constitution. A statesman has recently discovered that the only solution of this Negro problem is the removal of the Negro to Africa. I say to this man that we Negroes have made up our minds to stay just where we are. We intend that the American people shall learn the great lesson of the brotherhood of man and the fatherhood of God from our presence among them. During the war we were eyes to your blind, legs to your lame, shelter to the shelterless among your sons. Have you forgotten that now? Today we are number 8,000,000 people. Today a desperate effort is being made to blacken the character of the Negro and to brand him as a moral monster. In 14 states of this Union wild mobs have taken the place of law. They hang, shoot, burn men of my race without justice and without right. Today the Negro is barred out of almost every reputable and decent employment. We only ask to be treated as well as you treat the late enemies of your national life. We love this country and we want that you should treat us as well as you do those who love only a part of it. You fawn to the South and they despise you for it. They don't love you. You say you don't fawn to the South. Well, sometimes it seems to me that you do something very like it when you put us aside and under to please or to gratify the South. But stop. Look at the progress the Negro has made in 30 years! We have come up out of Dahomey unto this. Measure the Negro. But not by the standard of the splendid civilization of the Caucasian. Bend down and measure him—measure him—from the depths out of which he has risen."

Leading Citizens

I suppose my first introduction to Black Society came at the breast of Mrs. Austin Curtis. My mother, Mae, died when I was born on July 28, 1894, and her sister, Maude Powell Lawrence, took me to raise. Since she was childless, she became a mother to me, and I, a daughter to her.

Nama Curtis (her maiden name was Namahyoka Sockume) was the wife of Dr. Austin M. Curtis, who had been one of Dr. Daniel Hale Williams's chief assistants. She was one of the popular young society matrons in Chicago during the 1890s. They had two sons, Arthur and Maurice, who were older than I, and Merrill, who came along after me, so I suppose she was in a constant state of lactation. I am told that Nama Curtis, who had been a close friend of Mother's, nursed me until I was able to take a bottle with regular milk. In 1894 the advanced art of prepared formulas was still a way off.

Dr. Curtis had finished medical school at Northwestern in 1891, and Dr. Dan took him into Provident Hospital, which had just opened, as its first intern. Dr. Williams and Dr. Curtis were very close in those days, and when Curtis completed his internship, he became a surgeon on the staff of Provident also carrying on a private practice. He was apprenticed to the surgical staff of Cook County Hospital in 1896, the first of his race to be selected.

When Dr. Dan graduated from Northwestern University Medical School in 1883, there were no hospitals in Chicago where a colored physician could take his patients. Even worse, there was no place in the whole country where a colored girl could get nurse's training. There was a great deal of opposition to the idea of a colored hospital by those who thought it would be pandering to segregation. In the end Dr. Williams, Dr. Charles Bentley, Edward Morris, Lloyd Wheeler, James Madden, and S. Laing Williams were able to raise the funds to open a private colored hospital. Some of Dr. Williams's best friends were white physicians, like Dr. Frank

Billings and Dr. Christian Fenger who became consulting physicians and surgeons for the new hospital.

The issue of Negro doctors on the staff created the first serious problems for Provident Hospital. In selecting the staff for this new and innovative hospital with its interracial team of physicians and the first training school for black nurses, Dr. Williams made it very clear that he would only accept men with impeccable medical credentials. Dr. Charles Bentley, a graduate of the Chicago College of Dental Surgery and professor of oral surgery at Harvey Medical College, became the staff oral surgeon. Dr. Allen Wesley, another colored physician with an excellent background, was named head of gynecology and obstetrics.

However, Dr. Dan Williams turned down the application of Dr. George Cleveland Hall, whose background was not what he considered first class. He had come out of an eclectic school, one that Williams considered inferior. Dr. Hall may not have had the highest quality training, but he did have a number of friends. They appealed his cause to Dr. Williams, who weakened and permitted him to be named to the staff of Provident in the Pediatrics Department, but Hall was furious. By attempting to uphold high professional standards, Dr. Dan had made a lifelong enemy of Dr. George C. Hall.

When Provident opened on May 4, 1891, it had twelve beds but shortly took over the nurses' quarters to enlarge the capacity to twenty beds. Rented quarters adjacent to the hospital at 29th and Dearborn were secured for the nurses.

Provident Hospital had become a real community project, and many socials and afternoon teas were arranged to raise funds and gifts of equipment. Even Jesse A. Binga, later a banker and realtor but then a vegetable huckster, brought all of his unsold produce as a donation to the new hospital.

On July 9, 1893 James Cornish, a black laborer, was stabbed. He was brought to the hospital emergency room where Dr. Williams, with little to guide him but his knowledge of anatomy and the thoracic cavity, operated and repaired the rupture in the pericardial sac. The operation was historic; one of the first of its kind to have been performed. The patient lived more than forty years after the operation.

Our community in Chicago in the nineties was small in number and much less concentrated than it is now. There were many fine and well-to-do people who lived in Englewood, Woodlawn, Hyde Park, and on the North Side in the Lakeview section. Most, however, did live on the South Side in the area south of 22nd and State Streets. Prairie Avenue to the east and north was the most fashionable street in the city, with mansions occupied by the Pullmans, the Marshall Fields, and other millionaires.

Our leading citizens were doctors, lawyers, or other business and professional men. Certainly, Lloyd Wheeler was foremost in this group. He was the first black lawyer admitted to the Illinois bar on April 20, 1869 and was a leading citizen on several other counts. The Wheelers had been active in the Ohio Underground Railroad and, after the 1850 "anti-slavery" act, had been forced to migrate to Canada-West. Lloyd Wheeler was raised in Detroit, where he read law before coming to Illinois. Also, he was married to (Sarah) Raynie Petit, the adopted daughter of Mr. and Mrs. John Jones, Black Chicago's *first citizens*, and was a business partner of Mr. Jones in the flourishing tailoring shop they had downtown. John Jones, a free black, had opened the shop, catering to Chicago's wealthy gentry, in 1841 and later built a four-story office building at 119 S. Dearborn Street. He had been a county commissioner in 1874 and a close friend of John Brown and Frederick Douglass during the time of slavery. Their first home at 116 Edinah Street (now Plymouth Court) was the Chicago headquarters for the Underground Railroad. At the time of his death in 1879, Jones left his widow and family, including his daughters, Lavinia Jones Lee and Raynie Petit Wheeler, an estate in excess of $70,000; a magnificent sum.

Dr. Dan Williams had opened his office at 30th and Michigan, which was still a white area. Attorney and Mrs. Edward Morris moved into their first home after they were married in 1896, at 2712 S. Dearborn Street. Before their marriage, Jessica Montgomery Morris was one of the first of our girls to graduate from Cook County Normal School in 1892. At the time of her marriage, she was a secretary for William H. Tagge, the city prosecuting attorney for the city of Chicago.

Dr. Dan Williams roomed with the Jones family when he first came to Chicago to attend medical school. Lavinia Jones Lee's daughter, Theodora Lee, was married in her grandmother's house at 49 Ray Street in one of the really social weddings of the year I was born, 1894. She married Dr.

William Whipper Purnell of Washington, D. C., and when her baby Lee Julien was born in 1896, elegantly engraved announcements were sent from the Purnell residence on N. W. New Jersey Avenue in Washington, D. C. to signal the event. Dr. Purnell was the nephew of the great abolitionist and moral reformer, William Whipper.

I guess if the Wheeler and Jones families were considered the first families, then closely associated with them were the Bentleys (Dr. Charles Bentley and his wives, Traviata Anderson and then Florence Lewis); James B. Madden; Attorney S. Laing Williams and his very social wife, Mrs. Fannie Barrier Williams; Attorney Franklin Denison and Edna Rose Denison; the Archibald Carey, Sr. family; and the Edward Morrises.

Dr. Williams was becoming famous, and later in the same year President Grover Cleveland offered him the position as surgeon-in-chief of Freedmen's, the 200-bed federally supported hospital in Washington, D. C. He was to succeed Dr. Charles B. Purvis who had been associated with Freedmen's and Howard University Medical School since their inception after the Civil War. It was a challenge that the brilliant physician, not yet forty, could hardly resist and one that he had quietly courted by permitting his name to be placed in contention by President Cleveland's Secretary of State, Walter Q. Gresham. A Chicago judge, Gresham had been a friend of Dr. Williams and was one of Provident's early benefactors.

Freedmen's Hospital and Howard University Medical School in tandem had been Charles B. Purvis's private fiefdom since their days of crisis during the depression of the early 1870s. Purvis had been surgeon-in-charge at Freedmen's since 1881. He also served on the faculty of the medical school where his influence with the trustees had been cemented by his gracious action in 1873 when Howard University was unable to meet its payrolls. Three of the leading white faculty members resigned rather than accept half-pay, but Purvis wrote to General O. O. Howard:

> "While I regret that the University will not be able to pay me for my services, I feel the importance of every effort being made to carry forward the Institution and to make it a success. I accept my appointment believing it to be my duty to assist the University to regain its feet. This is no time to criticize and no true friend of the University will."

As a "true friend" of the university, Purvis, though ousted from his position at Freedmen's, retained his status at Howard. Daniel Hale Williams was not offered a faculty position at the university, which was the teaching arm of the hospital. This, added to the resentment felt by the local physicians against Williams, who was an outsider, was exacerbated by some of his not-too-diplomatic innovations when he took over the reins of Freedmen's.

Dr. Furman L. Shadd, assistant to Purvis, was displaced from his campus home to make a place for the new surgeon-in-chief. Shadd, of course, was related to the old and prestigious Wormley and Shadd families. The fact that Dan Williams kept him on his reorganized staff as *one* of the attending gynecologists did not lessen the insult of being downgraded from house physician, the post he had held under Purvis.

Dr. John R. Francis, one of the District's most influential colored physicians, had been acting head in the interim period between the time Purvis was relieved and Williams arrived for duty. Francis was kept on staff as one of the obstetricians, clearly a reflection upon his years of service to the institution and his ability. Before 1894 was out, Dr. Francis had severed his long connection with Freedmen's and opened the Francis Sanitarium, his own private hospital.

One of Dr. Williams's innovations was in reorganizing the surgical service and establishing a nurses' training program in the hospital. Purvis had started a nursing school at Howard University with which Williams's project clashed from the outset. Dr. Dan attempted to establish a new sense of routine and decorum among the hospital personnel and insisted that the interns wear uniforms when they were on duty. One of these interns, William Warfield, became Williams's protégé and close personal friend. Fair with dark hair and eyes, Warfield was strikingly handsome and equally ambitious. At the end of his first year of internship, he had parlayed his personal relationship with the "chief" into a staff position as second assistant surgeon and shortly afterwards into first assistant surgeon over the heads of Shadd and Francis. Warfield had failed the Maryland licensing examination on two different occasions, and this was quickly pointed out by Williams's critics. They also pointed to the fact that Warfield was the acting executive whenever Dan Williams was absent from Freedmen's. Dr. Dan's problems at Freedmen's did not end there. Purvis was successful in blocking his faculty appointment at the medical school, and although the death rate went down, the agitation against him continued.

The critics of Dr. Dan's professional behaviour and lack of sensitivity did not hesitate to attack him on a personal level. As a bachelor, he and Warfield frequently double-dated. That was acceptable, but the mother's whose eligible daughters did not find fancy in the eye of the young chief of Freedman's were only too ready to cast aspersions on the background of his most frequent companion, the daughter of an inter-racial union, sans wedlock. Irregular relationships of that nature were unacceptable in Washington's colored society. It was too reminiscent of the days of slavery, and spoke too directly to the origins that many sought to forget by ultra conservatism and propriety.

Independent and unconcerned about any benefits that might accrue as the result of an alliance with one of the *old* families, Dr. Dan became engaged to the lady, Alice Johnson, a Washington school teacher, in 1896. Her mother's illness and subsequent death, plus the problems that he was encountering with hearings relating to some of the practices he had instituted at Freedmen's, caused the wedding to be delayed, temporarily.

Finally, there was the move to place the position of surgeon-general under the U. S. Civil Service. The national administration changed in November, 1896, and with the new Republican president, William Mc-Kinley, came a new secretary of the interior, Cornelius Bliss. McKinley also appointed Blanche K. Bruce as Register of the Treasury and Richard T. Greener as consul to Vladivostok, Russia. Since the death of Frederick Douglass in 1895, Bruce and John Mercer Langston had been the recognized spokesmen for the colored community on national issues. Langston died after a short illness, November 15, 1897. This left only Bruce, and he died four months later, March 19, 1898, leaving a void at the highest level of leadership. The stage was set for new actors and a new script.

Booker T. Washington, principal of Tuskegee Institute, had been soundly condemned for his speech at the Atlanta Cotton States Exposition, September 18, 1895, when he made his famous "separate as the fingers of the hand" remark. Characterized as an "apostle of General Armstrong who felt that a common school education was good enough for a Negro," Washington was denounced from the forum of the Bethel Literary Society in

Washington for making "servile and unnecessary concessions to Southern prejudice." Said William H. Ferris, a Washington critic, "He [Booker T. Washington] grovels in the mud and mire of Southern prejudice to gratify an itching palm and please the white man in the South." He charged that Washington had created a climate of opinion which made it easy for the Northern white man to feign lost confidence in the efficacy of higher education for blacks taking place in institutions such as Fisk, Atlanta University, and Howard, and that by concentrating on the ignorance of the masses, Washington ignored the "culture refinement, intelligence, and education which prevails in Washington and other Southern societies.

A public announcement of a civil service examination was made for the position of surgeon-in-chief of Freedmen's Hospital, and Dr. Dan Williams, who was serving in the position, was dismayed. In spite of verbal assurances by the secretary of the interior that a replacement was not being sought for his position, the examination was held in Chicago, Washington, and Newark, New Jersey of all unlikely places. The resulting list placed Washington's Dr. Charles I. West at the top with a 91.50 score. Williams, not a candidate, was backing West, a native Washingtonian of old family. Trailing far behind were Dr. Austin M. Curtis of Chicago with 79.10 and James A. Wormley, the physician son of Garrett Smith Wormley, who had settled in Newark. His score was 76.05.

Dan Williams did not wait to see what would happen next. He resigned and in spite of public statements that the appointment of his successor would be apolitical, Dr. West was passed over, and Dr. Austin M. Curtis, Dr. Dan's former intern and assistant at Provident, was named as his replacement. It was rumored that the appointment had been secured because of Nama Curtis's work with Illinois Senator Mark Hanna's organization and the colored women's groups in Chicago. Women did not have the vote yet, but they were beginning to wield influence.

Nama Curtis had been one of the most active women in Chicago during the 1890s. She had been a key participant in arranging for Colored American Day at the World's Columbian Exposition in 1893, and her role was written up in one of the leading white papers, the *Chicago Record*. At the time of Dr. Curtis's appointment to the Freedmen's post, a contemporary columnist, J. W. Rawlings, wrote:

"And as for his wife, she is one of the brilliant women in America, capable of filling any position and as to whether she accepts one on the Democratic National Committee should not be made a matter of unholy comment in order to lessen her husband's chances of becoming the next surgeon-in-chief of Freedmen's Hospital."

Some years after the Curtis family went to Washington, Dr. Curtis's sister Eleanor married a young Chicago physician, Dr. Ulysses Grant Dailey. Dailey, later an eminent surgeon, was another of Daniel Hale Williams's disciples. So, in a sense, the connection between the Curtis family and Chicago was never really broken.

Meanwhile, Dr. Dan Williams and Miss Alice D. Johnson were married in a private ceremony in Washington, D. C. before he returned to Chicago to take up his work at Provident Hospital.

During the years when Dr. Dan had been absent in Washington, Dr. and Mrs. George C. Hall had been extending their influence, both in Chicago and nationally. When Williams returned in 1898 with his bride, he found that Dr. Hall was on the executive board of Provident Hospital and considered himself to be the Chicago connection for Booker T. Washington's increasingly powerful group of alliances.

Williams had sought an accommodation with Washington during his Freedmen's Hospital experience, but it had not gone well. Now back in his home community, he found Hall more than ever worthy of his contempt. Sides were taken, and Theodosia Hall was snubbed openly by those stalwarts who had rallied to Dr. Dan's side. There were any number of incidents, and in most of them, Dr. Hall contrived to see that Dr. Williams was embarrassed and placed in a position in which he came off as a caste-conscious, color-conscious snob. Gossip had it that one afternoon when Alice Williams arrived at a meeting of the prestigious Ladies Whist Club, she saw Theodosia Hall already seated. Without removing her hat or gloves, Mrs. Williams turned on her heels and left the card party. They say she never played cards with that group again, nor did she forgive what she considered an act of grave disloyalty. Finally, it became impossible for social activities to be planned including both the Hall and Williams factions.

Theodosia Hall was a statuesque woman, though certainly she did not have the fair patrician beauty of Alice Williams. Dr. Hall was a rotund and cheery dark-skinned man. There were those who believed it was his dark color and not his lack of credentials that set Dr. Dan against him. None of Williams's protégés were dark-skinned, not Austin Curtis, William Warfield, or U. G. Dailey, so maybe there was some truth to the allegation. At any rate, the war continued for years, with Dr. Dan finally being forced to resign from the staff of the hospital that he had founded, simply to keep it from being destroyed by the personal clash between himself and George C. Hall.

Women Unite

In August of 1899, under the presidency of Mary Church Terrell, the Association of Colored Women's Clubs met at Chicago's historic Quinn Chapel AME Church. Celebrating its fifty-second anniversary that week, the church offered a warm welcome to the women who assembled. Among them were Mrs. Blanche K. Bruce, widow of the man who had served as U. S. senator, recorder of deeds, and register of the treasury; Mrs. Booker T. Washington, wife of the Tuskegee president; Mrs. Josephine St. Pierre Ruffin of Boston, widow of Judge George L. Ruffin, one of the first black graduates of Harvard Law School, a member of the Massachusetts legislature, and Charlestown, Massachusetts municipal judge.

Mrs. Bruce was the houseguest of Mrs. Daniel Hale Williams, and Mrs. Terrell was the guest of Mrs. John B. French. Miss Ethel Mitchell from Wilberforce University stayed at the home of Reverend and Mrs. Reverdy Ransom, and Miss Hattie Curtis, Dr. Austin M. Curtis's sister, stayed with the George Cleveland Halls.

As the tentacles of segregation had drawn tighter and public accommodations less desirable, Black Society extended a network of relationships across the country. A visitor from New York or Boston or Washington was always someone's houseguest. And in the same way, when their sons and daughters traveled for education or pleasure, they stayed with someone they knew or who was a relative of a friend. It was, therefore, relatively easy to determine the status of the visitor by knowing whose hospitality they accepted.

The ladies who had come to Chicago for that national convention represented the highest levels of education and family background.

The first call for a national convention of colored women had come from Mrs. Josephine St. Pierre Ruffin, president of the Women's Era Club of Boston, in 1895.

She said in the Call:

> "The coming together of our women from all over the country for consultation, for conference, for personal exchange of greetings, which means so much in the way of encouragement and inspiration has been a burning desire in the breasts of the colored women in every section of the United States."

She reminded them that the time had come for colored women to "step across the threshold of home into the wider arena of womanhood."

There had been active women's organizations as early as the 1830s, and many more had been formed in the days before the Civil War when the needs of the refugees from the Fugitive Slave Law became critical. Women's groups were among those who came together to bring food, clothing and to raise money for the needy travelers on the Underground Railroad.

Ida B. Wells, a young school teacher in Memphis, had taken up the pen to write against injustice, racism, and murder under the pen name of Iola. Losing her teaching position because of her militancy, she became half-owner of a small newspaper, the *Memphis Free Speech,* in whose columns she advocated selective boycotts and migration to the Oklahoma territory. Following the lynch murder of three Memphis businessmen in May, 1892, she wrote that the crime of rape, which was attached to most lynchings, was a cover-up for the real crime—racism. The blacks had been killed, she charged, because black consumers had been patronizing their businesses rather than those of the white town merchants. The murders had been instigated and planned by the white business community. While at a church conference in Philadelphia, her print shop and newspaper office were sacked and burned by a mob, and the word went out that if Ida B. Wells wanted to live, she had better not come back to Memphis.

T. Thomas Fortune, then editor of the *New York Age,* offered his paper for her exposé of lynching, and the *Red Record* was published for the world to read. This was the first documentation of lynching published in the country. Ida B. Wells had become famous. She accepted speaking engagements all over the United States and England. In Chicago for the World's Columbian Exposition, she had met the widower lawyer, Ferdinand

Photographs

*Hobson Reynolds (above, l.), Grand
Exalted Ruler of the Elks, has been
the 500,000-member fraternity
head since 1960.*

Reynolds, born in 1898, the founding year of the Elks, and his wife, Evelyn, a member of the Josettes Club, reside in Philadelphia.

(Below) Family
of Simeon Booker, Jr.
Nieman Fellow and
Washington Bureau Chief
for Johnson Publications
(l-r) Beth Holland,
Dorothy Waring Howard,
Booker, Carol McCabe
Booker, James Booker,
Carolyn Booker Howard,
Simeon Booker, 3rd.

Raynie Pettit Wheeler,
grandson Lloyd, 2nd.
She was adopted daughter
of John Jones. Her
husband, in later years,
was associated with
Booker T. Washington at
Tuskeegee.

Dr. Henry Fitz-butler father of Dr. Mary F. Waring, pioneer physician, founded Louisville Medical College.

Painter Laura Wheeler Waring, gained fame with her portraiture.

Laura Wheeler's mother, Mary Freeman, was Oberlin graduate, '73. Father, Robert F. Wheeler, Howard U. Theologian. Husband, Walter.

Niece, Madeline Murphy Rabb with husband Dr. Maurice Rabb and sons, Christopher and Maurice, Jr. is artist, also.

James Monroe Trotter (l.) married the granddaughter of Thomas Jefferson, Anna Elizabeth Issacs. Their son was militant Boston newspaper editor, William Monroe Trotter. Their daughter was Maude Trotter Steward, well known Boston socialite, shown at right with Joseph Nelson and Josephine Williams.

Attorney Frederick Hamilton, Sr. (left), of Cincinnati, is the great grandson of Sallie Hemmings, the mother of five of Thomas Jefferson's mulatto children.

The Dammond family of New York City (bottom l.) are descended from Maude and William Monroe Trotter's sister, Bessie, and Henry Craft, grandson of escaped slaves William and Ellen Craft. They are Ellen Craft Dammond, Pearl Fallings Craft, Henry Craft, Donald Dammond, Margaret Trotter and Henry Craft Dammond. Jefferson's great grand-daughter, Bessie Curtis (r.), studies a portrait of her father, Peter Fossett.

M. Johnson (l.) and with Judge Sidney Jones, Albert Dent, James E. Stamps

Former Howard University President and Mrs. Mordecai Johnson (above) with five children and 14 grandchildren. Following wife Anna's death, Johnson was married to Mrs. Alice King, (l.) a widow. (opposite) David Jones, wife, Dr. Barbara Wright Jones, daughters Alison, Jane.

President of Bennett College and Mrs. David Dallas Jones (above); their son, David, married Mordecai Johnson's daughter, Anna. Below are Mrs. Ralph Bunche, Eleanor Roosevelt and Mrs. Louis T. Wright.

Dr. Louis Wright, daughters Jane, Barbara

Judge William Hastie, Arthur Spingarn, the former NAACP president, Dr. Louis Wright, Walter White.

Samuel Pierce is sworn in as judge of New York Court of General Sessions. His wife Barbara and then-Gov. Rockefeller look on.

Dr. James Nabrit, Jr. (above), former Howard
University president (1960-67), with wife
and family and (below) with brothers.

Mordecai Johnson, the first black president of Howard University, served from 1926-56 (above) with wife and present Howard president James E. Cheek and his wife, Celestine. Dr. Cheek (left) with wife and children and his mother Mrs. Lee Ella Cheek (r.). Cheek has served as president since 1969.

Dr. Charles Spurgeon Johnson
(near left), the first Black
president of Fisk University,
married Marie Burgette (far
left). One of their sons is
Charles, Jr. (center left).
Their son-in-law is Dr. Maurice
Clifford (below), former
director of Philadelphia's
Mercy-Douglas Hospital.

Patricia Johnson Clifford
(left), the only daughter
of Dr. and Mrs. Charles S.
Johnson, is the wife of
Dr. Clifford. Johnson's
other son, Jeh Vincent
Johnson, a New York City
architect, is shown with
his wife, Norma Edelin.

Charles S. Johnson, one of the South's foremost race relations experts, was a friend of Harlem Renaissance writer Arna Bontemps (top r.). Horace Cayton (center l.), of the Annual Fisk Race Relations Institute, was the grandson of Hiram Revels. Johnson delivered commencement address at Lincoln University.

Educator Horace Mann Bond, father of Julian Bond, speaking to 1962 graduates of Fort Valley State College of which he was formerly president. Before his death in 1972, he was also dean of Atlanta University's School of Education, dean of Dillard Univ., and president of Lincoln Univ. (Pa.).

Horace Mann Bond with (l. to r.) Franklin H. Williams, Robert Carter and Thurgood Marshall and addressing a group of educators including Dr. Zelma George, Michael Olatunji, and Samuel Allen.

Georgia State Representative Julian Bond with wife Alice and two of their four children, with Manhattan borough president Percy Sutton (l.), and preparing for opening day in the Georgia House.

Barnett, who also published the *Conservator,* a weekly newspaper. They were married in 1895, and Ida B. Wells Barnett soon added motherhood to her busy schedule. She did not stop lecturing, writing, and urging colored women to do something concrete about the slaughter of their husbands and sons. Organization and unity were the weapons at their disposal. She preached, and all across the country colored women heard her and came together in clubs whose mission was service to those less fortunate; the children of working mothers, the working girl alone in the city, and the migrant worker without a home.

Other women had also decided to use the power of their numbers by organizing. In 1893 Hallie Q. Brown from Wilberforce University had been rebuffed by Mrs. Potter Palmer, wife of the Chicago tycoon, when she sought a place on the Women's Board of Managers at the World's Columbian Exposition. Mrs. Palmer had dismissed Hallie Brown's request by telling her that membership on the board came through organizations and not on individual merit.

Following Hallie Brown's report of this meeting, a group of Washington, D. C. women organized in 1893 as the Colored Women's League of Washington, D. C. John F. Cook's wife, Mrs. Helen Appo Cook, was the president. Mrs. Ruffin called the Boston meeting on July 29, 30, and 31, 1895. The following December, a Congress of Colored Women met at the Atlanta Exposition.

Recognizing that there was no room, at that point in time, for two separate national women's groups addressing the same issues, committees were named from the National Federation of Afro-Americans Women and the National League of Colored Women. On July 21, 1896, they met in Washington, D. C. and agreed to drop their separate identities and be known as the National Association of Colored Women, with the motto "Lifting as we climb."

They were given a mandate to harmonize the differences between the two groups and to develop a program that would make it possible for colored women to come before the country with one national organization. The meeting in Chicago was the second of the combined group, and there were still evidences of factionalism and organizational strife. As black women, they could and would agree on larger goals.

Let Down Your Buckets

When I was little, my Grandmother Powell would scold me if she caught me playing with dark-skinned children. She said that ALL black men were crazy. I was still a child when I realized that most of my friends and relatives were different from the majority of colored people. For the most part they were fair-skinned. Almost all of the women were light enough to be taken for white, with "good" hair. This realization came to me very early in life because my father, Herbert Hodges, was dark and all of his people were dark. My mother's people who raised me were all fair-skinned.

My father had remarried after my mother's death, and his second wife was German. My mother's family disapproved. They did not like his being dark, but they liked even less his having a white wife. There were strong feelings about white women who were married to colored men. So, I seldom got to visit my father's family who lived on Wentworth Avenue in the thirties. The lot they owned had two houses on it, one at the front of the lot and the other at the rear. My father and his wife had the front house, and my grandmother and aunt lived in the back house. The only times I remember visiting my father's people were when it was time to wash my hair. My mother's people all had dead straight hair, but my hair, which was long and thick, always had a "crimp" in it.—those small waves that were never fashionable. My mother's people never knew what to do with "Baby's" hair, so when hair washing time came they'd send me to Father's folks, who were not fazed by my uncontrollable locks.

Hair has always been a very important factor in the lives of black people in the United States. Because of its importance, one of black America's early fortunes was built upon the desire by masses of black women to have straight hair.

First, and by far the most fabulous pioneer in the field of beauty culture, was Madame C. J. Walker, one of the first "outsiders" to break into black society. Born in a Louisiana delta cabin, widowed by age twenty, with a small child to support, she concocted a salve which softened hair and devised a metal comb which, when heated and run through the greased hair, left it soft, lustrous and straight.

Poor, black, illiterate, and orphaned at seven, Sarah Breedlove Walker had taken seriously Booker T. Washington's admonition to "let down your buckets where you are." She took in washing to support herself and her young daughter, A'Lelia, moving first to Denver then to St. Louis, where she continued as a washerwoman until she "had her dream." In her dream, she received "the magic formula," and with it still fresh in her mind, concocted the hair preparation which, within a decade, had started her on the road to fabulous wealth.

Recognizing that familiarity breeds contempt, Sarah Walker added "Madame" to her name and used only her late husband Charles J. Walker's initials. By 1910 she had built up a substantial mail order business and a door-to-door sales force, with main offices in Pittsburgh. Madame Walker later moved to Indianapolis, where she built her factory. By 1917 she was a millionaire.

Madame Walker was not alone in heeding Booker T. Washington's call to the common man. All over the country, and particularly in the Southland, the Tuskegee principal's message had been heeded. DuBois's "talented tenth" notwithstanding, the message of "lifting as we climb" had been passed on to many whose background of slavery, poverty, and deprivation made them willing apostles of the Booker T. Washington creed, which placed the highest priority upon economic security.

By 1905, Washington was unequivocally the spokesman for the mass of black people in the United States. A primary example of the efficacy of his philosophy was to be found in Durham, North Carolina, where the North Carolina Mutual and Provident Association, along with a group of related black enterprises, had come into being since Washington's speech at Atlanta.

In 1898, a group of young black men in Durham, North Carolina, heeding the gospel of self-help, had formed an industrial insurance company, offering health, accident and life insurance at reasonable rates to the colored community, which had been deprived of reliable insurance protection. This group was headed by John Merrick, a Durham barber whose six shops and real estate business placed him firmly in the class of fiscally responsible black entrepreneurs. Merrick was a former slave with only basic education. Three of his barbershops were for black customers, three for white customers.

With Merrick were Dr. Aaron McDuffie Moore, in whose office the first organizational meeting was held, William Gaston Pearson, Edward A. Johnson, James E. Shepard, Pinckney William Dawkins, and Dock Watson. All of these men were active in either the black educational or business community. Earlier, they had all had political ambition of one sort or another, but a wisdom based on survival led them away from politics into the more acceptable channels of behavior.

Booker T. Washington's tremendous influence on the founding of North Carolina Mutual was documented by C. C. Spaulding, general manager and the man credited with having been the driving force of the company. Spaulding told a 1910 meeting of the National Business League in New York that Booker T. Washington's Durham speech in the fall of 1896 had been the inspiration, "the result of which can be seen today in the North Carolina Mutual and Provident Association."

The National Business League, which had been founded by Booker T. Washington in 1900, defined its purpose on the premise that "through the promotion of commercial achievement, the race could be led to a position of influence in American life and thus pave the way to economic independence." The NBL is the major trade and commercial association of black businesses three-quarters of a century later.

This philosophy has certainly played a significant role in the development of black business. The existence today of such lists as the Top 100 Black Businesses in the United States recognizes that an entrepreneurial class, catering to the needs and seeking the support of the black consumer as well as competing on a national level for the total consumer dollar, is necessary to a viable community.

The Talented Tenth

While many applauded and jumped on the Washington bandwagon, including some of the leading colored citizens, others in the black establish-ment charged Booker T. Washington with ignoring the culture, refinement, intelligence and education of the colored community while concentrating on the ignorance of the masses. They had been mobilized into action by the fiery William Monroe Trotter and his fellow Bostonian and co-editor of the *Boston Guardian,* George W. Forbes. Later, they were joined by W. E. B. DuBois, who had made quite a name for himself at Harvard and at the University of Pennsylvania and then at Atlanta University, where he had held conferences on the state of black institutions like the family, the church and higher education. Booker T. Washington even tried to hire him to come to Tuskegee at one time.

Trotter and DuBois, both Harvard graduates and scholars of the first magnitude, did not agree on methodology but did agree on the folly of Washington's position. In the view of Trotter and DuBois, Washington had given up everything that the black man and woman had fought and died for over the preceding century without a struggle. Blacks' hard-won gains in civil rights were taken away, while Washington pacified black people by urging that they first get the tools for living, like industrial education, farms, property and business. Trotter and DuBois argued that the concessions Washington gained from the white community in support of his programs were at the expense of the total black community.

In the ten years following the death of Frederick Douglass, Booker T. Washington had become the most powerful black man in America. He was acceptable to the white world and they made him the spokesman for the entire group. He had access to the highest reservoirs of power, including the White House. Almost simultaneously with the departure of the last black representative from the U.S. Congress, George H. White, Booker Washington was invited to dine with President Theodore Roose-velt. Later, when Roosevelt dishonorably discharged an entire regiment of black soldiers for alleged involvement in the Brownsville, Texas affair, Washington had nothing to say.

Increasingly, opposition to them solidified among the intellectuals. DuBois and Trotter were accused by his black supporters of being jealous rabble-rousers. Almost everything involving power, money or political favors had to be cleared through Booker T. Washington between 1900 and 1915, the year of his death. The protests of Trotter, DuBois and Ida B. Wells were muted in the overwhelming approbation that he seemed to receive from the mass of his black constituency.

DuBois had delineated his opposition to apparent material prosperity at the expense of social and political advancement. He reminded the country that large and important segments of "Washington's own race . . . , the spiritual sons of the abolitionists, seek . . . that self-development and self-realization in all lines of human endeavor which they believe eventually will place the Negro in his proper role, not in front of, or behind, but beside other races." Said DuBois, "The opponents of Washington believe in the higher education of Fisk and Atlanta Universities; they believe in self-assertion and ambition; they believe in the right of suffrage for blacks on the same terms with whites . . ." Supporting DuBois were such highly respected people as Kelly Miller, the educator, poet Paul Laurence Dunbar, artist Henry O. Tanner and novelist Charles W. Chesnutt. There were many other leaders who were silent.

DuBois pointed out that under Washington's leadership, the Negro had been disfranchised; the legal segregation of the races had been accomplished, creating a distinct status of civil inferiority; and the steady withdrawal of aid from institutions of higher education for Negroes had taken place, thereby committing the black man to a hopelessly subordinate status, while Washington preached "thrift, patience and industrial training for the masses." DuBois was accused of being a partisan "for the favored few," . . . the black aristocracy, which though more favored than the rest was yet shut out from social and political equality with the white man. Yet, he continued to sharpen his theory of the role of the black aristocrat, the person he placed in "the talented tenth". It was his opinion that the black race, like all other races, would be saved by its exceptional people, who therefore had to be trained to a knowledge of the world and of man's

relation to it. Teachers, ministers, professional men, spokesmen, the exceptional few, must come first. To "attempt to establish any sort of system
of common and industrial school training without first providing for the
higher training of the very best teachers," said DuBois, is "simply throwing your money to the winds." He would single out a select group, enrich
them with the finest education and then charge them with the responsibility for leading and serving the masses. These would be "the culture
bearers, the people who would set the ideals of the community where they
lived, direct its thoughts and head its social movements."

From Atlanta in 1905, DuBois issued a call for "organized determination and aggressive action on the part of men who believe in Negro
freedom and growth." In July, twenty-nine business and professional men
met secretly at Niagara Falls, Ontario and organized the germinal Niagara
Movement, demanding total and immediate integration. The following year,
the group met in open sessions at Harper's Ferry, West Virginia. At the
Harper's Ferry meeting were members of the group which DuBois characterized as "the very best class of Negroes." The elite tone of this pioneer
"talented tenth" group disturbed some of the observers, particularly the
white ones, such as Mary White Ovington, who asked DuBois to permit
her to speak on "the Negro and the labor problem" at the 1908 meeting
in order to "hammer that side (Ovington was a socialist) of things into
some of the aristocrats in the membership."

The Niagara Movement became a national organization and provided
the framework out of which grew the National Association for the Advancement of Colored People. It did not survive, primarily because it had
at its head men like Trotter and DuBois, neither of whom could sublimate
to the leadership of the other. Trotter unhappy over the increased participation of whites in the organization's programs and what he considered an
increasing orientation to social work attitudes rather than political action,
broke and in 1908 organized the National Equal Rights League.

The National Urban League was organized in 1910 in New York
City as an interracial organization to deal with the social problems of the
increasing number of rural blacks migrating to the cities without an aware-
ness of urban lifestyles and habits.

George Edmund Haynes, the first graduate of color from the New York School of Social Work, and Eugene Kinkle Jones were its first executive officers.

The NAACP was founded on May 30, 1909, as the result of a call sent out by Mary White Ovington, DuBois, Oswald Garrison Villard, Bishop Alexander Walter and William Walling, a white Southerner. DuBois resigned his position at Atlanta University and, as the only black officer of the new organization, became the Director of Research and Publicity and the editor of The *Crisis*.

The Way It Was

I don't remember any hardships in my childhood. We lived in a border-line, racially-mixed community on Wabash Avenue where the fraternity houses for Armour Tech (now Illinois Institute of Technology) were located. There were only one or two black families. I went to the Douglas School (named for Stephen A. Douglas, not Frederick Douglass), where there were only two colored children; Anabel Carey and myself. Anabel, the daughter of Reverend Archibald Carey (later AME bishop), looked like she was white. I did not. My difficulty was not that I stood out prominently among the students, but because my name, Hodges, was different from my aunt's. The school officials tried to insist that I didn't belong in the school because I didn't really live in the district—that I was just using the address. It was aggravating, but not for long, because my aunt made them understand that I was "her" child, and we did live in the school district.

It was funny. Years later, when I was doing my practice teaching, I was assigned to that same school as a clerk, and I still had problems with the white principal, Miss Bonfield. The day I was assigned she would not let me come behind the railing which separated parents, many of whom were black, from staff personnel. I was assigned no duties. I sat all day outside that railing in the public section. I remember going home absolutely crushed. I told Aunt Maude I didn't want to go back, but she said, "Well, darling, you can't run away. You have to go back, so just go on back and sit." So I went back and sat outside the railing. Finally, the principal asked me to do something simple, like taking a message to a classroom, and gradually the ice broke and we became friends. Miss Bonfield simply did not want a black student-teacher in her school, and she always insisted that I wasn't a Negro. I had to be something else for her to accept me. White people simply don't understand why anyone would want to be Negro.

My Aunt Maude and Uncle David were very active in civic and social affairs. Aunt Maude was avant garde even before the twenties when it became stylish. She was one of the first ladies in her group to drive an electric auto. Because my aunt and uncle were both professional people, we ate out a lot in restaurants and hotels, and waiters put books on the chairs to get me up to the table.

Aunt Maude belonged to Saint Thomas, a very fashionable Episcopal church. I liked the organ music and the handsome and solemn altar boys. They never looked at anyone or smiled during the processional or recessional. Father Massiah, the priest, was a friend of our family. The Episcopal church has always been noted for the light complexions of the congregation and their level of economic and social acceptability. An unfortunate thing happened to me the day I was to be confirmed. I became too ill to attend the confirmation, even though I had faithfully gone to instruction and had made my own decision to become Episcopalian. All of my life I have become ill whenever anything was pressing me. I would become nauseated, run a temperature and really be sick. I was not faking, but I don't know how psychosomatic my illnesses may have been. I finally ended up being confirmed in a white church on the West Side. I've forgotten the name of the church because it was the only time in my life I was there.

Quinn Chapel (AME), Grace (Presbyterian), and Institutional (non-denominational) were the other churches we attended. In those days, so much activity was centered in the church, especially for the children and young people. Sometimes, on Easter Sunday, we went to as many as three churches. I always insisted on having a red hat for Easter. It was usually very cold, but still we dressed up in our Easter finery, even though we were freezing. We always wore our new clothes to the Amateur Minstrel Association's Easter Monday benefit for the Old Folks Home.

There were so many blacks in Chicago at that time who, if they had desired, could have "passed for white" without difficulty, keeping their miniscule amounts of pigmentation to themselves. They would not have been betrayed by those who knew. Indeed, many families were divided by the invisible barrier that kept those who had "gone over" from those who had stayed behind. People knew, but rarely talked about those who had "left the race."

Some, who "passed" on their jobs but not after working hours, always skated on thin ice because of the danger of recognition. Still others, like the Franklin Denisons, easily could have left the black community but chose to make their contribution to the race, instead.

The whole question of who is a Negro has been defined and redefined so often that it finally reached the point where it was almost safe to say that Negro is a state of mind. Walter White, who was fairer-skinned than his second wife, the well known Poppy Cannon, was a primary example of this point of view.

Up until 1910, the state of Virginia defined as colored a person with one-fourth Negro blood. In 1910, the statute was amended so that a person with one-sixteenth Negro blood was considered "non-white." In 1930, there was another revision which stated that you were Negro if you had "any ascertainable quantum of Negro blood." The fact is that there are probably in excess of eight million Americans in the United States who, while apparently white, actually, possess a determinable quantity of "colored blood."

The case of Laurence Dennis, a prominent pro-fascist during the period of World War II, comes to mind. Dennis, the author of *Is Capitalism Doomed?* and The Dynamics of War and Revolution, had been raised in Washington, D. C.'s colored community, but got lost to the black world after attending Exeter and Harvard University. He married a white woman and moved in the best white circles, working in a responsible State Department position. It was not until after his fascist theories received so much notoriety in the press that Dennis was revealed as a colored person.

In 1910 there were 2,050,686 mulattoes listed in the decennial census. By 1920, the figure had dropped to 1,660,554. Whether the missing mulattoes had "passed" into the mainstream of white America, or whether the census-takers had failed to enumerate a full half-million people who had been counted ten years earlier, is hard to say. It is sufficient to note that the subject has really become unimportant as black consciousness and anti-discrimination laws make passing, for the most part, a passé way of life for the fair-skinned American of African descent.

The year 1912 was a very big year for me socially, because it started out with one of my close friends, Bertha Mosely, making her debut at a reception at her home in Englewood. Her father, Attorney Beauregard Mosely, was very active in political and civic affairs, and Bertha was one of the few exceptions to the "light and bright" rule. She was brown-skinned, but she very much belonged to our circle. She was extremely popular. She had everything, it seemed; wit, charm, and an inner warmth and vivacious-ness that made her a natural leader. Her brother, B. T., Jr., died of tuber-culosis while we were at the University of Chicago. "T. B." took so many young people in those days. She married Carey B. Lewis the same Christ-mas that I was married to Binga Dismond.

That year, I was eighteen. My people had been very protective while I was growing up, as were all of my chums' parents. We met boys at in-vitational dancing parties sponsored by the churches, like St. Thomas (Protestant Episcopal), Grace (Presbyterian), Quinn Chapel (AME), or Institutional (nondenominational). Some were given by the men's clubs like the Assembly, the Appomattox, or the officers of the Eighth Regiment. We went to dancing school on Saturday afternoon, which was by sub-scription and invitation. All of our friends participated, and we had a chance to meet new boys who were invited. We were always chaperoned. Aunt Maude and Uncle David were quite often chaperones, because they had no children, except me, and loved young people.

Following my graduation from Wendell Phillips High School, which at that time had only about fifteen percent colored students, it was natural that I would make my debut during that summer. We decided on a dancing party to be held the evening of my eighteenth birthday. Aunt Maude had selected the Oakland Music Hall, a private clubhouse available for parties and affairs of this sort, for my coming-out party. It was a very beautiful old mansion which had been occupied by wealthy whites. We added our personal touches by taking our Oriental rugs and some fine crystal to be used for the punch, and there were lots of fresh flowers, gifts from admirers. My dress, with a short train, was made to accentuate my tiny waistline. Aunt Maude, Uncle David, and I received, and later the younger guests danced while the older ones visited and reminisced.

I must admit that I had more fun at Ethel Mitchell's debut that sum-mer than my own. I didn't have to be on my Ps and Qs. Ethel was the niece of Julius Avendorph, who was the *major domo* of Chicago's black society. Her reception and dancing party was at the Appomattox Club, at 35th Street and Wabash Avenue. The club rooms were beautifully decorated with jack roses and carnations, and Ethel was lovely in a white embroidered marquisette with blue satin trimmings and pink sweet peas.

Anabel and Eloise Carey, Bertha Mosely, Pearl Mayo, Gertrude Barbour, Vivian Harsh, Lovelyn Miller, Helen Perry, Ruth Boger, Swerzie McGooden, and Bennie Stovall were some of the girls who were there. Among the fellows, I remember Alfred Anderson, Guy Allen, Walter Abernathy, Tom Boger, Clarence, Herbert and Bennie Byron, Dr. U. G. Dailey, Carey B. Lewis, Ripley Meade, Ahrue Feaman, Fenton William "Pritt" Harsh, and Macon Huggins. We had a gay old time on nothing stronger than our youth, because only frappé was served.

That summer Lillian and Gertrude Perry gave a party for my cousin Marie, who was visiting from Mishawaka, and their friend, Mamie Lewis, from Washington, D. C. The Perry girls invited about fifty young people to dance at the Appomattox Club. Lillian and Gertrude lived in Evanston, so some of their Evanston friends, like Leslie and Ruth Pollard, came. William Hale and Mordicai Johnson, both graduate students at the University of Chicago, added an intellectual tone since most of us were either in college or starting college that fall.

Eleanor Curtis was visiting that summer from Washington, D. C. and met Dr. Ulysses G. Dailey, one of our most eligible bachelors. I think that was when she decided to join her brother, Dr. Austin Curtis, and his wife "Nama" in Tuskegee where they were all attending a medical convention. They became engaged that summer.

Also that same summer, Jesse Binga and some of the local black businessmen sponsored a State Street Business Exposition. Just to show there is nothing new under the sun, it is the same concept that Rev. Jesse Jackson is now using with Black Expo, but it was on a very small scale with the *Chicago Defender* and the *Chicago Broad Ax* both backing it. Mr. Taylor's paper, the *Broad Ax,* was older than Mr. Abbott's, but lots of people were reading and talking about the *Chicago Defender*.

Robert S. Abbott was dirt poor when he first started the *Chicago Defender;* he had graduated from Hampton Institute and Kent Law School before starting the paper. Rooming with Mrs. Henrietta Lee, Benote and Edward Wimp's mother, on South State Street, Abbott put the first papers together in her kitchen. Selling them up and down State Street, he picked up a lot of news. As he became known to the business people, they recommended the paper to their customers, and the *Chicago Defender* was on its way.

The other paper in those days was the *Broad Ax*. The editor and publisher, Julius Taylor, had come to Chicago from Salt Lake City, where he
had published the *Broad Ax*. He was outspoken and much more political
than Mr. Abbott in those days. He even backed Woodrow Wilson, a
Democrat, for president. Both papers had carried an item about my debut.

The summer of 1912, there was lots of excitement in Chicago about
the "Queen of State Street" contest. Today, this would not be thought
of as the kind of thing in which *nice* girls would participate. It is to the credit
of men like Jesse Binga, Beauregard Mosely, and Mr. Anthony Overton
(who had recently come to Chicago from Kansas City with his flourishing
Overton Hygienic Products business) that such a promotion involved the
very finest young women in the colored community.

I dropped out of the contest in the early weeks. Bertha Mosely got
over 1300 votes, but the winner was Hattie Holliday, the eldest of the
beautiful Holliday girls. They were Catholics, and Hattie had the backing
of all of St. Monica's Church. She got over 3,000 votes and was crowned
"Queen of State Street" in a big parade during the end of August. She was
also presented with a one-hundred dollar bill by Mr. Binga. Hattie later
married Colonel James C. Hall, who was very active in the Eighth Regiment and was commanding officer of Binga Dismond's company during
the war. Hattie's younger sister Mamie married Vincent Saunders from
Milwaukee. Vincent was Marie Burgette's brother, and Marie married
Charles S. Johnson.

Early that year, Mr. Binga, who was a very popular banker, broker
and real estate businessman, had married Miss Eudora Johnson. While their
wedding was talked about and written up in both the *Broad Ax* and the
Chicago Defender as a "society" event, you could tell from the people
who were *not* there just how *society* it was. It was not that anyone had anything against "Miss Dora," who was very wealthy and well educated.
Money notwithstanding, "Miss Dora" did not belong to Chicago's black
society, and that was that. Mr. Binga was what my aunt called "a self-
made man," and I remember talk that he had sold vegetables as a huckster
in the street when he first came to Chicago.

Actually, he was the youngest of ten children and had been born in
Detroit, Michigan in 1865. His father, William W. Binga, was a native
of Amherstburg, Ontario, and his mother, Adelphia Powers Binga, was

from Rochester, New York. Jesse was educated in the Detroit public schools, but he dropped out before completing high school. His mother owned a number of rent houses in Detroit on what was known as "Binga Row." They were what we would consider tenements today, but in those days the vast number of black migrants coming through Detroit on their way to and from Canada had to have a roof over their heads.

Jesse Binga collected rents for his mother and helped her keep up the repairs on the run-down property. For a period, he also worked in the law office of Thomas Crisup, the first black graduate of the University of Michigan at Ann Arbor. He was restless, however, and when he was twenty years old he left Detroit, heading West. Before he finally settled in Chicago around 1898, he had worked as a barber in San Francisco and Oakland, California and on the Southern Pacific Railroad as a Pullman porter. When the Indian reservation in Idaho was opened for settlement, he purchased twenty lots in Pocatello for twenty dollars, so the story goes, and a few years later sold them at a handsome profit. When he entered the real estate business in Chicago, he used his limited capital to secure leaseholds on property in the rapidly changing South Side. At one time, his leaseholds on property amounted to over 1,000 flats and homes. If he had bought, instead of leasing, it would have taken millions of dollars in capital investment to handle the property he controlled. At that time whites were fleeing the South Side, moving to South Shore and the Gold Coast, and blacks were desperate for desirable apartments and decent neighborhoods.

Miss Eudora Johnson was not a young woman at the time of her marriage to Mr. Binga. She looked like a caricature of a "big, fat, black mammy," but she was the first black person I ever knew to stay at the Plaza in New York. She was the sister of "Mushmouth" Johnson, a notorious Chicago gambler. When he died in 1906, it was reported that Eudora Johnson inherited $200,000 from his estate. Mr. Binga was a distinguished looking gentleman. I would not say that he married Miss Dora for her money, but $200,000 in those days was an awful lot of money. Mr. Binga could probably have chosen anyone he wanted.

The wedding was very elaborate, with the bride wearing a gown of Marie Antoinette gold brocade silk, embroidered with silver leaves. That spring, Miss Dora had a surprise birthday party for Mr. Binga. It was a stag affair. The society matrons had no opportunity to refuse her invitation.

Later, after I was married to Binga Dismond, Mr. Binga's nephew, I got to know Miss Dora. I knew what a sweet, delightful woman she was. The Bingas very seldom went out socially, as she explained, and they were not the entertaining kind. Although they had a large Christmas party every year, it was like a public relations *soiree,* meant to pay obligations. They probably could have gone wherever they wanted, but whether they stayed to avoid the opportunity for snubs, I don't know. They never had any children, and somehow I felt it was very sad that they were so alone.

In September, I entered the University of Chicago. Some of my friends were more fortunate. They were going to Howard and Fisk and Spelman, which were the best schools for contacts.

Edith Hardin, Dr. Robert Hardin's daughter, was one of the lucky ones who went to Howard University in Washington, D. C. We all automatically thought that the girls who went to Howard would marry doctors and lawyers from the Howard Medical or Law Schools. A girl who went to Fisk had a chance at the fellows from Meharry Medical School. Spelman girls met men from Morehouse or graduate students from Atlanta University. At the University of Chicago, there were more girls than fellows— that is, there were more colored girls than colored fellows, so we could not be accused of husband hunting.

I had applied to all three schools, but while I waited hopefully to hear from one, I received a work-study scholarship from the University of Chicago—the result of the interest of Harold Ickes's (Secretary of the Interior during the Roosevelt administration) mother-in-law, who was a friend of Aunt Maude. The four-year grant of full tuition was in return for services as a cataloging assistant in the university library. That ended my dream of being a belle on a black college campus.

The University of Chicago on the Midway was then, and still is, one of the most beautiful college campuses I have seen. It's awe-inspiring. There was not too much overt prejudice on the campus—none, noticeably, in the classrooms—and the only incident I recall occurred in the cafeteria. One day I took my luncheon tray to a table occupied by three white students, and they immediately picked up their trays and moved to another table. This was early in my first year, but it did not dampen my enthusiasm for the University of Chicago.

Photographs

Black resorts, which sprang up after the Reconstruction, were the social enclaves of the elite.

Highland Beach on Maryland's Chesapeake Bay, Oak Bluffs in Cape Cod, and Idlewild in Michigan were top resorts of the day.

Dr. Binga Dismond (l) and second wife on board cruiser. Teen cyclists enjoying summer hiatus on Martha's Vineyard.

Friendships started early for tots who gathered from across the country. Idlewild residents organized volunteer fire crew.

309

A garden party was the setting for the debut of Chicago's Earl and Katherine Dickerson's daughter Diane (above). Detroit debutante Gail Burton dances with her father Dr. DeWitt Burton and is escorted (near right) by Clifford Alexander and Ronald Harper. Dr. Percy Julian (far right) at daughter Faith's debut.

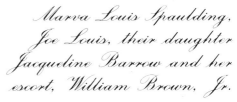

Marva Louis Spaulding,
Joe Louis, their daughter
Jacqueline Barrow and her
escort, William Brown, Jr.

Bride is the daughter of late
Dr. Douglass Stubbs of
Philadelphia, other daughter,
maid of honor, Fredericka
Turner Stubbs

Nearly one thousand guests attended the 1958 wedding of Marion (Patsy) Stubbs to market analyst-writer Harold S. Fleming, Jr. in Detroit.

(Opp.) Mother of the bride, Marian Turner Thomas, assists her youngest daughter, Linda Thomas, the junior maid of honor. (Above) Rehearsal buffet hosted by the Samuel Thomases, brother of stepfather, Dr. Alfred E. Thomas, Jr. Wedding was held at St. Paul's Cathedral, Reception on family owned island.

y School, Suite D,
Calumet Ave.,
Chicago, Ill.

nt Atlanta
Solemnized

Ga., Dec. 28, 1925.—
most brilliant social
Yule-tide season was
of one of Atlanta's
g women, Miss Orie
Mae Kelly and Mr. J. Julius Flood
of Tuskegee   which was
solemni   ce of the
       Fair St.,
       ber 26th.
       decorated
       ar poin-
       P. M.,
       ccompan-
       is, sang
       e first to
       Wynell
       as rib-
       epe de
       e, and
       Craw-
       bride, dressed in
georgette with hand made
applique of pastel shades. Then
entered Miss W. Verdelle Day, who
wore a pink georgette, followed by
Miss Johnie Kelly, maid of honor,
wearing a lovely georgette. The
bride's attendant carried bouquets
of pink roses with tull
       aster Howard Goodlet was
       the wedding ring; fol-
       little Miss Dorothy
       flowers in the
       to the
       from
       on the
       ride was
       te geor-
       beads, her
       to a long
       th orange
       bouquet of
       only orna-
       pearls, the
       As the bride
       of the living
room,   panied by his
best man,   h N. Davis of
Tuskegee Institu   entered from a
side door, joining the bride. The

Chicago
By MRS. BER

CHICAGO, Ill., Jan. 7.—The
Forty Club's dance on Saturda
night at the Appomattox Club wa

one of the jollies
affairs of the hol
idays. Wil
Brown's orches
tra furnished
music. The dec
orations were
beautiful and fa
vors many
added to the joy
of the occasion
There seemed te
be just a little
more real fu
among the Forty
"boys." An add
ed attraction o
the evening wa
the appearance o
Mr. White's quin
tette of Al John

Mrs. H. M. Lewis

son's show now at the Apollo The
atre in the "loop." Their singin
was sweet, harmonious and joyous
The guests went wild with enthus
iasm. Charming women, beautifu
gowns and glorious dance musi
were enjoyable features of the func
tion. The officers of the club are
Benjamin Martin, Pres.; Dr. F. G
Trapp, 1st Vice Pres.; Dr. J. A
Harper, 2nd Vice Pres.; W. A. Moli
son, Secy.; Rufus Sampson, Asst
Secy.; and F. W. Harsh, Treas. R
Walter Abernathy, chairman of th
entertainment committee. Chicag
has been crowded with large an
small dances but the Forty Clu
made an enviable reputation thi
season for giving, perhaps, th
swellest and most enjoyable dance
of the season. The Snakes, howeve
this week are expected to do som
real entertaining at its annu
dance at the Vincinnes Hotel.

Quite a large number of societ
people attended the basket ba
classic last week at the Coliseum be
tween the Wendell Phillips Hig
School and Central of Louisvil
Wendell Phillips won over Louisvil

In organizing the Boule (Sigma Pi Phi),
Dr. Henry Minton explained that it was . . .
"to bind men of like qualities, tastes and
attainment into close sacred union, that they
might know the best of one another." Even
as fraternities have, men's clubs have existed
for this primary purpose. In Chicago, among
the oldest and most prestigious are The
Assembly, The Royal Coterie of Snakes and
The Forty Club. Over the years as older
men move off the scene, young ones who are
like-minded are asked to join the select
company.

Mrs. Eunice Walker Johnson, secretary-treasurer of the Johnson Publishing Company, participates in candle lighting ceremony with fellow members of the Gay Northeasterners club (left).

The woman's clubs which sprang up around the turn of the century were service rather than social oriented. However, they did sponsor social events.

Girl Friends, Gay Northeasterners, and the Women's Boards of groups such as the National Urban League and the NAACP, have developed programs based upon community service and philanthropy.

During lighter moment at a national conclave, members are joined by males for festivities, above Earl B. Dickerson, Mrs. Norris Davis, Judge James Parsons, Mr. and Mrs. Theodore Jones.

The Chicago chapter of the Girl Friends (right) arrived in Louisiana to install popular New Orleans club into the National Sisterhood. Another national social club is the Links (below and bottom right).

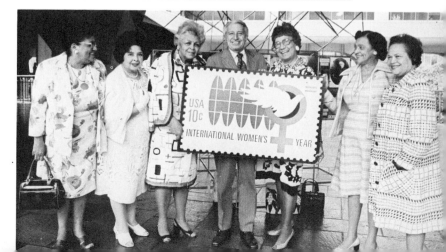

Gerri Major (above) with Senator Edward Brooke and Andrew Hatcher and (below) with Guilford Dudley, Jr., Mrs. Gloria Jackson, and Leroy Johnson in Copenhagen.

Ms. Major strolling (left) with long-time friend Jake Henderson at Acropolis in Athens, Greece, and with Rose Morgan (above) and Gladys Johnson enroute to Far East via Hawaii. Gerri, (below,) with William P. Grayson, former executive vice-president Johnson Publishing Co., Inc. in New York office.

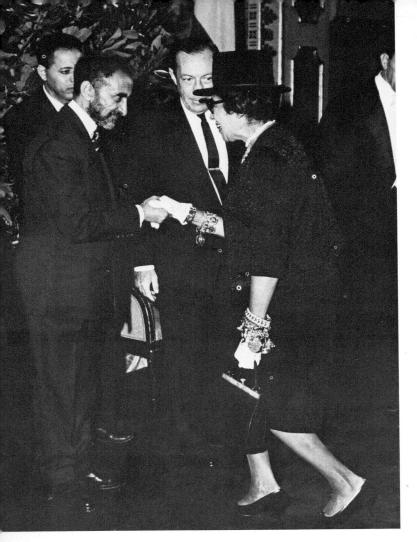

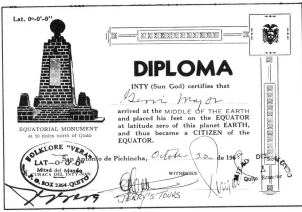

DIPLOMA

INTY (Sun God) certifies that

Gerri Major

arrived at the MIDDLE OF THE EARTH and placed his feet on the EQUATOR at latitude zero of this planet EARTH, and thus became a CITIZEN of the EQUATOR.

Lat. 0°-0'-0''

EQUATORIAL MONUMENT
at 10 miles north of Quito

FOLKLORE "VERA"
LAT-0°-0'-0'
Mited del Mundo
CURACA DEL INTI-ÑAN
P. O. BOX 2364-QUITO

San Antonio de Pichincha, October 22 de 1965 Quito Ecuador

WITNESSES

JERRY'S TOURS

Gerri Major crossed the equator many times during her travels as Jet magazine's society editor for which her first assignment was Queen Elizabeth's coronation in 1953. Emperor Haile Selassie (above, l.) and Haitian President Paul Magloire were among those dignitaries Ms. Major met and about whom she wrote during the 1950s. As the emerging nations of Africa came into national prominence, Ms. Major (top, opp.) with Atlanta University President Clement greeted Prime Minister Balewa and President Azikiwe (c., far right photo), both of Nigeria.

320

Ms. Major and Jay Clifford, a member of the international jet set, on French Riviera.

Gerri Major, (far r.) with Dominican Republic's Rafael Trujillo; Major Robinson, Era Bell Thompson, Ebony editor with Gerri.

321

322

Like-Minded People

Colored students who attended predominantly white colleges and universities had little opportunity for social life, nor as individuals did they have any mechanism for making their needs felt by the faculty, administration, or the general student body. Often, the few colored students on a large campus with thousands of whites did not even know each other, since there was nothing to bring them together.

Whites had always had fraternities, or at least back to the middle 1900s there had been active chapters of national fraternities on New England and Middle Western college campuses. These fraternities, and later sororities, rarely included colored students in their ranks.

Clubs, lyceums, and literary societies had been the kinds of groups developed to provide social contact, intellectual stimulation, and cultural enrichment for the Negro college student. This, of course, went back to the early 1830s when Philadelphia and most of the larger cities boosted lyceums and reading clubs.

Dr. Henry M. Minton spelled out the rationale for black fraternities when he organized Sigma Pi Phi, or the Boule, the first of the Greek letter fraternities among black people. Minton said,

> "This organization should be a fraternity in the true sense of the word; one whose chief thought should not be to visit the sick and bury the dead, but to bind men of like qualities, tastes and attainments into close, sacred union, that they might know the best of one another."

The Boule was for the man of achievement and accomplishment. It was for those who had already arrived at a certain position in terms of professional accomplishment and economic status.

It was also for friends. Dr. Minton had organized a Chicago chapter of Sigma Pi Phi in 1909, and Dr. Daniel Hale Williams was one of the charter members. Dr. George Cleveland Hall was never a member. But the feud which had divided Chicago society into two camps had extended to the Boule, and as long as Williams was active, Hall did not cease his agitation to become a member. Williams finally resigned from the group. In later years, Dr. Williams sent his books to Minton in Philadelphia to start a library for Mercy Hospital. "It only takes a small room and some chairs and some shelves . . . It will add much to your hospital," said the Chicago physician to his old friend.

Running almost concurrently with the establishment of the Boule in the fall and winter of 1905 and 1906 at Cornell University in Ithaca, New York, a number of young colored men, all students in different colleges at the university, got together to talk about organizing for their mutual benefit. Henry A. Callis, Vertner W. Tandy, George B. Kelley, Charles Henry Chapman, Nathaniel Murray, Robert H. Ogle, Morgan T. Phillips, and George Tompkins were all undergraduates. One, C. C. Poindexter, was a graduate student in the Agricultural College. They organized a social studies club in the beginning, and on October 27, 1906 the club became Alpha Phi Alpha Society, with the first initiation taking place October 30, 1906. By December 4, 1906, the decision had been made that Alpha Phi Alpha would become a fraternity. Mr. Poindexter, who had been one of their early leaders, resigned and expressed the feeling that, at that point in time, the black man in America had no cultural background upon which to build the framework of a college fraternity. He suggested this should take place at a later time. His resignation was accepted with regret, as was Mr. George Tompkins's. The fraternity had become a reality.

As early as 1903, a group of colored students at Indiana University had come together, forming a club to which they gave Greek letters, designating it Alpha Kappa Nu. The club did not last much beyond the time of the students who organized it, and it was not until 1911 that another group of young men at Indiana University, remembering the earlier group, came together with the idea of establishing a fraternity. They were chartered as Kappa Alpha Nu, which became Kappa Alpha Psi Fraternity incorporated May 15, 1911. The founders were Elder Watson Diggs, Byron Armstrong, Edward Irvin, Marcus Blakemore, Henry T. Asher, Ezra T. Alexander, Guy L. Grant, and John M. Lee.

At the University of Illinois, students had formed a club called the *Illia,* with Earl B. Dickerson as president. They were approached to become the second chapter of the fraternity. Byron and Irvin Armstrong, Guy Grant, John Lee, Frank Summers, and Elmer Mosle went to Urbana, Illinois, where they established Beta Chapter of Kappa Alpha Psi chartered on February 8, 1913. Members, Earl B. Dickerson, George C. Ellis, Byron K. Kenner, Frank L. Williams, William J. Prince, H. L. Burnham, T. H. Harpole, and C. L. M. Cooper. Dickerson became the first polemarch; Prince first keeper of the records; and Ellis, the first keeper of the Exchequer. After graduation, June 1916, Dickerson accepted a professorship at Tuskegee, and Prince succeeded Dickerson as polemarch.

The school year 1907-1908, a group of junior and senior women at Howard University, under the leadership of Ethel Hedgeman, a junior from St. Louis, came together with the idea of organizing a sorority. After seeking and receiving the approval and best wishes of Howard University's administration, Alpha Kappa Alpha Sorority was formed, and the first members were Beulah and Lillie Burke from Hertford, North Carolina, Margaret Flagg from Greensboro, North Carolina, Lavinia Norman from Montgomery, West Virginia, Marie Woolfolk from Atlanta, Lucy Slowe from Baltimore, Anna Easter Brown of Orange, New Jersey, and Marjorie Hill who died during the first year of the organization. At the suggestion of the organizer, Ethel Hedgeman, Lucy Slowe, a senior, was elected first president of Alpha Kappa Alpha. The Burke girls, Lavinia Norman, and Marie Woolfolk were products of Howard University Prep School, while Margaret Flagg came from M Street School to Howard.

In 1912, Beulah Burke, one of the founders of AKA and at that time a teacher at Sumner High School in Kansas City, Missouri, contacted a group of us who were students at the University of Chicago about forming a chapter of Alpha Kappa Alpha on our campus. In spite of the fact that AKA had been organized at Howard four years earlier, no new chapters had been organized on other campuses.

Under Beulah Burke's leadership, Eva Overton, Bertha Mosely, Louise Corbin, Beatrice Lee, Virginia Gaines, and I became charter members of the Beta chapter of Alpha Kappa Alpha, the second chapter in the first sorority for black college women in 1913. Later, in 1922, we organized Theta Omega Chapter for graduate women in Chicago.

Delta Sigma Theta, the other of the "old-line" sororities, was founded in 1913 by twenty-two Howard University undergraduate students who emphasized the service aspect of their activity rather than the social. A high level of scholastic achievement was necessary for both AKA and Delta. The twenty-two women founders were Winona Cargile Alexander, Eliza P. Shippen, Florence L. Toms, Myra Davis Hemmings, Osceola McCarthy Adams, Ethel Cuff Black, Bertha Pitts Campbell, Zephyr Chism Carter, Vashti Turley Murphy, Fredericka Chase Dodd, Ethel Carr Watson, Jimmie Bugg Middleton, Wertie Blackwell Weaver, Madre Penn White, Edith Mott Young, Pauline Oberdorfer Minor, Naomi Sewell Richardson, Marguerite Young Alexander, Jessie McGuire Dent, Edna Brown Coleman, Mamie R. Rose and Olive Jones. Sadie Tanner Mossell Alexander was first national president of Delta Sigma Theta.

Those years at the University of Chicago went by very quickly. I completed the four-year course in three and one-half years by attending summer sessions, graduating in 1915. I kept busy with the sorority, classes, studying, and the routine social life around the house where Aunt Maude and Uncle David often entertained.

Our cousin, Farrow Raymond Powell, and his friend, Nelson Glover, were living at the house we now had at 3308 S. Rhodes Avenue. Raymond had finished Fisk, after being turned down at Notre Dame because he was a Negro. He was now studying dentistry at Northwestern University Dental School. He and Nelson, a medical student, always had lots of friends by the house, one of whom was Bill Dawson, later the congressman from Illinois. At that time, Bill, who had spent a year at Harvard University Medical School, was going to Northwestern University Law School.

I was not an ardent track fan before Binga Dismond came to the university, but shortly after he joined the track team, I found that it was fun to watch his practice sessions. Binga was much more worldly than the fellows with whom I had grown up. His family was one of the FFVs (First Families of Virginia). He had attended Virginia Union University in Richmond where he was born and Howard University, before transferring to the University of Chicago. Binga was impetuous. He had eloped during his days at Howard with socialite Narka Lee of Boston. Narka was older than Binga, and the marriage soon fell apart. However, he was still a married man when he came to Chicago, and therefore absolutely beyond the pale, as far as I was concerned. The Lees were very prominent people in Boston, and the publicity about their marriage had come west with him. As far as my family was concerned, he was just not eligible. For over a year he was not permitted to call at my house, and we saw each other only at the home of friends and at school and group affairs. My folks didn't have anything personal against him. They simply did not want me dating a married, though separated, man. When his divorce finally came through, my family was still opposed to his calling on me, but I prevailed upon them and won. He became my "official beau."

After my graduation, because Aunt Maude thought it best for Binga and I to separate for a while, I accepted a teaching position at Lincoln Institute, an all-black school in Jefferson City, Missouri. Lincoln had been founded by colored soldiers who had served in the Civil War and felt that many of the benefits which had come to them as soldiers would be cut off once they returned to civilian life. Many had learned to read and write in the 62nd and 65th Colored Infantries. One of these soldiers, First Lieutenant Richard B. Foster, called a meeting of the men from all of the ranks and discussed starting a school in Missouri for freed blacks. They took up a collection from among themselves and then started soliciting funds from interested persons in Missouri. By the middle of 1866, they had six thousand dollars, and on June 25, 1866, Lincoln Institute was incorporated. R. B. Foster was the first principal. One of the many contributors to the school was outlaw Jesse James, who gave two separate donations, one of five and the other of ten dollars.

At that time in the state of Missouri, unless you lived near one of the larger cities like St. Louis or Kansas City, there was almost no place a colored child could acquire even an elementary school education. For many years, Lincoln Institute was the only place in the state where Negroes could go for education after high school.

When I arrived at Lincoln, I had never been away from home before, nor had I ever been to an all-black school. There I was in this little country town in Missouri where many of the students were older than I, and certainly larger. From the beginning, it was a nightmare. I was assigned to teach college English and physical education. I had a Ph.B. from the University of Chicago, but I was totally unprepared to be a teacher. However, I decided to stick it out.

There were many rules and regulations governing the conduct of the faculty and students. Among them:

> Every student was required to observe Sunday by attendance at both church and Sunday school. All preparations for Sunday observance had to be performed on Saturday.

> Any form of association between males and females without permission was strictly forbidden, as was the use of alcohol, tobacco, firearms or any other deadly weapon.

> No woman student or faculty member could board at a disreputable house and retain connection with the Institute.

Benjamin Franklin Allen was president during my tenure at Lincoln. President Allen, fair-skinned, balding, wearing wire-rimmed pince-nez, was a graduate of Atlanta University and a Georgia gentleman. He had been president of Lincoln since 1902. His field was English and pedagogy, the latter being the term used for education courses.

President Allen sought to walk the thin line between the Booker T. Washington industrial education zealots and the W. E. B. DuBois "talented tenth" view of higher education. Allen felt the main problem "befogging the brains of the Negro people, dividing and directing them away from the leading issues of education, was the misconception that labor was degrading; that book learning and fine clothes and dignified leisure belonged to a favored few; that it was not possible for the man who worked with his hands to be cultured and refined." Dr. Allen wanted Lincoln to show that it was not what one did, but the spirit in which he approached the task that determined the cultural value of that which one happened to undertake. His policy was to emphasize education for usefulness whether it was industrial or classical higher education.

Lincoln was a boarding school where teachers were on duty almost twenty-four hours a day, seven days a week, although technically they were to report at eight in the morning and remain on duty until four o'clock in the afternoon with the exception of noon recess. They were expected to prepare for their classes after four o'clock and before reporting for 8 a.m. classes. Many were like I, young for the responsibility placed upon us.

My problems began when I identified with the students and they responded by falling in love with me. That might have been all right, but the male professors fell in love with me, too. That created problems. When I arrived, President Allen's administration was under fire from the alumni, the trustees, and the state officials who really controlled the institution. He was constantly under attack and as a result was either defensive or defiant, depending upon the source of the criticism. Whenever the president left the campus in his auto, he found a reason to take me with him, and that added to my problems. The excursions were innocent enough, but every day we had chapel, and every day it seemed the chapel sermon would be directed to me. No names were called, but the innuendoes were thick and heavy. ". . . You must not do this . . . you must not do that . . ." One day, President Allen was looking for his car, and his chauffeur had taken me into town to do some shopping. What a row ensued!

Since I was very good at elocution, I was given charge of the class play. Believing, as I did, in realism, it was natural that when the script called for a character to smoke a cigar, I gave the student a cigar to smoke. That bit of realism was too much. When the puffs of real cigar smoke drifted up to the balcony where the white trustees were sitting, poor President Allen came running down to the stage to take the cigars away from the boys and to chastise me.

So I came home for the summer, and when it was time to go back to Lincoln in the fall, I became ill. It was the same kind of illness that I got when I was to be confirmed at St. Thomas Episcopal Church—nausea, cold sweats, and weak limbs. I realized, and so did Aunt Maude and Uncle David, that the experience at Lincoln had been too much for me. I sent a letter saying that I could not return for the fall 1916 academic year.

A very tragic thing happened after I left Lincoln. A member of the faculty, Mr. R. A. West, was killed by Mr. T. E. Martin, the steward of the Boarding Department. President Allen left Lincoln in 1918. I suspect the killing on the campus that he loved so much was the last straw. I believe he returned to Georgia.

I returned to Chicago Normal College, for a teacher's certificate, which I received in 1917. Meanwhile, Binga had earned his B.S. degree from the University of Chicago in 1917. We were still in love.

World War I

In April 6, 1917, the United States declared war on Germany. Binga volunteered as soon after his graduation as he could. A training camp for colored officers had been established at Fort Des Moines, Iowa. Binga went to Des Moines in June. A number of fellows we knew were there; Earl Dickerson, Bill and Julian Dawson, Austin and Merrill Curtis from Washington, Percy Piper, Oscar Brown and Charles Garvin from Cleveland. For a time it must have seemed like an extension of college days. So many of them were Alpha Phi Alpha men, too.

After being commissioned a second lieutenant, Binga was assigned to the 370th Infantry Division (the old Eighth Regiment, Illinois National Guard) and was sent to Houston, Texas. Colonel Franklin Denison, our family friend, was the officer in charge. He was the highest ranking black officer on active duty in World War I.

One of the tragedies of that period was the treatment given to Colonel Charles Young, the West Point graduate who was denied active duty on the basis of "high blood pressure." Colonel Young dramatized his physical fitness by riding horseback from his home in Xenia, Ohio to the nation's capital, but to no avail. He was not assigned to active duty.

As Christmas, 1917 approached, I decided to accept Binga's plea that I marry him before he left for France. Aunt Maude helped me shop for my trousseau elegant lingerie and simply tailored daytime outfits.

I had planned to travel to Houston with the Denison family. As it turned out, I found myself traveling alone and being "Jim Crowed" for the first time in my life. Everything went well until we arrived in Kansas City. We got off the train for a change of engines and I went to the Harvey House for something to eat. While eating, the friendly porter who had been in my car came to say that he had moved my luggage into the coach set aside for "us." I understood, so I didn't argue. He was trying to spare me embarrassment. I gave him a tip and allowed him to show me to my new seat which was behind the engine. The porter told me that if anyone molested me, I should go to the engineer for help. That certainly wasn't reassuring, but the coach was empty except for me. I did my best to make myself comfortable on the antiquated straw seats and soon fell asleep.

When I woke up, it was to the most ungodly racket I had ever heard. The car was filled with men, women and children of all ages and sizes, and all very black. They had food, it seemed, by the tons, and they passed it back and forth, over and around me. The smell of the fried chicken began to get to me. It was night, and I was unable to see out of the window. I tried to rest but that was impossible because the man who was sitting next to me kept excusing himself to go to the toilet. I finally realized he didn't have a weak bladder, but he was going to drink from his paper bag-wrapped bottle of whiskey. The car finally settled down and I slept. I had put my money in a little flannel sack pinned inside my brassiere as my Aunt Maude suggested so I wasn't afraid of being robbed. As it turned out, I had no need to call on the engineer for assistance. We arrived in Houston early the next morning.

Binga and I agreed that a formal dress wedding would be inappropriate in Texas and wartime. On December 15, 1917, the same day I arrived, I was married in a soft green wool suit to Lieutenant Henry Binga Dismond. Colonel Spencer Dickerson, an old family friend, gave me away, and Edna Rose Denison was my matron of honor. Reverend William S. Braden, the chaplain, officiated. I was so nervous that I began to weep as I started down the aisle. Little George Denison, blue-eyed and tow-headed, was the ring bearer. He was all dressed for the wedding when he fell and cut his forehead. It made him so shaky that Edna fastened the ring to the cushion with a safety pin to keep it from falling off. I had the first and possibly the only big wedding at Camp Logan, Texas. It was military from start to finish with flags and crossed sabers and a wedding supper in the Officers' mess. My wedding night was spent in a rooming house in the colored section of Houston which catered to the families of colored officers. The floorboards were so far apart that we could see clear through to the ground below. To compensate for the primitive accommodations, the landlady, a lovely, warm black woman, mothered us and warmed us with thick eggnog that we ate with spoons and which was spiked with what must have been the best pre-Prohibition bourbon in Texas.

I returned from Houston via New Orleans with Edna Rose Denison and her four children. Jacqueline, the Denison's last child, had not yet been born. The older children, Franklin and Dorothy, were very obedient, but Denise and George were at the age where they didn't do whatever you wanted them to do, and vice versa. We stopped for a few days in New Orleans in the lovely home of the LaPerres. Mr. LaPerre was a prominent contractor from an old Creole family. The hospitality was superb, and the change of atmosphere from Texas was welcome.

The day we were to leave, Mr. LaPerre took us to the train station shortly before our scheduled departure. We had purchased first-class Pullman accommodations in advance, so expected to board and go to our Pullman immediately. To our chagrin, we discovered that the train had been delayed due to bad weather. Mr. LaPerre had settled us in the "white" waiting room, because no Negroes could purchase first-class accommodations. So we waited uneasily, the fair Edna Denison, the darker Geraldine Dismond, and the four children. People entered the waiting room and took no notice of us, but we were apprehensive. Edna removed the sailor hat from Georgie's golden-crowned head, which he would quickly replace, determined not to show one strand of straw-colored hair. On the other hand, Denise, with her fly-away curly hair, reminiscent of her dark ancestors, would not keep her bonnet on as she chased Georgie from one end of the station to the other. However, we were not challenged, and the questioning looks we received may have been because the children seemed so exuberant.

We were relieved when our train finally arrived, and we took our seats in the Pullman car assigned to us. The knowledgeable black porter was all politeness and detached formality as he readied the berths for our occupancy. The conductor took our tickets without comment. The next morning a new conductor came through and again examined our tickets and reservations. We were very calm and, to all intents and appearances, quite unperturbed. After looking at the children and me, the conductor went immediately to the Pullman porter to question him about the two women and four children. We waited. Nothing happened. When we crossed the Mason-Dixon line, we breathed deeply, happy that the silent subterfuge was over. As we moved further from the South, the dining car waiters and Pullman porters surrounded us with care and attention; the cool formality that they had previously exhibited having vanished with the advance into Northern country. It was then we learned that the white conductor had questioned my presence in the Pullman car, indicating that I was "pretty dark." The porter had reassured him that since we boarded in New Orleans, I could be "Mexican or something." Anyone was acceptable, except an American of African descent. As we pulled into the Central Station, just to know we were back in Chicago made me happy. Geraldine Hodges, post debutante, was now Mrs. H. Binga Dismond, matron.

For the first time in my life, I had been exposed to naked race prejudice. I suppose that social consciousness had never been my long suit, and somehow or other, the realities of which others around me may have been aware just had not penetrated me. Even the experience in Jefferson City had not really rubbed off on me. Our families had worked hard to protect us from the damage resulting from prejudice. They had succeeded. In an effort to spare us from the pain, we were left more vulnerable.

In Houston I became aware that the Eighth Regiment with which I had grown up was really something quite special. It was under the command of Colonel Franklin A. Denison, with Lieutenant Colonels Otis B. Duncan and James H. Johnson, Majors Charles L. Hunt, W. H. Roberts, Rufus M. Stokes, James R. White and Arthur Williams, and with a total complement of captains and first and second lieutenants, including my Binga. The 370th Infantry was the only unit in the entire army under the command of black officers. It was organized as a single battalion in 1891 and increased to a regiment and sent to Cuba in 1898. They had seen service in the Mexican border campaign of 1916 and had never had a white officer. The Eighth Regiment was a matter of pride to the men, the officers, and to the entire Chicago community.

Before being called to duty, the regiment, which was composed of approximately 1,000 officers and enlisted men, was increased to about 2,500 as the result of a recruiting campaign. When they arrived in France in April 1918, every single man had voluntarily enlisted. They had been called up in July 1917 and attached to the 33rd Division. It was made up of all Illinois soldiers. Because of the racial situation in Texas, they were not permitted to go to Camp Logan until October 12. From July until they left in October, they drilled in the streets of Chicago and in the Armory. The officers were determined that the unit would not be made to look bad because of a lack of discipline or training. The day that the group left, the entire community turned out to say goodbye. They came out of the

Armory with the band playing and the people cheering. The colored police under Lieutenant Childs, the only black police lieutenant, escorted them to the railroad siding where they boarded the troop train. Binga told me later that at every village and town through which the train passed, the one question which was always asked was "Where are the white officers?"

The regiment was in Houston for five months, and there was nothing but praise for the men of "Denison's Regiment." Their military appearance and discipline was superb, and they knew that the white population had never witnessed their likes before. There had been rioting in which members of the 24th Infantry had been involved, but the 370th Infantry remained vigilant and did not let their guard down during the entire stay in the Lone Star State.

I went back to Houston the first Sunday in March because I knew they were about to leave, and I wanted to see Binga again before they sailed. The camp was literally black with local people and folks from Illinois who had come to say their tearful goodbyes. Binga and I had only a few moments alone, and although I had promised myself that I wouldn't, I cried.

It actually wasn't the real farewell, because from Houston the 370th went to the port of embarkation at Newport News, Virginia. As soon as I could get some clothes in a bag, I went to Newport News. It was much worse in many ways than Houston, because there was a great deal of tension. The men from the 370th and the local MPs seemed to be having clashes all the time. The men were restless now and ready to go. Again, they were the cause of envy. Most of the other black soldiers who shipped out of Camp Stewart were stevedores or in labor battalions.

It was at Newport News that the 370th began to lose its black commanding officers. Lt. Col. J. H. Johnson and Capt. J. Nelson were ordered home because "they could not stand the rigors of trench warfare." It was heartbreaking for both men who had suffered so much to be able to go "over there."

The 370th was accompanied by men from the 371st and by a labor battalion, which was composed almost entirely of draftees. They were under the complete control of white officers and non-coms. There was not even a colored chaplain to whom they could relate. It was very sad.

Upon their arrival in France, they were soon assigned to the French 73rd Division in the San Mihiel sector. Binga's letters could not be too explicit. He told me later, that during that month, they really learned what trench warfare was.

They were relieved from San Mihiel on June 30 and after a week's rest marched to Rarecourt. On the 9th of July, Colonel Denison was ordered to move with the 36th French Division to the Chateau Thierry front. He indicated that to use his men in this manner, as shock troops, would be to send them to slaughter. They had been deprived of their American equipment and had been given French weapons. These were strange to them, because they had not had sufficient time to be trained in their use.

The next day, Colonel T. A. Roberts, who was white, arrived from General Headquarters and recommended that Colonel Denison be relieved in order to take a much-needed "rest." Colonel Roberts assumed temporary command on July 12, and for the first time, a white commanding officer was over the proud 370th Infantry, affectionately known as the "Old Illinois 8th."

Colonel Denison was recalled from France before the end of the war on a technicality and replaced by a white officer. Many said that Colonel Denison's race was not known to higher-ups, although it was no secret to anyone in the black community. Gossip had it that the "brass" discovered that the fair Colonel Denison was really black and, above all, protective of his men. When the 370th came back from France, they were again placed under the command of a black officer, Colonel Otis Duncan.

I knew nothing about all of this at the time, because when Colonel Denison returned to Chicago, I was still in Virginia. I had stayed to attend summer classes at Hampton Institute, temporarily living with Binga's aunt and uncle in Newport News. After Binga left, I moved to the Hampton campus to be close to classes and the library. In September I went back home and to teaching at Douglas School.

Harlem

After the war, Binga returned and entered Rush Medical College, a part of Northwestern University, and I continued to work at Douglas School. Because of the vast in-migration of blacks, many families had moved outside the old boundaries. Homes and churches had been fire-bombed, and the tension between whites and blacks in the summer of 1919 escalated as the thermometer rose. In July, it finally erupted when Eugene Williams, a seventeen-year-old black youth went swimming at the 31st Street Beach and strayed over the invisible line separating the black from the white sections of the beach. He was stoned by angry whites in Lake Michigan at the foot of 29th Street and, as a result, drowned. The Chicago riot had begun.

Negroes gathered in crowds and rumors flew. A black man was shot and killed by a black policeman and at every place whites and blacks met, a clash ensued. White mobs roamed in autos through the streets of black neighborhoods, stoning pedestrians and throwing lighted torches into homes. Uncle David, a chiropodist, was forced to remain in his downtown office as the white rioters took over street cars, pulling black men and women off to beat them. Oscar DePriest, the black alderman, went into the stockyards to bring men and women workers out to safety.

At the end of the three-day riot, twenty blacks were dead, fourteen whites were dead, hundreds were injured of both races, and countless thousands of dollars were lost in property damage, primarily in black communities where the rioters had roamed, burning and destroying homes and businesses.

Governor Frank Lowden appointed a commission to investigate the riots, and Charles S. Johnson, who had been a graduate student at the University of Chicago and research director for the Chicago Urban League, was named assistant director of the investigative staff. During the summer, I worked on the staff of the commission. Their report, *The Negro in*

Chicago, remains today a landmark in investigative research and analysis. As a result of his brilliant work in Chicago, in 1921 Charlie Johnson and his wife, Milwaukee's Marie Burgette, moved to New York City where Johnson became the national director of research and publicity for the National Urban League. He also edited *Opportunity,* the League journal and published a fine anthology of black writing called *Ebony and Topaz.*

After finishing medical school, Binga interned at Provident Hospital in Chicago and then practiced briefly in Danville, Illinois, a small city south of Chicago. We alternated weekends between Danville and Chicago for a short time, and then in 1922 Binga was invited to New York to set up practice. The invitation came from a group of black physicians practicing in Harlem. Dr. U. Conrad Vincent, Dr. Godfrey Nurse, Dr. Chester Booth and others urged Binga to relocate where the opportunities for a man interested in specializing in electro-therapy and x-ray would have greater scope. He joined the medical staff of the out-patient department at Harlem Hospital. Dr. Booth, a dentist, helped us to locate our first apartment on 135th Street, and it was there, with a single nurse as staff, that Dr. H. Binga Dismond opened his first office in New York City.

A Virginian and an easterner at heart, Binga was immediately at home, and was even more so when he joined the New York Sons and Daughters of Virginia. I joined the Chicago Club in New York, as well as the New York chapter of AKA and the NAACP. Binga felt the best way for him to make the kind of contacts necessary for his success was to belong to everything, and so he was a member of the Elks, Masons, Knights of Pythias, Foresters, as well as the Alpha Phi Alpha fraternity.

I started writing very shortly afterwards, and my first columns appeared in the *Pittsburgh Courier* under the head, "Through the Lorgnette." I also wrote a column for the *Chicago Bee* called "In New York Town." In 1928 I organized the Geraldyn Dismond Bureau of Specialized Publicity where I did various public relations and promotions jobs. In 1928, I became managing editor of the *Interstate Tattler,* a job I maintained until 1931. The *Tattler* had a magazine-type format and covered society news, theater and entertainment stories, gossip, sports and politics. As the managing editor, I had to make up dummies, handle hot type, read it up-side down and know the different type faces and sizes for layouts. I used to take the copy to press and stay with it until it rolled off completed. The *Tattler* was one of my most exhilarating experiences as a journalist.

I did two columns for the *Tattler,* "Social Snapshots of Geraldyn Dismond" and "Between Puffs by Lady Nicotine." I also started writing "New York Social Whirl" for the *Baltimore Afro-American* in 1928. I wrote my columns for the local readership, whether it was Baltimore, New York, Pittsburgh or Chicago, and that was how I really developed a national following.

The first house we owned in New York was at 252 W. 135th Street, next door to the police station. We had not been in it very long when the city wanted the house to build a garage for the police station. So we bought the house at 245 W. 139th Street on "Striver's Row." Abe Hill later wrote a play about the street and called it *Striver's Row.* The homes on 139th, between 7th and 8th, were designed by the famous architect, Stanford White, when Harlem was still lily-white. Of course, after blacks moved in, the whites ran, and those gorgeous homes went into black ownership. We bought ours from Harry Wills, the famous boxer. Vertner Tandy, the famous black architect, Dr. Louis T. Wright and many other professional people and well-to-do socialites lived there.

Harlem was the Mecca of black life and activity in the 1920s. The NAACP's James Weldon Johnson and his brother, J. Rosamond Johnson, had published their *Book of American Spirituals;* Walter White, his novel, *Fire in the Flint;* and W. E. B. DuBois, *The Gift of Black Folks* and *Dark Princess.* Miller and Lyles were playing in *Running Wild;* Sissle and Blake were appearing in *Shuffle Along;* Gilpin was starring in *Emperor Jones;* Countee Cullen had published *Color;* and Jean Toomer had written *Cane.* Claude McKay and Langston Hughes were publishing their slim volumes. Langston's *Weary Blues* was being quoted on street corners. Toomer was the grandson of P. B. S. Pinchback, the Reconstruction governor of Louisiana, and Hughes was the nephew of John Mercer Langston. Duke Ellington opened at the Cotton Club in Harlem in 1927, and Florence Mills, who stole everyone's heart in *Blackbirds,* then broke them when she died that year. Her funeral was the largest and most spectacular Harlem had seen, larger even than Bert Williams's, who died in 1922. Then there were the Stellar parties at A'Lelia Walker's Harlem townhouse, Dark Tower.

Photographs

Marion Lewis Cook, sons John H. Jr., Will Marion, Hugh O.

Louise Peters, Abbie Mitchell, Dasie Jackson below husbands

Louise, Lenoir,   Mercer, Marion,   Kathleen, Hugh Jr.

Vashti Smith and Dr. Mercer
Cook Jr. and their sons
Mercer Jr. and Jacques.

Ann Dibble Cook, Nancy Goldberg Cook

Jacques, Robert (right)

Eleanor, Hilda, Gregory

Antoinette, Mercer, Jackie, Janice

Descendants of Lomax Cook, who migrated from Fredericksburg, Virginia to Detroit in the early 1840s, have been quite illustrious. John Hartwell Cook Sr., a graduate of Oberlin College (1864), was in the first graduating class of the Howard University Law School. Elected to the board of trustees in 1873, he became professor and dean of the law school in 1876. Two years later he died, leaving his widow, Marion Lewis Cook (top, far left), to rear their three sons, John Jr., Will Marion and Hugh Oliver. John was a researcher in the U.S. Patent Office, Will became a successful musician, composer and producer, and Hugh became an accomplished educator.

Vincent, Rinda, Hugh O. III

341

Wilkins's sons are Chicago attorneys John and Julian (middle) and J. Ernest, Jr., youngest University of Chicago Ph.D. at 19. Mrs. Wilkins (r.) at the Howard Univ. Mother's Day program.

J. Ernest Wilkins's appointment as Under Secretary of Labor in 1954 made him the highest-ranking government official and the first black to attain cabinet status.

344

Author-syndicated columnist and former ambassador to Finland (1963) Carl Rowan (opposite) with wife and children, (above) with colleague, Sid Davis, and (below) with Federal Communications Commissioner Benjamin Hooks.

The first black woman ambassador, Patricia R. Harris, and her husband, Washington attorney William B. Harris, entertained such guests as Roy Wilkins (opposite) during her service to Luxembourg.

Hobart Taylor Sr. (left) aided Lyndon Johnson's favorite-son presidential bid as a delegate to the 1956 Democratic Convention in Chicago. Wayne State University bestowed doctor of laws honors on (below) Sen. Philip Hart, Governor George Romney, LBJ, and Hobart Taylor Jr. who was associate counsel for Pres. Johnson before assuming directorship of Export-Import Bank.

At Democratic Fund Raiser
with the late Billy Simpson,
Washington restaurateur.

Below, with sons Albert and Hobart III and wife Lynette, executive secretary of Delta Sigma Theta, Taylor is on the board of directors of several
companies. Above, he meets Dr. and Mrs. Clarence Hinton's daughter Barbara.

Birmingham businessman Arthur G. Gaston, Sr. (above) with wife, and Gaston home (l.). Gaston's enterprises include Booker T. Washington Insurance Company.

Gaston building (above) houses the
insurance company, the Citizens Federal
Savings and Loan, and a business college.

THE ART OF
ENRY O. TANNER
1859 - 1937

*Works of Henry O. Tanner were displayed
in a 1969 one-man show sponsored by the Frederick
Douglass Institute and the National Collection of Fine Arts.*

Tanner's "Thankful Poor, lost for many years, was found in a Philadelphia school's basement.

Eighty paintings and drawings were exhibited at the Washington show of the black American who achieved fame in Europe at the turn of the century.

Above, Mr. and Mrs. Clifford Alexander, (right) Brother of the late Dr. Horace Mann Bond, J. Max Bond (r.), with wife and John Kinard, curator of the Anacostia Museum.

In spite of the glitter and gaiety and apparent well-being in Harlem, in other places, race riots continued, lynchings continued, and blacks were still intimidated when they moved out of ghettoes into so-called white communities. In Detroit, Dr. Ossian Sweet, his wife and family were all placed on trial in a case where a white man had been killed by a gunshot from the Sweet home after a white mob had advanced against them. Clarence Darrow entered the case as attorney for Dr. Sweet. Mrs. Sweet died before the end of the ordeal, and Dr. Sweet's life was virtually ruined, although he was ultimately freed in the case. We did get a lift when Oscar DePriest was elected to Congress from Chicago's First Congressional District in 1928. He was the first black man in Congress from the North ever, and the first in the nation since George White in 1901. We felt maybe we were on the way back, politically.

Marcus Garvey's Universal Negro Improvement Association had been at the height of its influence when we first arrived, but the movement was dealt a stunning blow when Garvey was imprisoned for mail fraud and then deported to Jamaica by the federal authorities in 1929.

October, 1929. The stock market crashed. Black people who had been very comfortable and well-to-do were very much affected. My Aunt Maude was practically wiped out. She had placed most of her capital in the stock market on the advice of our good friend in Chicago, Attorney Edward Morris. She had been closely associated with Morris for years. He was one of the receivers when the Binga Bank failed. The failure of Jesse Binga's bank, followed closely by the closing of Anthony Overton's Douglass Bank in Chicago, was a real blow to thousands of substantial middle-class black people. They had put a few dollars aside for a rainy day only to have it wiped out before their eyes. It was a wonder that as many blacks did not commit suicide and jump out of windows as did whites. Perhaps, they had been wiped out before and so they knew how insecure their "security" had been. Many remembered their families having been wiped out with the failure of the Freedmen's Bank. Many old folks who had never given up their cache to banks, continued to rely on the safety of the cigar box.

I persuaded Aunt Maude to come and visit us in New York for the Christmas holidays in 1931. I thought it would be good for her morale. We entertained quite a lot and she was the recipient of a number of other invitations from our friends and old friends of hers. I gave a small luncheon for a half-dozen guests, and we had a big Christmas Eve party at our house. Hazel Alexander, an old friend from Indianapolis, was in town, so we had more than enough reason to entertain. It was, as I recall, the last big party that Binga and I gave during our marriage. Our living room was huge with a baby grand piano, so we set up space for dancing to the music of David Fontaine, Carrol Boyd and Carol Taite. The black rug with the large silver swan planters and the holly and poinsettia arrangements all around the room, made it very festive. There were gifts for all of the guests, men and women, under the silver Christmas tree, and they were opened before the buffet supper.

Among the guests were Dr. and Mrs. Louis T. Wright, Dr. and Mrs. Vertner Tandy, Dr. and Mrs. Marshall Ross, Mr. and Mrs. Flournoy Miller, Mr. and Mrs. Sol Johnson, the Harry Austins, Chester Harding, Howard and Bessie Bearden, Dr. Gertrude Curtis, Norman Cotton, Olivette Miller, Rev. Shelton Hale Bishop, Edward Perry, Harold Jackman and so many others that I cannot recall. Auntie was thrilled and, for the moment, forgot that she was nearly broke. When she went back to Chicago, I promised to come for a visit during the summer.

That summer, I went to Chicago to see Aunt Maude and stayed a rather long time. When I returned to New York, I didn't move my trunk out of the foyer of the 139th Street house. I had decided I wanted a divorce. Binga was excessively jealous, and yet he could race around with a half-dozen women and no one should say anything about it. Binga believed that every man should have as many women as he could support. After sixteen years, I was tired of being Wife Number One.

While I was in Chicago, I discussed the situation with Mr. Morris. He advised me to return to my home and my husband, but I knew it was only a temporary arrangement. One day I told Binga I was leaving him. He didn't believe me, but I left, taking with me only a few personal things and leaving the house and furnishing to him. I didn't ask for any money and wanted none. I wanted out, without any hassle.

In spite of the Depression, I got a job immediately on the Daily Citizen, a newspaper edited at the time by G. James Fleming. I had been with them only about six months when they folded. I then got a job as a writer with the New York Bureau of Public Health.

Meanwhile, I married again. My second husband was Gilbert Holland, a Canadian who, although he was colored, did not identify with black people. Binga came to the wedding reception and got drunk on my champagne. The marriage lasted less time than it takes time to write about.

My next matrimonial adventure was my last. John Major, a solid and secure Philadelphian whose business as an undertaker had made him most sensitive to human beings and their suffering, persuaded me to marry him and move to Atlantic City where he maintained his funeral business.

In order to help him, I took up undertaking, although it was not my cup of tea. We were very happy for the brief period of our marriage, but death intervened. John had children from a previous marriage, and after all of the business details had been worked out, I accepted Dr. C. B. Powell's offer to take over the women's pages of the *Amsterdam News*. I returned to New York City and Harlem and home.

I guess the '50s saw Black Society at its peak in many respects. The barriers which kept the black community as one had only begun to be broken down, and there was still a spirit of *family* among us.

During those days, no one in America was closer to the pulse of colored life than the society editors of the black press. Through their columns and news items about the most intimate phases of black life, they did more to interpret the social patterns of the community than the sociologists or psychologists. They also did more to dignify colored womanhood than all of the other media specialists put together.

The personality of the society editor and her own social status are the keys to the quality of "society" news carried by a paper. Names make news, and people want to read about their activities. If the society editor or woman's editor knows her people, her columns, her pages, and her paper she will develop a following loyal to the death. That's why society editors usually have the greatest amount of job security even in the black newspapers which are notorious for their turnstyle personnel changes.

There is little about the state of the black nation-within-a-nation that society editors don't know—and much that they can't print. To watch society in action might seem a lark to the average layman, but actually these ladies of the press work hard, long hours for little pay. At that time, depending upon the employer, it could range anywhere from $25 to $90 weekly. They chronicled the gay activities of the caviar and Cadillac set. *The Pittsburgh Courier's* ace society editor, Toki Schalk Johnson, once said, "To be a social editor, you must have a strong constitution, cast iron stomach, a private income, lots of good clothes, and the ability to say 'dahling'."

In the years following World War II, several trends appeared which reflected the changing times. Paramount, and the one with the most serious long-range consequences for blacks, was the increasing number of affairs in white hotels and ballrooms. Fashionable weddings in New York and Chicago began to be held at Manhattan's Little Church Around The Corner and the University of Chicago chapels. Downtown hotels got the society business that once went to the Parkway and the Terrace Room communities.

Toki Schalk Johnson got started in Boston where she wrote a "Beantown" column for several years before being promoted to full editorship in the early forties. A professional writer, Toki once wrote for the pulps and confession magazines. Her trademark became her incredible hats.

Ora Brinkley, who was the Houston-born society editor of the *Philadelphia Tribune,* for years ran an annual fashion show. "Teesee", Theresa Fambro Hooks, was doing the same thing a score of years later as a part of her job as woman's editor of the *Chicago Defender* newspaper.

Marion B. Campfield ran the *Chicago Defender* women's page for a decade, where the diminutive newswoman was known to her readers as "Campy." She entered the newspaper field as a teen-aged bride by marrying into the Mitchell family of the *St. Louis Argus.* She later was city editor for the Overton-owned *Chicago Bee,* whose managing editor was Olive M. Diggs. Often, a society editor had a straight news background.

Jessie Beavers of the *Los Angeles Sentinel,* had four sisters and her mother to assist in gathering social items. Still she managed to eat home on an average of one night a week during the peak of the social season.

The late Lula Jones Garrett for years edited women's pages for all editions of the *Afro-American* and wrote two society columns as well.

Under the direction of Myrtle Gaskill, a former Atlantan and mother of three, the *Michigan Chronicle* women's pages were *must* reading for Detroiters and those who wanted to keep up with the scintillating motor city set. A former teacher, Myrtle gathered most of her copy by phone. Without a staff to help keep pace, the black society editor is generally dependent upon family, friends, and telephone to see that no part of her constituency is neglected.

Pearl Cox began "Pearlie's Prattle" with the *Washington Tribune* in 1933 and continued the column when the paper was purchased by the *Afro-American*. Known as one of Washington's best-dressed women, the ex-law student admitted her weakness for hats. There was a practical reason for it, because black society reporters have learned that basic suits with eye-catching hats can expand a wardrobe to far-out limits.

Odile T. Elias, who recorded New Orleans social events for the *Louisiana Weekly* during the '40s, believed that the busiest time of the year for her was Mardi Gras season.

Before the sad demise of the *New York Age*, Betty Granger, the Long Island tennis-playing, socialite editor carried an extra change of clothes in her car when she left for work in the city. Later, she did a theatrical column for the *Amsterdam News* and covered the doings of the Long Island social set. I covered Manhattan.

When I came to *Jet* magazine in March 1953, Betty extended her "Conversation Piece" to include the greater New York area. At the time the transition was made, she wrote a column that I have cherished for years.

> "With our next edition of the *Amsterdam News*, our column moves over to the women's pages . . . and by the time you read this, we will have moved over to the desk formerly occupied by our pal, Gerri Major. Also, by that time, we'll be missing Gerri, her subtle sense of humor, her madder than madder hats . . . more and more with each passing minute . . . For Gerri will have moved her editing pencil into other journalistic postures downtown and the *Gerri-Go-Round* will be circling this and other countries with an eventual pause at that event-of-events, the coronation of the Queen of England."

The Jet Set

*T*he pièce de résistance offered me by *Ebony* magazine publisher John H. Johnson had been the opportunity to cover the coronation of Queen Elizabeth II of Great Britain in June 1953 for Johnson Publishing Company.

My column, entitled "Gerri Major's Society World," made its debut in *Jet* magazine, April 9, 1953. The first columns name-dropped Nancy Bullock Woolridge, an English professor at Hampton whose plans to attend the Queen Elizabeth II coronation in England included house-guesting with her godmother, Lady Astor.

Finally, the time came, and I checked in at New York's International Airport for the trip to London via B.O.A.C. There, arrangements had been made for me to join the international press corps handling the coronation, which usually happened only once in a generation. The last one had been the crowning of King George VI and Queen Elizabeth following the abdication of his brother, King Edward VIII, to marry the divorced American Wallis Warfield Simpson. All people of whatever color and station in life are somewhat taken by the magical quality of what was then the British Empire with all of its pomp and grandeur.

I was met on arrival at London's Heathrow Airport by Bill Houghton, a charming young Jamaican who had been a Royal Air Force gunner. He was now attached to the British Information Office, and one of his assignments was to expedite my activities during the busy days ahead. Arrangements had been made for me to cable my weekly column, from London and later, Munich, Rome, Madrid and Paris.

I was lodged at a small family-type hotel, typically British, located near the Marble Arch. Most of the guests were elderly people, and I seemed to provide the most excitement they had had in years. The doors were locked promptly at midnight, and since I rarely made it in by that time, the grandfatherly doorman took it upon himself to admonish me for my late hours and hectic pace.

Howard K. Smith, ABC's anchorman, was in charge of all U. S. corre-
spondents, and I reported to him in order to secure my press credentials,
my Scotland Yard pass, and the numerous invitations to galas and other
scheduled activities.

Africa and the West Indies were well represented in London. There
were twenty West African chiefs and tribal officials watching the ceremonies. One who did not attend was the Ashantiene of Kumasi, who was
voted 30,000 pounds by his tribal council to attend but decided not to go
because one local organization objected. He had written the Gold Coast
commissioner that if all of his people did not approve his trip, he would
not make the journey. The fabulous 60-year-old ruler was supposed to have
had so many jewels that he seldom went out because it took him too long
to dress. . . . Prince Osayande Akensua of Benin, Nigeria and his constant
companion, Rebecca Solomon of the Gold Coast, stopped London traffic
and were eye-catchers at the Queen's Garden Party. Both wore native
dress. Native costumes complete with huge umbrellas created a truly international atmosphere at the garden party. . . . It cost the Gold Coast
chieftain, Nii Kwabena Bonne, an extra 12 cents taxi fare to transport his
umbrella, which was six feet in diameter. It was purple and green with a
silver fringe and topped with a gold pineapple. . . . The 16-year-old
Princess Goinapi from Swaziland was dressed in a yellow, scarlet and black
striped blanket. Her coronet was of red feathers plucked from the wings of
the Liqwalaqwala bird—feathers which only members of the Swazi Royal
Family are allowed to wear. . . . Upon the arrival in London of the Oto-
lorin of Ife, members of the Nigerian delegation prostrated themselves in
obeisance before their chief, gathering quite a crowd of curious spectators.
. . . In the motor car procession of representatives of foreign states were
His Imperial Highness, the Crown Prince of Ethiopia; His Excellency, Love
O. Leger of Haiti; and the Honorable William R. Tolbert, Jr. of Liberia.
. . . In addition to the official representatives of Jamaica, which included
Chief Minister William Alexander Bustamante, his private secretary,
Gladys Longbridge, Colonel A. G. Curphey, president of the Legislative
Council and his wife, and Lady Edris Allan, widow of the late Sir Harold
Allan, about twenty visitors from the island had seats along the coronation
route. The P. M. H. Savorys of Tarrytown threw a party for members of
the Jamaican delegation to the coronation. Heading the honorees was the
Honorable William Bustamante. . . . One of the first persons of color I
saw in London was Blanche Strickland of Los Angeles and Dallas, Texas

being escorted about London by the Leslie Hutchinson family. Her greatest thrill, after the coronation pageant, was the dog racing at White City, the Madison Square Garden of London. . . . Dr. Gertrude Curtis Thompson of Los Angeles came in from Paris the day after coronation. Said she hates crowds. Her hostess was Adelaide Hall who was appearing at the Saville Theater in *Love From Judy*. The doctor was loaded down with fine leather goods which she had picked up in Italy. . . . The Stanley Mileses and Harry Waters of New York City had no hotel worries while in London. They arrived on the S.S. Nassau Coronation Cruise and used their ship as a hotel. . . . The Ralph Youngs, also of New York City, commuted from Bristol on Coronation Day. In Bristol, they were the house guests of a British couple whom they had met the previous year in Europe. . . . Geneva Valentine, the Washington realtor, arrived in London for the coronation as official representative of the National Association of Business and Professional Women. . . . Two members of Harlem's smart Bridgettes, Ida May King and Alberta Osborne, arrived in London via the S.S. Veedam for the coronation weekend and a tour of France and Italy. . . . Aboard the S.S. United States when she docked to disembark coronation guests were Willa and Dr. Edmund Goode and Olga Hill of Manhattan, and Helen Hill Green of Brooklyn. They, too, will visit on the continent. . . . Earliest arrival from the States was Helen Ivy, wife of the *Crisis* editor, James, who came over in April for a long holiday with her relatives who are scattered through Alfretton, Derbyshire, the Midlands, and London. . . . John Velasco of New York and points around the world did London's top clubs with a lady from Mexico. . . . Millicent Hines of Brooklyn arrived in London after a holiday in Florence and Paris. . . . Ruth Khama, whose love cost her husband, Seretse Khama, the leadership of his tribe in Bechuanaland, was none too popular with his colored friends. They said her affected Oxford accent was particularly annoying. . . . Dinah Lee, one of the best known Americans in London, was the only shop owner of color in the "Royal" borough of Kensington. She operated a women's specialty store, but that did not keep her from taking an active part in the civic life of the town. Coronation Day she conducted a street party in Beaversbrook Road where she lives. Among Americans present were Geneva K. Valentine and Blanche Strickland of Dallas, who was vice-president of the Excelsior Life Insurance Company. The night before, she had given a cup, the Dinah Lee coronation trophy, to the Jamaican team which won the open table tennis championship. . . . Boston-born Emma Layton, who has lived in London so many years with her husband, the famous Turner Layton,

and daughter A'Lelia, would like to come back to America. "You live aw-
fully alone over here," she said, "not because you want to, but because you
have to. English people are very stand-offish—even with each other. They
can be very clubby outside but seldom invite you to their homes." The Layton family was the only colored American family then in London society.
. . . Hardest person to catch up with in London was Rose Stevens of the
Lincoln School for Nurses. Her day started early in the morning and ran
through to early the next morning. . . . Doris Anderson, widow of actor-
author Garland Anderson, and herself author of *Nigger Lover,* claimed
that she often spoke with her departed husband through seances at Ronald
Strong's, the famous British medium. . . . Bill Houghton, the former Royal
Air Force gunner, was to be godfather for the first child of the John Shaws.
The expectant father was a member of England's landed gentry and captain
in the Horse Guards swanky British regiment known as The Blues. The
two men began their friendship in Frisco's Mayfair Club, the former
meeting-place of aristocracy. . . . Among admirers of Marian Bruce's
torchy singing at Churchill's was multimillionaire Maharajah of Cooch
Behar who used to drink a potent combination of pernod and whiskey but
at that time took only Coca Cola, straight. . . . Danish Count Peter Rabin
and an American GI tangled in Alex Graham's Sugar Hill Club. The latter
failed to stand when the club's cabaret closed with *God Save The King.*
. . . At an informal supper party, Herbert McDermot, who once lived
in New York but was then selling prefabricated houses in Africa for a
British firm, served up pigs' "trotters" to add a homey touch for American
visitors. Josephine Baker and some African guests won eating honors. . . .
At the plus ultra British-American Ball, Muriel Smith, a guest star on the
ball's cabaret, was introduced to the American ambassador and his wife,
the Honorable and Mrs. Winthrop Aldrich. Before the conversation ended,
Miss Smith mistakenly addressed the ambassador's wife as "Mrs. Gifford."
Later, Douglas Fairbanks, Jr., master of ceremonies, commented: "Dear
Muriel, you are living in the wrong administration." . . . Portia Tren-
holm, wife of the president of Alabama State College, H. Councill Tren-
holm, stopping at the Charing Cross Hotel for the coronation, planned to
tour Europe until mid-July. . . . I ran into Fleur Cowles, associate editor
of *Look* magazine and then wife of *Look* magazine publisher, Gardner
Cowles, at Epsom Downs racetrack. We were members of the "working
press" covering the coronation. I won a few pounds at the Derby by
betting on a long-shot simply because I liked his name. It was really something to see the British gentlemen in their high silk hats at the racetrack.

. . . Shortly after returning from Queen Elizabeth's coronation garden party at Buckingham Palace, Enid Margaret Cripps, the daughter of the late Sir Stafford Cripps, who was known to her friends as Peggy, and Joseph Emanuel Appiah, a law student from the Gold Coast, announced their engagement and disclosed to the press their plans for a July wedding. The engagement ring Appiah presented to his fiance was antique rose gold design, circa 1760. Appiah was the personal representative in London for Gold Coast premier Kwame Nkrumah. They planned to have three homes—one at Kumasi, the tribal seat of the Appiah family; another at Accra, the Gold Coast capital; and an apartment in London. . . . The news reached London that South African A. J. Luthuli, president-general of the African National Congress, had been banished from public life by Prime Minister Daniel Malan's nationalist government. Accused of stirring up hostilities between Europeans and non-whites, Luthuli was ordered to remain out of twenty-one magisterial districts for a year. He was also banned from attending any public meetings in South Africa. . . . Marie Bryant, the American entertainer, responded by singing nightly a song at London's Hippodrome which poked fun at Malan and had the nationalist government leader fuming in London. The tune, "Don't Malign Malan," stirred up as much talk as coronation pageantry. *Die Transvaaler,* the Johannesburg newspaper of the Malan regime, called the tune "shocking," and claimed that it had "palace" approval. Despite the controversy, Hippodrome producer Stephen Mitchell said the song would stay in the show. In the song, Miss Bryant sang:

> *Don't malign Malan because he dislikes our tan.*
> *We know that it's wrong to have a skin that's all brown,*
> *And wrong to be born on the wrong side of town.*
> *It is quite right that our filthy old homes be burned down,*
> *Malan is a wonderful man. Don't malign Malan.*
> *He's doing the best he can.*

. . . Alexander Bustamante, fiery chief minister of Jamaica, British West Indies, accused the British of committing "robbery without violence" in taxing Jamaica's poor. As he prepared to leave London after the coronation, the white-thatched labor boss said he got little or no satisfaction in talks with colonial, treasury, and food ministers over British purchases of Jamaican sugar. Bustamante complained: "The treasury does not care one bit more about the colonies than I do about a grasshopper." He said he would ask his legislature for new laws which would enable islanders to retain some of the taxes paid by British companies in Jamaica. . . . The Honorable Alfred Francis Adderley, chief justice of the Nassau (Bahamas Islands) Supreme Court, died aboard a British airliner en route home from London of leukemia. Adderley, a Bahamas envoy to the coronation, became ill during the ceremonies. A veteran government official and one of the Bahamas's top criminal lawyers, he was Crown prosecutor in the famous Alfred deMarigny murder trial when deMarigny was accused of murdering his father-in-law, Sir Harry Oaks. . . .

. . . .

Mrs. Virginia Reid Bruce, former wife of Eldridge Bruce, who married Marshall Field heiress Bettine Field Bruce, was suing to have the marriage between her former husband and the new Mrs. Bruce voided on the grounds that their divorce was gained without her knowledge. Bettina Bruce was suing her former husband, Dr. McChesney Goodall, for custody of their nine-year-old daughter. The Bruces make their home in England where interracial marriages find more acceptance.

. . . .

Soprano Mattiwilda Dobbs, of the prominent Dobbs family of Atlanta, Georgia, married a Spanish radio announcer named Don Luis Rodriguez Garcia de la Piedra in Genoa, Italy where she was appearing at the San Carlo Opera House. She was the first Negro to sing at La Scala in Milan.

. . . .

Marie Brown Frazier and husband Professor E. Franklin Frazier returned to Washington after a two-year stint in Paris. While there, the Howard University sociologist published *Le Bourgeoisie Noir,* later published in the United States as *Black Bourgeoisie.*

. . . .

I noted upon my return to the states that "The most beautiful women in Negro Society" were:

—Mrs. Charlotte Harris of Richmond, Virginia, an auburn-haired beauty who liked to spend her spare time painting.
—Mrs. Grace Gladden of Washington, D. C., olive-complexioned wife of orthopedic surgeon James Robert Gladden.

—Mrs. Ouida Williams, wife of Attorney David Williams and mother of two sons, David Jr. and Vaughn, spent time in activities ranging from cub scouting to Urban League.

—Mrs. Barbara Barland, wife of Detroit physician Herbert Barland, was voted one of Detroit's six most glamourous women and had a "coy Creole charm."

—Mrs. Vera Abels of San Francisco, an accomplished soprano who once sang in the San Francisco Opera.

—Mrs. Frances Parrish, wife of sociologist Dr. H. C. Parrish and a popular society matron whose looks were enhanced by grey-green eyes.

—Mrs. Vivian Allen of Houston, Texas, author, described by a Swiss professor as "the most exciting woman I have met in America."

—Mrs. Lois Lowe, striking blonde wife of Chicago insurance executive Walter Lowe, was actively interested in the United Negro College Fund.

My columns for *Jet* magazine had always had a heavy sprinkling of items about the international set—items about black Americans travelling abroad and activities of foreigners, particularly Third World people, Africans or West Indians, in local happenings. Column items ranged from such incidental intelligence as the fact that Chuma Azikiwe, at that time a Harvard University freshman, had spent the Christmas holidays in New York City with the Clarence Holtes, close family friends. Chuma was the son of Nnamdi Azikiwe, the prime minister of Eastern Nigeria and a former student at Lincoln University. Azikiwe, known familiarly as "Zeke," was extremely popular with the black community.

I wrote items that reinforced the breadth and scope of the black traveller . . . Ann Burns Stepto and husband, Dr. Robert Stepto, with good friends and fellow Chicagoans Edward and Katherine McDonald Wimp, were vacationing in St. Thomas in the American Virgin Islands. New York attorney, Pauli Murray (whose book about her family, *These Proud Shoes,* made us all proud), was off to Accra, Ghana, where she was to teach in the law department of the University College of Ghana and at the Ghana School of Law, as well as assist in the revision of Ghana's legal textbooks. Pauli's 22-pound Shetland sheep dog, Smokey, sailed with her on the Ghanaian jaunt.

Frequently, the route that the news took to get to my column was as interesting as the item itself. It was news when author Chester Himes cabled Mollie Moon from Paris that *Paris Match*, the famous French magazine, would be covering with a writer-photographer the Annual Beaux Arts Ball that Mollie ran as a benefit for the New York Urban League. *Paris Match* was coming to New York because the fabulous Josephine Baker was to be the guest of honor. What made the item really news to those in the know was the fact that Chester Himes, whose amusing (and shocking for those days) novel, *Pinktoes*, had allegedly been based on Mollie Moon.

When the young Aga Khan IV, a Harvard University student, became a life member of the NAACP and his name headed the New York NAACP Honor Guard, it was in my column.

I had met the old Aga Khan when I was in Paris following the coronation. He had a horse at Longchamps, the famous Paris race course, and I had gone there to cover a story on the famous black trainer, Jimmy Winkfield, who trained horses for the Aga Khan and others. The Aga Khan, for all of his huge size and pompous bearing, was a very pleasant man.

I met Ali Khan when I went down to cover the Federation of the West Indies. I happened to be at the airport trying to arrange for a trip through the West Indies to the United States when the debonair Ali Khan disembarked from his plane. All of the press people had left the airport terminal, and when I saw that no one seemed on hand to meet him, I introduced myself and told him that I was representing *Ebony* magazine at the Federation ceremonies. He was most gracious and kissed my hand. At that moment, a white woman rushed up. She had been called and told that there was no one at the airport to meet him, and amid profuse apologies, she went rushing off with him in tow. After that, every time we met, he smiled a greeting or went out of his way to speak. I was the first person that he had met in the West Indies and he did not forget.

During the period when General Trujillo was interested in improving his image in the black American community, he employed a friend of mine, Bill Alexander, to handle this kind of public relations. One of Bill's ideas was that Trujillo take a lifetime subscription to *Ebony* magazine and that I come down to present it to him. This would have a two-fold purpose: *Ebony* would do a story on the progress that the Dominican Republic had made under the Trujillo regime and, perhaps, counter the propaganda that American blacks were not welcome on that side of the island of Hispanola. The man in the street had the view that the Haitian side was "black" and the Dominican Republic, "white," although this was far from being liter-ally true. A large percentage of the Dominican population is black and many others are what we call mulatto or quadroon.

Era Bell Thompson, then co-Managing Editor of *Ebony*, our photog-rapher Moneta Sleet and I went down to Ciudad Trujillo. Everything was arranged for us to see. At one point, the generalissimo told me that I looked like his mother. I took that as a compliment.

I had met Trujillo's former son-in-law, Porfiro Rubiroso earlier. "Rubi," as he was called by his friends, was probably most entitled to be called the playboy of the Western world." His romances and marriages were legendary. He had been married to the two wealthiest women in the world, Doris Duke and Barbara Hutton. He had been married to one of the most beautiful French actresses, Danielle Darrieux. He had had a whirl-wind romance, which included planting a shiner on Zsa Zsa Gabor.

But in the days before his reputation became international, Rubi, the son of poor Dominicans, had been the husband of Flor Trujillo, the daugh-ter of the generalissimo. It was through Flor and the generalissimo that Rubiroso made it to the big time—the international circuit. He was assigned to the Dominican Republic's Paris consulate. Needless to say, I did not mention to the generalissimo that I was acquainted with the man who broke his daughter's heart.

Trujillo was very charming, but we never were able to forget that we were in a country that was under a dictatorship. Jose was our man, or rather Jose was in charge of us. Nothing was done without Jose, and when we planned a trip to a small village for a barbecue, we met Jose in the lobby of the hotel. He said, "The generalissimo wants you to come to a luncheon today." We told him that we were expected by our hosts at the barbecue in the village. Jose told us that we should forget the barbecue and come to the luncheon. It was a command performance. I was very uneasy at the luncheon, enough so that the generalissimo said to me, "I think you should go back to your hotel and take a rest." I did, but not before being formally presented to his son, which seemed to have been the only reason for the luncheon. We arrived late that night at the village where we had been expected at noon.

Batista, in exile from Cuba, was staying at the same hotel. One afternoon, while coming up on the elevator, I saw a gentleman who was smiling at me. When I got to my room, the telephone was ringing. "Are you Mrs. Major?" "Yes," I replied, and the voice said, "I am the man who smiled when you got on the elevator." "How did you get my name?" I questioned. Ignoring that, he went on, "I am here with Mr. Batista and we would like for you to come down and have cocktails with us." I remembered that Batista and Trujillo were having a little argument about what Batista should pay for permission to remain on the island. I didn't think it politic for me to have cocktails in public with Batista and the man with the smile. I knew that Trujillo knew everything that I did, so I invited them to come up and have drinks on our terrace. He came that afternoon, and the next afternoon we were invited to Batista's suite for cocktails, two floors above. While I am sure that Trujillo knew that we had had cocktails with Batista, he never mentioned it. Before I left, he sent by Jose a thirty-dollar gold piece with his likeness on it as a token of my visit. There was so much excitement when we left that I forgot the liquor I had bought and that was in bond at the airport. Just before take-off, I remembered and screamed to Jose, "My liquor, my liquor! I've forgotten my liquor!" He signalled for the door to be opened and the steps rolled back up, and while he went to get the liquor and put it on the plane, the other passengers were busy whispering. The stewardess asked Era Bell, "Who is she . . . a movie star?"

In spite of the fact that I had always been ready to grab a plane at a moment's notice and I kept my travel documents in order, I almost fainted the day that Mr. Johnson called me out of a clear blue sky and, without any preamble, told me that he wanted me to go to Paris to take over the Paris bureau. He was bringing Paris chief, Charles Sanders, a fine writer from Cleveland, Ohio by way of Texas, back to Chicago to be co-Managing Editor of *Ebony* with Hans Massaquoi. Era Bell Thompson would be the International Editor but would work on a schedule much less strenuous than the month-to-month hassle of putting out a major magazine. Herbert Nipson, a veteran editor and journalist on the *Ebony* staff who had shared managing editor chores with Era Bell, was named Executive Editor of the magazine.

Mr. Johnson indicated that he wanted me to stay in Paris at least six months, while he decided whether or not to maintain the office indefinitely. I was ill at the time, and my love affair with Paris had ended somewhere during the past twenty years. It seemed as though France was never quite the same after the German occupation as it had been before. Some of the warmth and joy had gone out of the French people and it had been replaced with a cold and withdrawn materialism.

The Parisian taxi driver had always been independent, and now he was argumentative, as well. They acted as though they didn't care whether you rode or not and would argue with you about where you wanted to go. I had taken Aunt Maude to Paris while she was still active. She had enjoyed renewing her old friendship with Ada DuConge Smith, whom everyone in the international set knew as "Bricktop," and with Beauford Delaney, the black artist, who was by now a part of Paris. My cousin Marie Moore and our friend Pauline Kigh Reed, were with us, they, Auntie and I managed to do all of the things that she had always wanted to do. We even took her to Monte Carlo, where Jay Clifford escorted her in style to the casino.

This was different. I was not being sent on a two-week assignment but for a minimum of six months. Mr. Johnson talked to me about five minutes regarding his proposal. I heard him say that I had been promoted to senior editor and that I had to go because he had no one else to send. I told him, "Let me talk to Marie about it and I'll give you an answer before the day is over." I left the office, which was located at Radio City Music Hall in Rockefeller Center and Sixth Avenue and went by taxi to my apartment at Fifth Avenue and 135th Street. I had been in the apartment only minutes before the telephone rang and it was Mr. Johnson again. Headache or no, I had to make a decision right then, so I told him, "Okay, I'll go." I hung up the phone, realizing then that I had not had a chance to call Marie or anyone else.

My first columns under the head, *Paris Scratchpad,* appeared in *Jet* magazine, December 14, 1967. It was unforgettable, because just about the same time, the first black American astronaut, Major Robert Lawrence Jr., of Chicago, was killed in the crash of an F-104 Starfighter while on a training mission. The war in Vietnam was in all of the Paris papers, and President Charles DeGaulle had earlier that year decreed that all American

Photographs

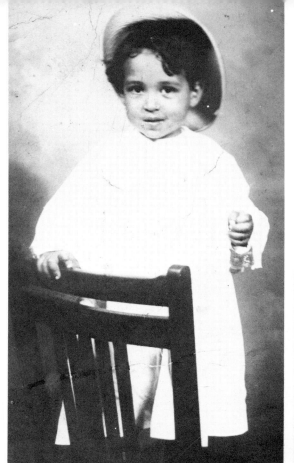

372

Justice Marshall with wife and sons, (below) accepting award from National Council of Women's Vivian Carter in 1958, and with other justices of the U.S. Supreme Court.

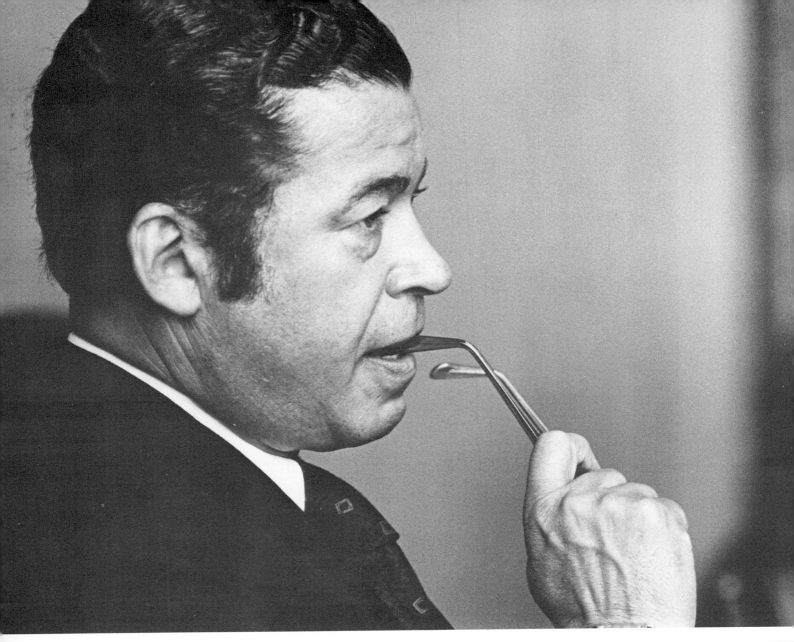

A pensive Senator Edward W.
Brooke: with daughters,
Edwina and Remigia, and
Italian wife, Remigia
and with mother, Helen.

Lt. Gov. Eliot Richardson swears Brooke in for second term as Atty. Gen. of Massa- chusetts. Mabel Sandridge, Col. Larkland Hewitt, Helen Brooke, Dr. David French, Atty. and Mrs. Brooke and Diamond Ball.

Brooke (above) at daughter Remi's wedding to Don Hasler, with political allys, and on Caribbean vacation. Edwina married Michel

Andre Lucien Petit, son of the mayor of Marigot, St. Martin, French West Indies.

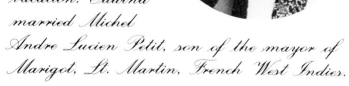

375

Reverend Andrew Young (clockwise from top) with Martin Luther King, Jr., and Rev. Ralph David Abernathy during civil rights movement; campaigning for Congress with Coretta Scott King; in Atlanta with Mayor Maynard Jackson; with "Daddy King"; and against Atlanta skyline.

At home in 1971 with his parents, Mr. and Mrs. Walter Young, wife Jean, and daughters Lisa, 12, Andrea, 14, and Paula, 6.

Congressman Andrew Young is shown (r.) with wife and son, Andy Jr., in the nation's capital and (below) in his Washington office. He was one of the first blacks to voice his support for former Georgia Governor Jimmy Carter (below r.) in his bid for President.

Secretary of Transportation William T. Coleman with Senator Edward Brooke (r.), Atlanta Mayor Maynard Jackson (below), and wife, Mrs. Lovida Coleman.

President Ford looks on
as oath is administered
by Justice Thurgood
Marshall in March,
1975. Coleman's
mother, wife, sons and
daughter attended
the White House
ceremonies.

The Reverend Benjamin L. Hooks is still active as a minister despite his heavy schedule as a Federal Communications commissioner. Hooks recently announced resignation to take position as executive director, National Association for Advancement of Colored People, upon retirement of long-time head Roy Wilkins.

Before his appointment by Richard Nixon in 1972, Hooks was the first black judge in Selby County (Memphis) Criminal Court.

Mrs. Benjamin (Frances) Hooks, (top l.) with Mrs. Walter E. (Vennetta Bullock) Washington, Benjamin L. Hooks (top r.), with family.

Mrs. Margaret Bush Wilson, chairman of the board of NAACP, with Hooks, Dr. Montague Cobb and Hobart Taylor.

381

Cosmetics manufacturer George Johnson, president of Johnson Products in Chicago, confers with special asst. Edwin Berry and Gail McGrady and vice-president Dorothy McConner.

382

Wife Joan and children, Eric, John, George Jr. and Joan, share family home at Runaway Bay, Jamaica. Eric married the former Renee Phillips.

Publishing executive John H. Johnson, president, publisher and editor of Johnson Publishing Co.

JPC publishes Ebony, JET, Black Stars and Ebony Jr! magazines. Affiliates are Fashion Fair cosmetics and travelling fashion show, Supreme Beauty Products and WJPC, the only Black-owned radio station in Chicago. Johnson is chairman of the board of Supreme Life Ins. Co. and is a member of the boards of The Marina City Bank of Chicago, Service Federal Savings and Loan of Chicago, Boston U., and Twentieth Century Fox, among others.

President John F. Kennedy appointed Johnson, a frequent White House guest, a special ambassador to Ivory Coast independence ceremony in 1961.

Mrs. Eunice W. Johnson (above and center r.) is secretary-treasurer of JPC and director-producer of the Ebony Fashion Fair. Mr. Johnson dines (r.) with his mother, Mrs. Gertrude Johnson Williams, the company's vice president, and cousin Mrs. Willie Miles Burns, another vice president and agency manager. Johnson is shown below with son, photographer John, Jr. (l.), and daughter Linda.

troops in France be withdrawn. Oriana Falaci the brilliant Italian journalist had written a very disturbing interview with H. Rap Brown, which seemed calculated to cause Europeans to run whenever they saw a black man heading in their direction. The Black Revolution in the United States, had hit the continent with some strange results.

Still, Paris, rather than London, seemed to be the focal point for all blacks travelling in Europe. Following World War II, many black people were associated with the military and were stationed in or around Paris or with easy access to The City of Light. Also many of the black Americans, Caribbean or Africans, familiar with America, and either travelling for pleasure or to their posts with any one of the many international missions and offices located on the Continent, came to Paris and found their way to the office at Number 38, Avenue George V in the Eighth arrondissement. Here they could expect to get the news and gossip from home, find out who was in town or had been or what was on the future calendar. It was a busy and exciting period and posed the greatest challenge that I had faced in quite some time.

I was not unhappy, however, when Mr. Johnson decided to close the Paris office because of the escalating cost of doing business in France. I was ready to return to Manhattan and my Harlem apartment.

The Second Reconstruction

*I*t was during January, 1817 in Philadelphia at Richard Allen's Bethel Church, that James Forten took the chair and spoke for the black assemblage to white America. He said at that time that our ancestors had, though not by choice, by virtue of their skill, resourcefulness and adaptability, been the first successful cultivators of the wilds of North America, or as it later became—the United States. He said that as the descendants of those pioneers "we are entitled to participate in the blessings of her luxuriant soil which their blood and sweat have manured; and that any measure or system of measures, having a tendency to banish us from her bosom, would not only be cruel but in direct violation of those principles which have been the boast of this republic."

He said further: "We [the free black population] never will separate ourselves voluntarily from the slave population in this country; they are our brethren, by the ties of consanguinity, of suffering, and of wrong; and we feel that there is more virtue in suffering privations with them than fancied advantages for a season."

Nearly a half-century later, a national convention of colored men met in Syracuse, N.Y. on October 4, 1864. The Civil War was raging. The Union had made overtures to the South stating that if they were to come home, all would be forgiven. The Union implied that the South could keep their slaves until the Supreme Court or Congress ruled on the issue. The Emancipation Proclamation had not been implemented but had only been used as a threat to secure an accommodation with the secessionists. Free blacks in the nation feared that should the South accept the Northern terms, the plight of free and enslaved blacks would be catastrophic.

One hundred and forty-four delegates were present at the Convention from 18 states, including Virginia, North Carolina, South Carolina, Florida, Mississippi, Louisiana and Tennessee. Frederick Douglass was the convention president. He spoke, as Forten had, to the Convention. His

remarks were also addressed to white America: "In surveying our future
. . . you will not blame us if we manifest anxiety in regard to the position
of our recognized friends as well as that of our open and declared enemies;
for our cause may suffer even more from injudicious concessions and weak-
nesses of our friends than from the machinations and power of our
enemies. . . . We have spoken of the existence of powerful reactionary
forces arrayed against us. . . . What are they? The first and most powerful
is slavery; . . . . The second is prejudice against men on account of their
color. . . . One controls the South, the other controls the North. Both are
original sources of power, and generate peculiar sentiments, ideas and laws
concerning us. . . . The agents of these two . . . influences are . . . chiefly,
the Democratic Party and the Republican Party. What we have to fear
from these two parties is—alas—only too obvious. . . . What do we want?
. . . First, the complete abolition of the slavery of our race in the United
States. We shall not stop to argue. . . . We cannot be free while our brothers are slaves. . . . The enslavement of a vast majority of our people extends
its influence over every member of our race; and makes freedom, even to the
free, a mockery and a delusion. . .

Further, . . . we want political equality. . . . Your fathers laid down
the principle that universal suffrage is the best foundation of government.
We believe, as your fathers believed, and as they practiced; for in eleven
states out of the original thirteen, colored men exercised the right to vote
at the time of the adoption of the Federal constitution. The possession of
the vote . . . is the keynote to the arch of human liberty, and without that,
the whole may at any moment fall to the ground. . . . Lastly, the power
to redress our wrongs and grant us our just rights is in your hands. . . .

We are among you and must remain among you; . . . it is for you to
say whether our presence shall conduce to the general peace and welfare of
the country, or be a constant cause of discussion and of irritation . . .
trouble . . . everywhere.

To avert these troubles and to place your great country in safety
from them, only one word from you—the American people—is needed, and
that is JUSTICE! Let that magic word be sounded, become all controlling
in all your courts of law, subordinate and supreme; let the halls of legislation, state and national, spurn all statesmanship as mischievous ruinous
that has not justice for its foundation. . . ."

Following the Civil War, for a brief decade and a few years, the nation had almost lived up to its promise. There were laws on the books to protect the civil rights and the political and social rights of black men and women. There were representatives in the state houses and in the national Congress, and, indeed, two black men sat in the Senate where only Edward Brooke now represents the entire national black community. Once before the pendulum seemed to have swung in the direction of equity for the man farthest down. But, now as in 1876, all of the signs and portents are present which indicate that this modern reconstruction period may be in for another long eclipse. It is dangerous to feel that the second reconstruction is any more foolproof than was the first.

Black Society? In the early pages of this book it was stated that Black Society, as it is generally regarded, is dead. What has remained is what there has always been . . . a class of people, who are as large, perhaps as ten percent of the total black population, and who are and have been in the vanguard of their people. They provide the leadership, the role models, the motivation and the dynamics which keep the central theme ever present and articulated before the larger community. They are in the United States Congress and the state legislatures, in presidential cabinets, on the U.S. Supreme Court bench and in the United States Senate. They sit on the boards of major corporations; they are the businessmen; the diplomats; the economists; the college presidents; the teachers; the preachers; the social workers; and the entertainers. They have spoken for the United States in the United Nations and have represented this international body on peace negotiations. They have been the recipients of the Nobel Peace Prize in the person of Drs. Ralph Bunche and Martin Luther King, Jr.

It is however, in the areas of politics and business that black accountability and responsibility are being most clearly demonstrated. As a result of the Voting Rights Act of 1965, sharp gains were registered in the numbers of blacks elected to public office. Nine times out of ten, the black elected official in office is there because of the feeling that it is the most viable method of bringing about the justice that the black American still seeks for himself and for his vast and voiceless constituency of Black Americans.

In Congress, for the first time since the height of the Reconstruction, there are more blacks than ever before. They are intelligent; they are forceful; they are hardworking; and, in the broadest sense of the term, they are dedicated public servants. Who can forget the spine-chilling effect of Barbara Jordan's ringing statements as she sat on the House Judiciary Committee during the Watergate Investigation? As the evidence was reviewed against Richard Nixon, she weighed whether or not to recommend impeachment for the President of the United States. Surely this was a potent and powerful position.

But because of the widening gulf between the black leaders and their followers today, it is difficult for the mass community to understand that it is the black elite that has been responsible, in large measure, for the survival of black people. They have provided the continuum that has permitted us to grow from a nation of 3,953,760 slaves and fewer than 500,000 free people into a nation with a purchasing power of 25 million people of 63 billion dollars. Nonetheless, these gains should not be taken for granted. The gap which was narrowing between the average black American and the average white American is widening again. While perhaps two percent of the black population can consider that they have tasted of the wine of democracy, more than half of the population are offered only the dregs.

Millions of black Americans have given up the pursuit of equality as a lost cause, and millions more have decided that the mainstream is not for them. While the numbers of those who gain entry into the upper echelons of the white power structure have increased; the Ed Brookes, the Thurgood Marshalls, the John H. Johnsons, the Hobart Taylors, the Patricia Harrises, the Barbara Jordans and the William Colemans; their numbers are not growing with the same momentum that the numbers at the base are multiplying.

Poverty has become endemic and self-reproducing. The vastness of the problem defies solutions proposed by theoretician and politician. Along with poverty, racism is growing. It is no longer even an illusion that racism is confined to the area of the nation below the Mason and Dixon line in the Old Confederacy. As the economic shoe tightens, the gulf between the haves and have-nots becomes wider. Recognizing the tenuous nature of the toe hold so recently obtained on the ladder of success, the black influential, as he inches up, ponders the strategy necessary to break the logjam that will surely catch him in the undertow if the rest of his people drown. Clearly until all blacks learn to swim, they must be taught to tread water.

Carl Rowan in his February, 1966 *Ebony* magazine discussion of "The Problems of the Black Elite" summed it up:

> Because we are a new era, Negroes are going to have to understand that everybody *talking* about equality ain't going there—and that some of the people striking the biggest blows for Negro freedom are those who never get around to boasting about it publicly.

> The simple fact is that it takes a lot less courage to stand up before a rally of angry Negroes in Harlem or an NAACP rally in Washington and give "Mr. Charlie" unshirted hell than it does to sit in a small meeting with a dozen powerful white men and tell them without compromise what you, the Negro, and the country will not stand for. But this is what the Louis Martins, the Cliffs Alexanders, the Ulric Hayneses are called upon to do frequently. Some Negroes in Washington do this "inside job" with superb skill and courage—and none can afford to pick up the phone an hour later and relate to *Jet* or The *Afro* how he "just told off Mr. Charlie."

> These are some of the facts of life that must be understood if the Negro is to make speedy progress in what is now the toughest part of his struggle—the effort to break down the vicious circle of social, economic and educational discrimination that stands to keep the Negro a second class citizen no matter how many laws may be on the statute books.

> Unlike the "kitchen cabinet" of the Roosevelt era, Washington's Negro leaders have continuing access to the President and to those other powerful men who make policy for this nation. How they use that access is going to go a long way toward determining how long and how many other Negroes must remain in that separate world of poverty.

It wasn't just by growing older that Lyndon Baines Johnson changed from a Texas senator who backed segregation to a President who dared tell the nation with eloquent emotion that "We shall overcome" the ravages of racism and bigotry. There had to be a few Negroes in the background, arguing cajoling, warning, disagreeing and influencing him in the myraid other ways that men are moved from one moral position to another.

The challenge of just that kind of influencing lies before the more fortunate Negro with a compelling urgency today. If he has the tact, the skill, the integrity that the times require, the next generation need not talk of either two Negro Americas or one. The white man's America can also be the only America known by black men.

July 29, 1974, I celebrated my eightieth birthday with a three-month round gala activities which began when I went to Rio de Janiero for Carnival and concluded only when my body could no longer keep up with my mind. I was entertained by friends Alger and Jessie Adams, Flo Thornley and Rose Morgan, Ruth Ellington, Morris and Ivy Steed all had parties for me. The Steed party was a two-day affair up at their Cape Cod home. Herman and Odile Russell, Freddye and Jake Henderson and Henry and Marian Shorter entertained in Atlanta, and there were other small and wonderful happenings all that year. My legs say they want to stop, but my heart and head say, "keep going", and I do. It is the spirit that has brought my people out of the darkness of slavery into the light of a brighter day. I am grateful for having been a part of it.

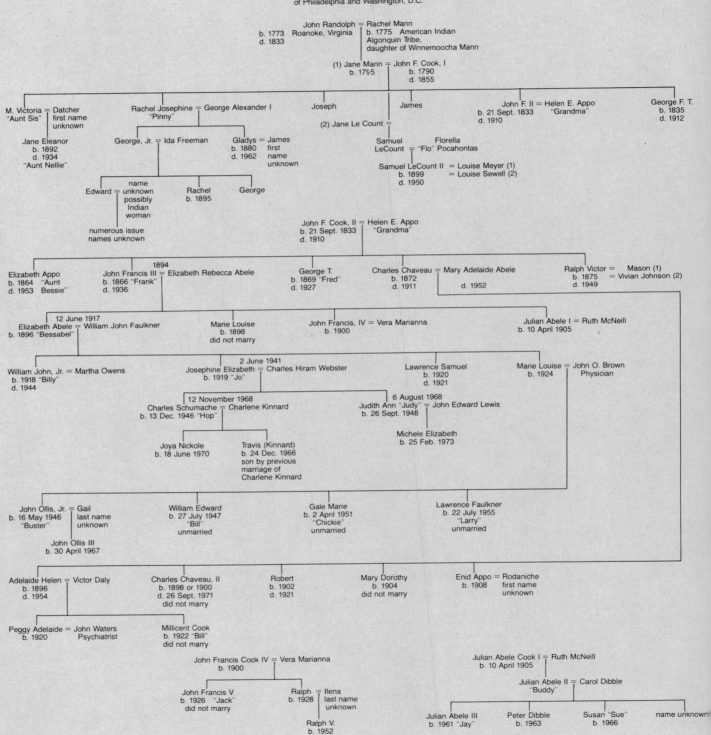

Cook—Jones—Abele Families
of Philadelphia and Washington, D.C.

John Randolph = Rachel Mann
b. 1773 Roanoke, Virginia b. 1775 American Indian
d. 1833 Algonquin Tribe,
daughter of Winnemoocha Mann

(1) Jane Mann = John F. Cook, I
b. 1795 b. 1790
d. 1855

M. Victoria = Datcher Rachel Josephine = George Alexander I Joseph James John F. II = Helen E. Appo George F. T.
"Aunt Sis" first name "Pinny" b. 21 Sept. 1833 "Grandma" b. 1835
unknown (2) Jane Le Count = d. 1910 d. 1912

Jane Eleanor George, Jr. = Ida Freeman Gladys = James Samuel Florella
b. 1892 b. 1880 first LeCount = "Flo" Pocahontas
d. 1934 d. 1962 name
"Aunt Nellie" unknown Samuel LeCount II = Louise Meyer (1)
b. 1899 = Louise Sewell (2)
Edward = name Rachel George d. 1950
unknown b. 1895
possibly
Indian
woman

numerous issue
names unknown

John F. Cook, II = Helen E. Appo
b. 21 Sept. 1833 "Grandma"
d. 1910

Elizabeth Appo 1894 George T. Charles Chaveau = Mary Adelaide Abele Ralph Victor = Mason (1)
b. 1864 John Francis III = Elizabeth Rebecca Abele b. 1869 "Fred" b. 1872 b. 1875 = Vivian Johnson (2)
d. 1953 "Aunt b. 1866 "Frank" d. 1927 d. 1911 d. 1952 d. 1949
Bessie" d. 1936

12 June 1917 Marie Louise John Francis, IV = Vera Marianna Julian Abele I = Ruth McNeill
Elizabeth Abele = William John Faulkner b. 1898 b. 1900 b. 10 April 1905
b. 1896 "Bessabel" did not marry

William John, Jr. = Martha Owens 2 June 1941 Lawrence Samuel Marie Louise = John O. Brown
b. 1918 "Billy" Josephine Elizabeth = Charles Hiram Webster b. 1920 b. 1924 Physician
d. 1944 b. 1919 "Jo" d. 1921

12 November 1968 6 August 1968
Charles Schumache = Charlene Kinnard Judith Ann "Judy" = John Edward Lewis
b. 13 Dec. 1946 "Hop" b. 26 Sept. 1948

Michele Elizabeth
Joya Nickole Travis (Kinnard) b. 25 Feb. 1973
b. 18 June 1970 b. 24 Dec. 1966
son by previous
marriage of
Charlene Kinnard

John Ollis, Jr. = Gail William Edward Gale Marie Lawrence Faulkner
b. 16 May 1946 last name b. 27 July 1947 b. 2 April 1951 b. 22 July 1955
"Buster" unknown "Bill" "Chickie" "Larry"
unmarried unmarried unmarried

John Ollis III
b. 30 April 1967

Adelaide Helen = Victor Daly Charles Chaveau, II Robert Mary Dorothy Enid Appo = Rodaniche
b. 1896 b. 1898 or 1900 b. 1902 b. 1904 b. 1908 first name
d. 1954 d. 26 Sept. 1971 d. 1921 did not marry unknown
did not marry

Peggy Adelaide = John Waters Millicent Cook
b. 1920 Psychiatrist b. 1922 "Bill"
did not marry

John Francis Cook IV = Vera Marianna Julian Abele Cook I = Ruth McNeill
b. 1900 b. 10 April 1905

John Francis V Ralph = Ilena Julian Abele II = Carol Dibble
b. 1926 "Jack" b. 1928 last name "Buddy"
did not marry unknown

Ralph V. Julian Abele III Peter Dibble Susan "Sue" name unknown
b. 1952 b. 1961 "Jay" b. 1963 b. 1966

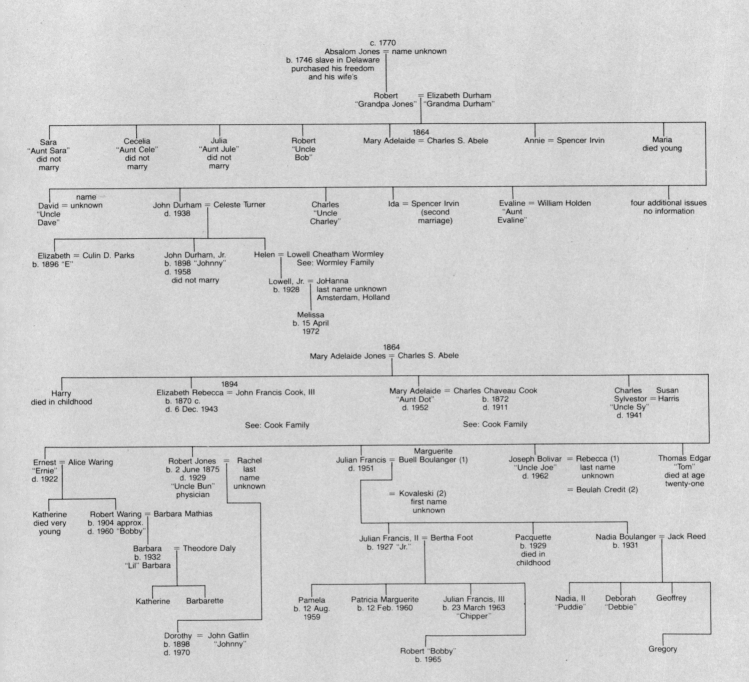

c. 1770
Absalom Jones = name unknown
b. 1746 slave in Delaware
purchased his freedom
and his wife's

Robert = Elizabeth Durham
"Grandpa Jones" "Grandma Durham"

1864
Mary Adelaide = Charles S. Abele

Sara
"Aunt Sara"
did not
marry

Cecelia
"Aunt Cele"
did not
marry

Julia
"Aunt Jule"
did not
marry

Robert
"Uncle
Bob"

Annie = Spencer Irvin

Maria
died young

David = name
"Uncle   unknown
Dave"

John Durham = Celeste Turner
d. 1938

Charles
"Uncle
Charley"

Ida = Spencer Irvin
(second
marriage)

Evaline = William Holden
"Aunt
Evaline"

four additional issues
no information

Elizabeth = Culin D. Parks
b. 1896 "E"

John Durham, Jr.
b. 1898 "Johnny"
d. 1958
did not marry

Helen = Lowell Cheatham Wormley
See: Wormley Family

Lowell, Jr. = JoHanna
b. 1928   last name unknown
Amsterdam, Holland

Melissa
b. 15 April
1972

1864
Mary Adelaide Jones = Charles S. Abele

Harry
died in childhood

1894
Elizabeth Rebecca = John Francis Cook, III
b. 1870 c.
d. 6 Dec. 1943

See: Cook Family

Mary Adelaide = Charles Chaveau Cook
"Aunt Dot"   b. 1872
d. 1952   d. 1911

See: Cook Family

Charles   Susan
Sylvestor = Harris
"Uncle Sy"
d. 1941

Ernest = Alice Waring
"Ernie"
d. 1922

Robert Jones = Rachel
b. 2 June 1875   last
d. 1929   name
"Uncle Bun"   unknown
physician

Marguerite
Julian Francis = Buell Boulanger (1)
d. 1951

Joseph Bolivar = Rebecca (1)
"Uncle Joe"   last name
d. 1962   unknown

= Beulah Credit (2)

Thomas Edgar
"Tom"
died at age
twenty-one

Katherine
died very
young

Robert Waring = Barbara Mathias
b. 1904 approx.
d. 1960 "Bobby"

= Kovaleski (2)
first name
unknown

Barbara = Theodore Daly
b. 1932
"Lil" Barbara

Julian Francis, II = Bertha Foot
b. 1927 "Jr."

Pacquette
b. 1929
died in
childhood

Nadia Boulanger = Jack Reed
b. 1931

Katherine   Barbarette

Pamela
b. 12 Aug.
1959

Patricia Marguerite
b. 12 Feb. 1960

Julian Francis, III
b. 23 March 1963
"Chipper"

Nadia, II
"Puddie"

Deborah
"Debbie"

Geoffrey

Dorothy = John Gatlin
b. 1898   "Johnny"
d. 1970

Robert "Bobby"
b. 1965

Gregory

395

Lomax Cook Family

of Fredericksburg, Virginia

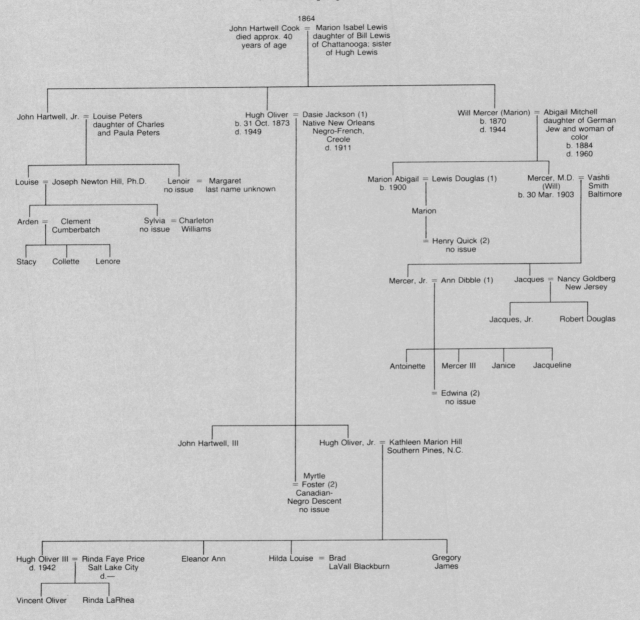

1864
John Hartwell Cook = Marion Isabel Lewis
died approx. 40   daughter of Bill Lewis
years of age   of Chattanooga; sister
                   of Hugh Lewis

John Hartwell, Jr. = Louise Peters   Hugh Oliver = Dasie Jackson (1)   Will Mercer (Marion) = Abigail Mitchell
daughter of Charles   b. 31 Oct. 1873   Native New Orleans   b. 1870   daughter of German
and Paula Peters   d. 1949   Negro-French,   d. 1944   Jew and woman of
                                                           Creole   color
                                                           d. 1911   b. 1884
                                                                                                      d. 1960

Louise = Joseph Newton Hill, Ph.D.   Lenoir = Margaret   Marion Abigail = Lewis Douglas (1)   Mercer, M.D. = Vashti
                                      no issue last name unknown b. 1900   (Will)   Smith
                                                                                                        b. 30 Mar. 1903 Baltimore

Arden = Clement   Sylvia = Charleton   Marion
        Cumberbatch   no issue Williams

Stacy   Collette   Lenore   = Henry Quick (2)
                                                                     no issue

                                                          Mercer, Jr. = Ann Dibble (1)   Jacques = Nancy Goldberg
                                                                                                    New Jersey

                                                                                          Jacques, Jr.   Robert Douglas

                                                   Antoinette   Mercer III   Janice   Jacqueline

                                                          = Edwina (2)
                                                            no issue

                   John Hartwell, III   Hugh Oliver, Jr. = Kathleen Marion Hill
                                                                Southern Pines, N.C.

                                     Myrtle
                                     = Foster (2)
                                     Canadian-
                                     Negro Descent
                                     no issue

Hugh Oliver III = Rinda Faye Price   Eleanor Ann   Hilda Louise = Brad   Gregory
d. 1942   Salt Lake City   LaVall Blackburn James
                  d.—

Vincent Oliver   Rinda LaRhea

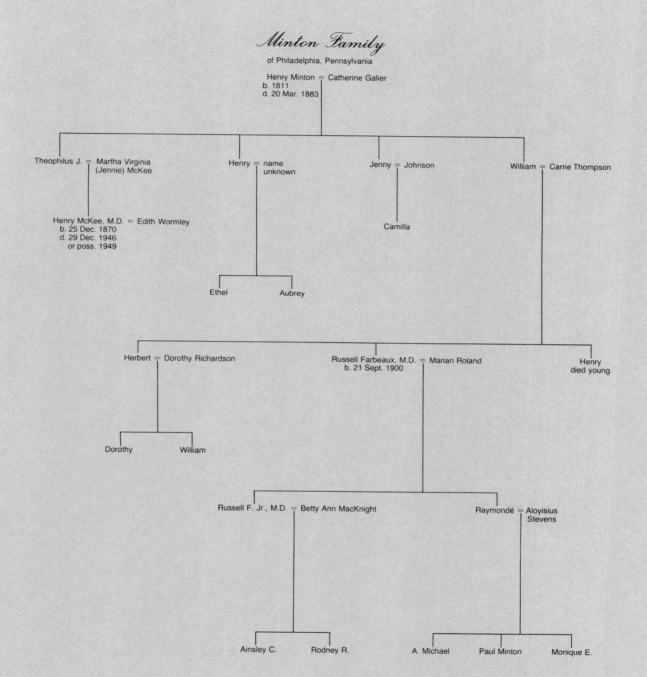

Minton Family
of Philadelphia, Pennsylvania

Henry Minton = Catherine Galier
b. 1811
d. 20 Mar. 1883

Theophilus J. = Martha Virginia (Jennie) McKee

Henry McKee, M.D. = Edith Wormley
b. 25 Dec. 1870
d. 29 Dec. 1946
or poss. 1949

Henry = name unknown

Ethel   Aubrey

Jenny = Johnson

Camilla

William = Carrie Thompson

Herbert = Dorothy Richardson

Russell Farbeaux, M.D. = Marian Roland
b. 21 Sept. 1900

Henry
died young

Dorothy   William

Russell F. Jr., M.D. = Betty Ann MacKnight

Raymondé = Aloyisius Stevens

Ainsley C.   Rodney R.

A. Michael   Paul Minton   Monique E.

The Syphax Family

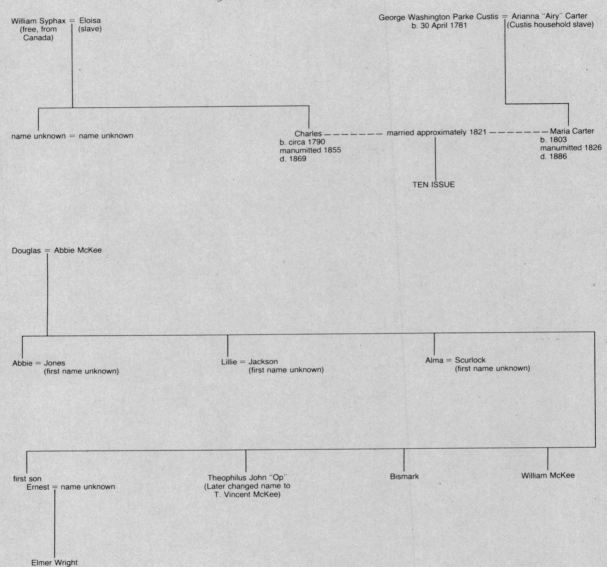

William Syphax = Eloisa
(free, from   (slave)
Canada)

George Washington Parke Custis = Arianna "Airy" Carter
b. 30 April 1781   (Custis household slave)

name unknown = name unknown

Charles ————————— married approximately 1821 ————————— Maria Carter
b. circa 1790   b. 1803
manumitted 1855   manumitted 1826
d. 1869   d. 1886

TEN ISSUE

Douglas = Abbie McKee

Abbie = Jones   Lillie = Jackson   Alma = Scurlock
(first name unknown)   (first name unknown)   (first name unknown)

first son   Theophilus John "Op"   Bismark   William McKee
Ernest = name unknown   (Later changed name to
                         T. Vincent McKee)

Elmer Wright

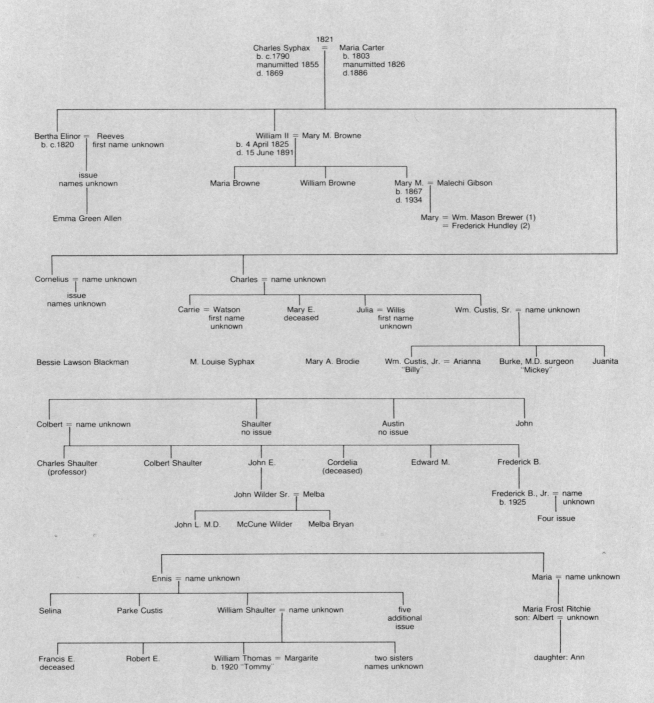

1821

Charles Syphax = Maria Carter
b. c.1790   b. 1803
manumitted 1855   manumitted 1826
d. 1869   d. 1886

Bertha Elinor = Reeves
b. c.1820   first name unknown

William II = Mary M. Browne
b. 4 April 1825
d. 15 June 1891

issue
names unknown

Maria Browne   William Browne   Mary M. = Malechi Gibson
b. 1867
d. 1934

Emma Green Allen

Mary = Wm. Mason Brewer (1)
= Frederick Hundley (2)

Cornelius = name unknown
issue
names unknown

Charles = name unknown

Carrie = Watson
first name
unknown

Mary E.
deceased

Julia = Willis
first name
unknown

Wm. Custis, Sr. = name unknown

Bessie Lawson Blackman   M. Louise Syphax   Mary A. Brodie   Wm. Custis, Jr. = Arianna
"Billy"

Burke, M.D. surgeon
"Mickey"

Juanita

Colbert = name unknown   Shaulter
no issue

Austin
no issue

John

Charles Shaulter
(professor)

Colbert Shaulter

John E.

Cordelia
(deceased)

Edward M.

Frederick B.

John Wilder Sr. = Melba

Frederick B., Jr. = name
b. 1925   unknown

John L. M.D.   McCune Wilder   Melba Bryan

Four issue

Ennis = name unknown

Maria = name unknown

Selina   Parke Custis   William Shaulter = name unknown   five
additional
issue

Maria Frost Ritchie
son: Albert = unknown

Francis E.
deceased

Robert E.

William Thomas = Margarite
b. 1920 "Tommy"

two sisters
names unknown

daughter: Ann

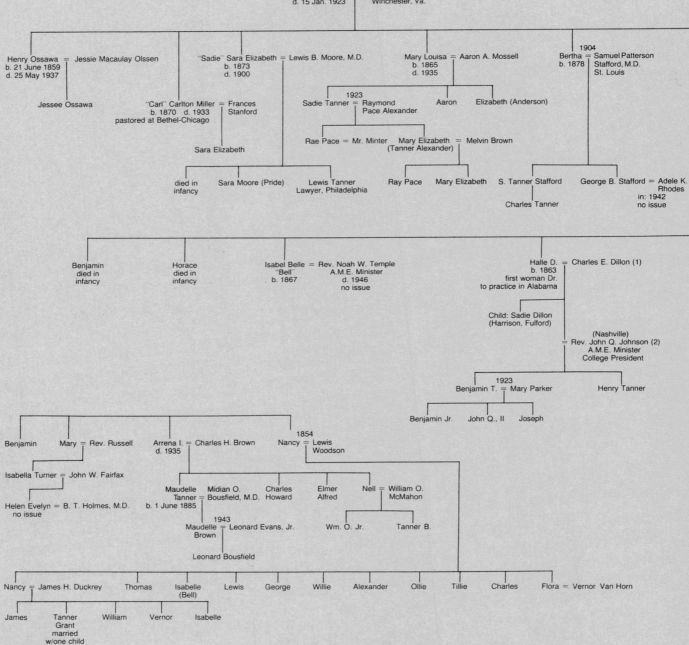

Richard Tanner

Free Negroes—Pittsburgh
19 Aug. 1858
Benjamin Tucker = Sara Elizabeth Miller
b. 25 Dec. 1835   b. 18 May 1840
d. 15 Jan. 1923   Winchester, Va.

Henry Ossawa = Jessie Macaulay Olssen
b. 21 June 1859
d. 25 May 1937

"Sadie" Sara Elizabeth = Lewis B. Moore, M.D.
b. 1873
d. 1900

Mary Louisa = Aaron A. Mossell
b. 1865
d. 1935

1904
Bertha = Samuel Patterson
b. 1878   Stafford, M.D.
           St. Louis

Jessee Ossawa

"Carl" Carlton Miller = Frances
b. 1870   d. 1933   Stanford
pastored at Bethel-Chicago

1923
Sadie Tanner = Raymond
              Pace Alexander

Aaron   Elizabeth (Anderson)

Sara Elizabeth

Rae Pace = Mr. Minter   Mary Elizabeth = Melvin Brown
                         (Tanner Alexander)

died in   Sara Moore (Pride)   Lewis Tanner   Ray Pace   Mary Elizabeth   S. Tanner Stafford   George B. Stafford = Adele K.
infancy   Lawyer, Philadelphia   Rhodes
                                                                                                                       in: 1942
                                                             Charles Tanner   no issue

Benjamin   Horace   Isabel Belle = Rev. Noah W. Temple   Halle D. = Charles E. Dillon (1)
died in   died in   "Bell"   A.M.E. Minister   b. 1863
infancy   infancy   . b. 1867   d. 1946   first woman Dr.
                                                     no issue   to practice in Alabama

                                                                                     Child: Sadie Dillon
                                                                                     (Harrison, Fulford)

                                                                                     (Nashville)
                                                                                     = Rev. John Q. Johnson (2)
                                                                                       A.M.E. Minister
                                                                                       College President

                                                                          1923
                                                                 Benjamin T. = Mary Parker   Henry Tanner

                                                                 Benjamin Jr.   John Q., II   Joseph

                                              1854
Benjamin   Mary = Rev. Russell   Arrena I. = Charles H. Brown   Nancy = Lewis
                                   d. 1935   Woodson

Isabella Turner = John W. Fairfax

Helen Evelyn = B. T. Holmes, M.D.   Maudelle   Midian O.   Charles   Elmer   Nell = William O.
no issue   Tanner =   Bousfield, M.D. Howard   Alfred   McMahon
                                     b. 1 June 1885

                                         1943
                                     Maudelle = Leonard Evans, Jr.   Wm. O. Jr.   Tanner B.
                                     Brown

                                     Leonard Bousfield

Nancy = James H. Duckrey   Thomas   Isabelle   Lewis   George   Willie   Alexander   Ollie   Tillie   Charles   Flora = Vernor Van Horn
                                      (Bell)

James   Tanner   William   Vernor   Isabelle
         Grant
         married
         w/one child

The Wormley Family

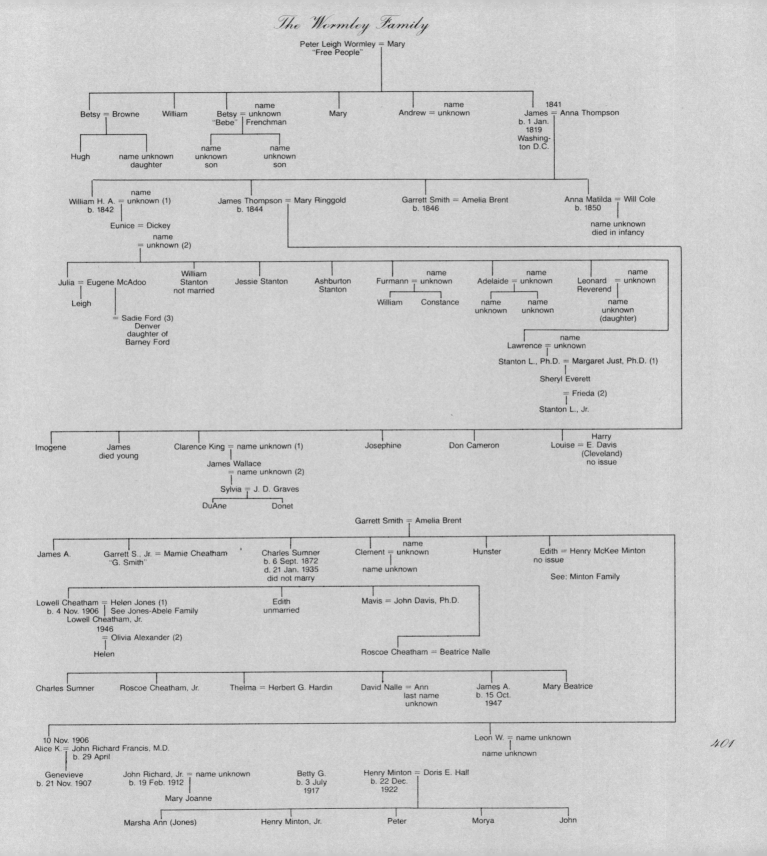

Photographic Sources

Mrs. Harry Anderson 221
Mrs. Maurice Clifford 286
Mrs. Thomas Coleman Collection 61, 156, 157
Will Marion Cook Family Collection 340, 341
George Denison 152, 190
Olive Diggs Collection 214
Josephine Faulkner Webster/Rev. William
J. Faulkner Collection 117, 127, 190, 223
First National Bank of Chicago 23
Dr. Adelaide Hill Gulliver 120
Janet Avery Hamilton 186
Mrs. J. Newton Hill 88
Oscar Hill 180, 221
Moorland-Spingarn Research Center, Howard
University 52, 89, 94, 116, 154, 155
Mary Gibson Hundley Collection 225
George E. Johnson Collection 382, 383
Mrs. John H. Johnson Collection 97
Johnetta Walker Kelso 252, 253
Gerri Hodges Major Collection 122, 214
Mrs. Russell Minton 93, 128, 157, 251
Byron Minor Collection 256, 257
Mrs. Herman Moore 192
Denise Denison Morris Collection 118, 126, 127, 158, 159
George Murphy, II 184, 185
Anthony Overton, II 180, 190
Dr. F. Raymond Powell Collection 123, 193
Mrs. Harvey Russell 152
John H. Sengstacke Collection 188, 189
William Custis Syphax 91
Williston Family Collection 124, 150, 151, 215
Dr. Stanton L. Wormley Collection 222
Mrs. Lawrence Young 184, 185

All other photographs courtesy of Johnson Publishing Company

Bibliography

American Guide Series, Federal Writers' Project of the Works Project Administration for the State of Florida. *A Guide to the Southernmost State.* Oxford University Press, 1939.

Bardolph, Richard. *The Negro Vanguard.* New York: Vintage Books, 1961.

Bennett, Lerone, Jr. *Black Power U.S.A.: The Human Side of Reconstruction, 1867-1877.* Chicago: Johnson Publishing Company, Inc., 1967.

Berwanger, Eugene H. *The Frontier Against Slavery: Western Anti-Negro Prejudice and the Slavery Extension Controversy.* Urbana: University of Illinois Press, 1967.

Billingsley, Andrew. *Black Families in White America.* Englewood Cliffs, New Jersey: Prentice-Hall, 1968.

Bontemps, Arna. *One-Hundred Years of Negro Freedom.* New York: Dodd, Mead & Company, 1961.

————; Conroy, Jack. *They Seek a City.* New York: Doubleday, Doran and Company, Inc. 1945.

Boykin, James H. *The Negro in North Carolina Prior to 1861.* New York: Pageant Press, Inc. 1958.

Bragg, George F. *History of the Afro-American Group of the Episcopal Church.* 1922. Reprint. New York: Johnson Reprint Corporation, 1968.

Brawley, Benjamin. *A Social History of the American Negro: Being a History of the Negro Problem in the United States.* New York: The Macmillan Company, 1921.

Brown, William Wells. *The Black Man: His Antecedents; His Genius, and His Achievements.* New York: Thomas Hamilton, 1863.

Butcher, Margaret Just. *The Negro in American Culture.* New York: Alfred A. Knopf, 1956.

Butwin, Miriam and Pirmantgen, Pat. *Protest I.* Minneapolis: Lerner Publications Company, 1972.

The Chicago Commission on Race Relations. *The Negro in Chicago: A Study of Race Relations and a Race Riot.* Chicago: The University of Chicago Press, 1922.

Cromwell, John W. *The Negro in American History: Men and Women Eminent in the Evolution of the American of African Descent.* 1914. Reprint. New York: Johnson Reprint Corporation, 1968.

Daniels, John. *In Freedom's Birthplace: A Study of the Boston Negroes.* 1914. Reprint. New York: Johnson Reprint Corporation, 1968.

Dann, Martin E. *The Black Press 1827-1890: The Quest for National Identity.* New York: G. P. Putnam's Sons, 1971.

Davis, Elizabeth Lindsay. *Lifting As They Climb.* Washington, D.C.: National Association of Colored Women, 1934.

Davis, John P., ed. *The American Negro Reference Book.* Englewood Cliffs, New Jersey: Prentice-Hall, Inc., 1966.

Detweiler, Frederick G. *The Negro Press in the United States.* Chicago: The University of Chicago Press, 1922.

Douglass, Frederick. *My Bondage and My Freedom.* 1855. Reprint. Chicago: Johnson Publishing Company, 1970.

Douty, Esther M. *Forten the Sailmaker: Pioneer Champion of Negro Rights.* Chicago: Rand McNally and Company, 1968.

Dreer, Herman. *The History of the Omega Psi Phi Fraternity: A Brotherhood of Negro College Men,* 1911 to 1939. Baltimore: Clarke Press, 1940.

DuBois, W. E. Burghardt, Ph.D. *The Philadelphia Negro: A Social Study.* Boston: Ginn & Company, 1899.

Edelstein, Tilden G. *Strange Enthusiasm: A Life of Thomas Wentworth Higginson.* New Haven: Yale University Press, 1968.

Foner, Phillip, ed. *The Life and The Writings of Frederick Douglass.* V. 1-4, New York: International Publishers, 1950.

Franklin, John Hope. *The Free Negro in North Carolina, 1790-1860.* Chapel Hill: The University of North Carolina Press, 1943.

Frazier, E. Franklin. *The Negro Family in the United States.* Chicago: The University of Chicago Press, 1939.
Black Bourgeoisie. Glencoe: Free Press, 1957.

Gibson, J. W. and Grogman, W. H. *Progress of a Race.* Atlanta: J. L. Nichols and Company, 1902.

Gordon, Taylor. *Born to Be.* New York: Covici-Friede, 1929.

Greene, Robert Ewell. *Black Defenders of America, 1775-1973.* Chicago: Johnson Publishing Company, Inc. 1974.

Haley, James T. *Sparkling Gems of Race Knowledge Worth Reading.* Nashville: J. T. Haley & Company, 1897.

Harris, M. A. ("Spike"). *A Negro History Tour of Manhattan.* New York: Greenwood Publishing Corporation, 1968.

Hughes, Langston. *The Big Sea.* New York: Alfred A. Knopf, 1945.

Hundley, Mary Gibson. *Dunbar Story: 1870-1955.* New York: Vantage Press, 1965.

Isaacs, Edith J. R. *The Negro in the American Theatre.* New York: New York Theatre Arts, Inc., 1947.

Johnson, James Weldon. *Along This Way.* New York: The Viking Press, 1933.

Lofton, John. *Insurrection in South Carolina: The Turbulent World of Denmark Vesey.* Ohio: The Antioch Press, 1964.

Logan, Rayford. *Howard University, The First Hundred Years: 1867-1967*. New York: New York University Press, 1964.

Meltzer, Milton, ed. *In Their Own Words: A History of the American Negro, 1619-1865*. New York: Thomas Y. Crowell Company, 1964.

Newbold, N. C. *Five North Carolina Negro Educators*. Chapel Hill: The University of North Carolina Press, 1939.

Nichols, J. L., and Crogman, William H. *Progress of a Race*. Naperville: J. L. Nichols Company, 1929.

Nowlin, William F. *The Negro in National Politics—Since 1868*. Boston: Stratford Publishing Company, 1931.

Ottley, Roi. *New World A-Coming: Inside Black America*. Cambridge: The Riverside Press, 1943.

Parker, Marjorie H. *Alpha Kappa Alpha Sorority: 1908-1958*. Published by Alpha Kappa Alpha Sorority, 1958.

Patterson, Caleb Perry. *The Negro in Tennessee, 1790-1865*. Austin, Texas: University of Texas Bulletin, No. 2205, February 1, 1922.

Payne, Daniel A. *History of the African Methodist Episcopal Church, V. 1*. 1891. Reprint. New York: Johnson Reprint Corporation, 1968.

Pipkin, Rev. J. J. *The Story of a Rising Race*. N. D. Thompson Publishing Company, 1902.

Quarles, Benjamin. *Black Abolitionists*. New York: Oxford University Press, 1969.

————. *The Negro in the American Revolution*. Chapel Hill: The University of North Carolina, 1961.

Range, Willard. *The Rise and Progress of Negro Colleges in Georgia, 1865-1949*. Athens: University of Georgia.

Richardson, Clement, ed. *The National Cyclopedia of the Colored Race, V. 1*. Montgomery, Alabama, National Publishing Company, Inc., 1919.

Robb, Frederick H., ed. *The Negro in Chicago*. V. 1. Washington: Intercollegiate Club of Chicago, 1927.

Russell, John H., Ph.D. *The Free Negro in Virginia: 1619-1865*. Baltimore: The Johns Hopkins Press, 1913.

Siebert, Wilbur H. *The Underground Railroad from Slavery to Freedom*. New York: Arno Press and The New York Times, 1968.

Siebert, Wilbur Henry. *The Mysteries of Ohio's Underground Railroad*. Columbus, Long's College Book Company, 1951.

Simmons, William J. *Men of Mark*. Chicago: Johnson Publishing Company, Inc., 1970.

Smith, Charles Spencer. *A History of the African Methodist Episcopal Church*. 1922. Reprint. New York: Johnson Reprint Corporation, 1968.

Spear, Allan H. *Black Chicago: The Making of a Negro Ghetto, 1890-1920*. Chicago: The University of Chicago Press, 1967.

Still, William. *Underground Rail Road*. 1871. Reprint. Chicago: Johnson Publishing Company, Inc., 1970.

Stuart, M. S. *An Economic Detour: A History of Insurance in the Lives of American Negroes*. New York: Wendell Malliet and Company, 1940.

Trotter, James M. *Music and Some Highly Musical People*. Boston: Lee and Shepard, 1881.

Virginia Writers' Project. *Negro in Virginia*. New York: Hastings House Publishers, 1940.

Washington, Booker T. *The Negro in Business*. Boston: Hertel, Jenkins and Company, 1907.

Williams, George W. *History of the Negro Race in America: 1619-1880*. New York: Arno Press and the New York Times, 1968.

Williams, William Hazaiah. "The Negro in the District of Columbia During Reconstruction." The Howard Review (1924) 1:97-148.

Bibliography

Wilson, Joseph T. *The Black Phalanx*. New York: Arno Press and The New York Times, 1968.

Woodson, Carter G. *A Century of Negro Migration*. Washington, D. C.: The Association for the Study of Negro Life and History, 1918.

Woodson, Carter G. *Free Negro Heads of Families in the United States in 1830*. Washington, D. C.: The Association for the Study of Negro Life and History Inc., 1925.

Workers of the Writers' Program of the Work Projects Administration for the District of Columbia. *Washington, D. C.: A Guide to the Nation's Capital*. New York: Hastings House, 1942.

Workers of the Writer's Program of the Work Projects Administration for the District of Columbia. *The Negro in Virginia*. New York: Hastings House, 1940.

Wright, Bishop R. R. *The Bishops of the African Methodist Episcopal Church*. Nashville: The A.M.E. Sunday School Union, 1963.

Wright, R. R. *The Negro in Pennsylvania*. Philadelphia: AME Book Concern, 1912.

Articles and Journals
Cobb, W. Montague, ed. *National Medical Association Journal*. 1950 to date.

The Colored American Magazine. V. 1-7. Boston: Colored Cooperative Publishing Company, 1901.

Negro History Bulletin. Washington: Association for the Study of Afro-American Life and History Inc., various issues.

Rowan, Carl. "The Problems of the Black Elite." *Ebony*, Feb. 1966.

Newspapers and Magazines

Afro-American
Amsterdam News
Chicago Defender
Color
Crisis
Ebony

Indianapolis Freeman
Jet
Negro Digest
New York Age
Pittsburgh Courier
Washington Bee

Index